GOD'S POWER, AMERICA SAVE OUR LEGACY

Vote Freedom Vote President Trump

By

Lisa Lucia Arden, MDIV

To my Mother and Father

Frank and Alvera

Trinity, Virgin Mary, Arch Angels, Angels of God, Saints

Table of Contents

Introduction   1

Chapter One: Karl Jasper Discussion   17

Chapter Two: Political Urgencies   43

Chapter Three: Emergencies America Save Our Legacy   109

Chapter Four: Ethics and Liberalism   133

Chapter Five: Brief Notes on the Eucharist   145

Chapter Six: Hitlerian World Controls Discussion of Karl Jaspers   163

Chapter Seven: Divine Message Leander Texas   179

Chapter Eight: Discussion on China Business   195

Chapter Nine: Military Comparisons   199

Chapter Ten: PILLARS OF PARADIGMS OF POWER   209

Chapter Eleven: Catholic Justice   237

Chapter Twelve: Nicomachean Ethics   267

Chapter Thirteen: Aristotle's Metaphysics   309

Chapter Fourteen: Dr. Professor Karl Jaspers   351

Chapter Fifteen: John Philoponus   367

Bibliography   389

Pope Francis on Solidarity

"Grace is not part of consciousness; it is the amount of light in our souls, not knowledge nor reason."

Divine Command: VOTE PRESIDENT TRUMP
Prior warning in Prayer
GOD FIRST, AMERICA OUR MIRACLE.
VOTE FREEDOM VOTE PRESIDENT TRUMP
God's Love can overcome all things. God loves all humanity.

In Jesus Christ's power in the Trinity, we can have Salvation.

Even with problems, in our world, we can live God's life of the most supernatural beauty and create the most extraordinary beauty in the Spirit of God in us and the gifts He gives us.

We, as Americans, are responsible for taking our country back NOW.

YOU HAVE THE POWER OF THE RIGHT ARM OF GOD STRENGTH AMERICA.
WE ALSO HAVE A COVENANT THAT GOD WILL PROTECT US WHEN WE SEEK HIM FIRST IN RIGHTEOUSNESS.

"And we have seen and testify that the Father has sent the Son as Savior of the world" (1 John 4:14). As Savior, Jesus is the only One Who can save us! Deliverer: "Him God has exalted to His right hand to be Prince and Savior, to give repentance to Israel and forgiveness of sins" (Acts 5:31).

I have been called for years to prepare America for the future. In 2011 and before, I wrote about the warnings of One World Controls. Warning that we could not lose our freedoms to the Communistic World powers and Secret highest tables of evil

Our Need To Give to the World, Heal America Love in God 2016

Arise to God's Truth, Restore and Keep America's Freedom 2020

Many articles of warning.

THE WAR AGAINST GOD AND EVIL IS THE WAR
WE NEED TO SAVE THE SOULS OF THE PEOPLE AND OUR

LEGACY AND AMERICA

ABORTION IS MUCH OF THE CAUSE OF THE BREAKING DOWN OF AMERICA
WE HAVE A COVENANT

We are not a pagan nation. We are a Judeo-Christian Nation and originally had a Covenant with Jesus Christ—the Prayer of the Continental Congress of 1774, the Constitution, and the Declaration of Independence.

Also, 300,000- 500,000 internationally from the Ukraine war and borders missing children and not foster parents interviewed

Before 2016, I was told in a prayer that God chose President Trump to be President, and I need to promote him and keep America's freedom and restoration.

I wrote this in before warning: ..

Democratic Party Elite Communistic Obama, Biden, Kamala America they want to destroy controlled by the higher elite world powers and the secrecy of the highest evil tables. Also, the United Nations wants Agenda 21 under Obama, Bush, Clinton, Biden, and Kamala.. Taking away ownership and control by the World Health Controls and World Economic Forum. Under Biden and Kamala. Also, the CCP virus was made to kill off the people and the CCP vaccinations.

Kamala and Biden, the weather disaster destroyed North Carolina, Tennessee, and Florida. Chemical Spraying and EMFs affect the brain.

CULTURE AND RELIGION TRYING TO BREAK DOWN THE JUDEO-CHRISTIAN NATION WITH LIBERAL AND

COMMUNISTIC CONTROLS Health de pollutions: - CCP VIRUS AND CCP VACCINATION TO KILL THE PEOPLE

UNDER KAMALA.BIDEN ALL THESE HAPPENINGS IN A MATTER OF 4 YEARS.

KAMALA OPEN BORDERS USES IMMIGRANTS AS A POLITICAL IDEOLOGY TO CONTROL THE VOTE FOR THE FUTURE AND TAKE AWAY THE LIVES OF AMERICANS. SAFETY HAS BEEN DESTROYED UNDER KAMALA OPEN BORDERS.

GEOPOLITICAL POWERS NOW IN THE WORLD WE HAVE TO PROTECT OUR BORDERS

I diligently sent social media, wrote books and articles, spoke, and Pod Casts and art… to many people. For years, I believed, and NOW they listened to America's Restoration EMERGENCIES and Solutions …I ask to get Elon Musk and all Democrats to come on the Republican's side to save America. For years, I have continuously given a list of necessary urgencies. As we can see, RFK also speaks of all the Health problems and Elon on the most urgent issues—beautiful, brilliant fighters Tulsi, J. D. Vance, Vivek, Tucker, Rogan, and Americans. I have been asking and promoting for years. And now we have a miracle.

Vote for our Covenant with Jesus Christ

Let us give our lives to Jesus Christ in America and nations.

America, did you know we have had a Covenant with Jesus Christ since 1774? We are a Judeo-Christian Nation

First Prayer of the Continental Congress, 1774

The Prayer in the First Congress, A.D. 1774

O Lord our Heavenly Father, high and mighty King of kings, and Lord of lords, who dost from thy throne behold all the dwellers on earth and reignest with power supreme and uncontrolled over all the Kingdoms, Empires and Governments; look down in mercy, we beseech Thee, on these our American States, who have fled to Thee from the rod of the oppressor and thrown themselves on Thy gracious protection, desiring to be henceforth dependent only on Thee. To Thee have they appealed for the righteousness of their cause; to Thee do they now look up for that countenance and support, which Thou alone canst give. Take them, therefore, Heavenly Father, under Thy nurturing care; provide them with wisdom in Council and valor in the field; defeat the malicious designs of our cruel adversaries; convince them of the unrighteousness of their Cause, and if they persist in their sanguinary purposes, of own unerring justice, sounding in their hearts, constrain them to drop the weapons of war from their unnerved hands in the day of battle!

Be Thou present, O God of wisdom, and direct the councils of this honorable assembly; enable them to settle things on the best and surest foundation. The scene of blood may be speedily closed; that order, harmony, and peace may be effectually restored, and truth and justice, religion and piety, prevail and flourish amongst the people. Preserve the health of their bodies and vigor of their minds; shower

down on them and the millions they represent such temporal blessings as Thou seest expedient for them in this world and crown them with everlasting glory in the world to come. <u>We ask for all this in the name and through the merits of Jesus Christ, Thy Son, and our Savior.</u>

Amen.

Reverend Jacob Duché
Rector of Christ Church of Philadelphia, Pennsylvania
September 7, 1774, 9 a.m.

America, we are God's people. Let us seek His Covenant of Power in His Salvation.

In God's Power, America Save Our Legacy

Revelation 19:11 And now I saw heaven open, and a white horse appear; its rider was called Trustworthy and True; in uprightness, he judges and makes war. 12 His eyes were flames of fire, and he was crowned with many coronets; the name written on him was known only to himself; 13 his cloak was soaked in blood. The name knows him, The Word of God. 14 Behind him, dressed in dazzling white linen, rode the armies of heaven on white horses. 15 From his mouth came to a sharp sword with which to strike the unbelievers; he is the one who will rule them with an iron scepter and tread out the wine of Almighty God's fierce retribution. 16 Name was written on his cloak and thigh: King of kings and Lord of lords.

Apostles' Creed

I believe in God, the Father almighty, Creator of heaven and earth, and in Jesus Christ, his only Son, our Lord, who was conceived by the Holy Spirit, born of the Virgin Mary, suffered under Pontius Pilate, was crucified, died and was buried; he descended into hell; on the third day he rose again from the dead; he ascended into heaven, and is seated at the right hand of God the Father almighty; from there he will come to judge the living and the dead. I believe in the Holy Spirit, the holy catholic Church, the communion of saints, the forgiveness of sins, the resurrection of the body, and life everlasting. Amen.

Nicene Creed

I believe in one God, the Father almighty, maker of heaven and earth, of all things visible and invisible. I believe in one Lord Jesus Christ, the Only Begotten Son of God, born of the Father before all ages. God from God, Light from Light, true God from true God, begotten, not made, consubstantial with the Father; all things were made through him. For us men and our salvation, he came down from heaven, and by the Holy Spirit, he was incarnated of the Virgin Mary and became man. For our sake, he was crucified under Pontius Pilate, he suffered death and was buried, and rose again on the third day by the Scriptures. He ascended into heaven and was seated at the Father's right hand. He will come again in glory to judge the living and the dead, and his kingdom will have no end. I believe in the Holy Spirit, the Lord, the giver of life, who proceeds from the Father and the Son, who is adored and glorified with the Father and the Son, who has spoken through the prophets. I believe in one holy, catholic, and apostolic Church. I confess one Baptism for the forgiveness of sins, and I look forward to the resurrection of the dead and the world's life. Amen.

INTRODUCTION

Articles Subjects of Emergency America

Prayer of Gladness and Love to the Supreme Maker of all things.
Jesus Christ

America is a Judeo-Christian nation, and with the principles under the Constitution, we have a covenant with God.

All now need to choose the light of God, the Most Highest God, the God of Abraham. I pray that many come to the Salvation in Jesus Christ.

We can work together for peace when we vote for leaders who respect the Judeo-Christian nation. We have a Covenant.

Our leader is Jesus Christ God's power:

Revelation 19:11 And now I saw heaven open, and a white horse appear; its rider was called Trustworthy and True; in uprightness . . .and is seated at the right hand of God the Father Almighty; he is the one who will rule them with an iron scepter, and tread out the wine of Almighty God's fierce retribution. 16 A name was written on his cloak and thigh: King of kings and Lord of lords.

America has God's power in His covenant and salvation to save America's legacy.

Let us have "gladness that enlarges our heart so that it runs in the way of God's Commandments." We hope and pray that they will see us helping others in the power of God's salvation, that it will overflow to their hearts, and that they will have a miracle to save their legacy of America and worldwide.

Even the most powerful who control the world will be saved with the eternal quintessential Spirit of God's living power to bring miracles in the heart of all America and even around the globe to save the legacy of humanity.

Even the most impoverished in the purse will be saved by the eternal quintessential Spirit of God's living power, which will bring miracles in the hearts of all Americans and even across the world to save humanity's legacy.

Even the sickest will be saved by the eternal quintessential Spirit of God's living power, bringing miracles to the heart of America and even across the world to save humanity's legacy.

"This same Christian teaching also commands us to honor God by faith, that is of the mind, by hope, that is of the will, by love, that is of the heart, and thus the whole man is subjected to the supreme Maker and Ruler of all things."

THE

SACRED POWER OF

CHRIST

Virgin Mary conceived the Christ Child, the Son of God. God is with us.

Isaiah 7:14

GIVES us the SPIRIT of LOVE WITHOUT MEASURE

teaches us to LOVE one another and saves us WITH his BREAD OF LIFE

FORGIVES our humanity and brings us to HIS HEART

UPHOLDS us IN THE JOURNEY OF THE QUEST OF LIFE DIRECTS our EYES TO SEE FROM STARS TO STARS THE ABSOLUTE TRUTH

gives us a mind of brilliance and beauty

GUIDES us THROUGH THE PERSEVERANCE to VIRTUE BRINGS forth DEEP HAPPINESS EACH SEASON CALMS ALL THE SEAS OF TRIALS

heals us with the mystery of

HIS HOLY SPIRIT

never forsakes us; Christ is always with us, listening and answering us. Christ thirsts for our love and All humanity to be his rock; the church in Christ gives us everlasting life and empowers us for the present in our humanness and future everlasting. Christ is our Lord and Savior and King OF ALL CREATION

Guide Virgin Queen Mary Mother of God

Did you know that President Washington had a vision and spiritual experience with a Virgin Mary (beautiful lady) who guided him to save America in 1776? [1]

I was struck by an incident in the book: Washington, fighting the British during the winter of 1777-1778, was in dire straits: his soldiers were ill-equipped, and supplies and ammunition were meager. As he prayed for divine intervention in his freezing quarters, Demi writes, "According to a popular legend…he had a vision of a beautiful and luminous lady. She foretold that the Americans would be victorious and that a new and great nation would be born."

Then, the temple of God in heaven opened, and the ark of the covenant could be seen inside his temple. Then came flashes of lightning, peals of thunder, and an earthquake and violent hail.

And now, in heaven, appears a great portent, a woman that wore the sun for her mantle, with the moon under her feet and a crown of twelve stars about her head. She had a child in her womb and was crying out as she travailed, in great pain of her delivery. Then a second portent appears: a great dragon, fiery red, with seven heads and ten horns… And he stood fronting the woman who was in childbirth, ready to swallow up the child as soon as she bore it. She bore a son, the son who is to herd the nations like sheep with a crook of iron, and this child of hers was caught up to God, right up to his throne, while the mother fled into the wilderness, where God had prepared a place of refuge for her, and there … she is to be kept safe.

Revelations 11

---

[1]   https://catholicherald.co.uk/did-george-washington-have-a-vision-of-our-lady/m,Did George Washington have a vision of Our Lady?

When I was correcting this book, I saw the moon's brilliance and shimmering strong in the daylight… Then I remembered the verses in the Book of Revelation, which say that the Virgin Mary will come at the Second Coming.

A guide, the Virgin Queen Mary, saves the world through Mary unto Christ. *"Ad Diem Illum"* expresses God's desire through Mary to renew all things in Christ." Just as Mary carried Jesus Christ in her womb unto the world, Mary held Jesus Christ to save the world. We need to be examples such as Mary to have Jesus Christ in the womb of our hearts, the Spirit of Christ, to others. And we must be examples of Joseph to protect Christ in the heart of His love…We must empower and defend America's Legacy and her people's country.

During President Trump's Presidency and his team, America was in her covenantal blessing like flowing living waters.

Here are a few miracles blessings President Trump

Highly ethical man of wisdom and love of humanity

International Diplomacy of the Greatest President

Defeated ISIS
No wars
Ninety-two percent approval Rating for Veterans
Tariffs President Trump Billions of Dollars
Building Manufacturing
Beginning the Infrastructure building
High morale for children and business
Fewer regulations for businesses for building
Protected the Boarders
Best Economy in the World
Billions from China
Energy Independent

We have liquid gold.
Energy Depended, and we were going to give it to.
Abraham Accords President Trump Built DR PETERSON SAID
PRESIDENT TRUMP SHOULD OF GOT A NOBLE PEACE PRICE
No inflation
Best Taxes
Highest employment
Building Military for protection
Protected the Steel Plants

As stated in my other books, America's life is a force of life in all nations worldwide that is ordained to be a force of God's justice.
We need to have a President of the following:

President Trump is at a businessman's and his team's highest diplomacy level.

In his actions to put America first and God first, he accepted the Covenant of Continental Congress 1774, our Constitution, and the Declaration of Independence.

President Trump and the team have a future that will allow all solutions to restore and free America and bring saving grace to our salvation through the power of God.

God's Power, America, save our legacy.

Vote President Trump, Vote for Freedom

Restore. America now

Today, the Judeo-Christian nation, the economy, traditions, safety, children's education, businesses, restoration, health, housing, all wholesomeness of human existence, stopping World Controls, and the

International Diplomacy situation in the USA need to be protected and restored. Please see the book *God First, America Our Miracle.*[2]

America .. President Trump and His Team and the Americans

We will save America. In God's Power

In God's Power, America will save our Legacy

On the other side, you have the globalized world powers of the Elite communists of Kamala and Biden using the immigrants as a human shield for political gain for the to-be Democrats. And other criminal reasons.

Over a million prisoners from other countries poured out of prisons into America.

This was a plan to take down America.

Many other terrible things are worsening, but they do nothing about it. Think of all the tragedies happening in their office.

Why did Democratic Elite Communist under Biden and Kamala give open borders to Geopolitical Criminals in the USA CCP, ISIS, Iran, international criminals, 60 billion to the immigrants, and 6 BILLION to the vets.

When we have all these urgencies, and these urgencies are only to name a few

1. 325,000 Children are missing in the USA. And .. 1000's in Ukraine.

---

[2] Arden Lisa Lucia, MDIV God First, America our miracle www.lisaluciaarden.com Note these chapters are articles. Hence, there will be some repeated information.;GOD first, America Our Miracle: Vote Freedom, Vote President Trump: Arden MDIV, Lisa Lucia: 9798345121887: Amazon.com: Books;www.arisetogodstruth.com; www.lisaluciaarden.com

2. The war with Russia and Ukraine under Kamala and Biden kept the war because of the making of military tools with three companies in the USA to get money for commodities from Ukraine. When Putin wanted to stop in 2022, I pleaded and pleaded and asked to trade commodities at the beginning of the war. Robert Francis Kennedy RFK stated that in Ukraine, we could have paid for all the homeless homes in the USA.

3. The initial stoppage of oil well drilling resulted in 140,000 job losses and almost doubled the number of people who did not hire other services because of their loss of income. Also, they needed help writing up the oil leases and could not fulfill them properly. Also, with the scrap oil, they could not make money? why did they not use President Trump and the teams' contracts?

4. Today, under Biden and Kamala, they printed the most American dollars in the existing time for any country. We paid the surplus checks to the citizens during CCP lockdowns. They did not need to do lockdowns.. We have the highest debt. Why would we open the borders and let immigrants in where their country has commodities to build and take care of them, and they let in more than a million prisoners? This is treason to our Constitution.

5. We owe 800 billion to China. We pay the debt through your taxes. China uses the money for the Red Army. See the military chart. China has the largest Army. [3]

6. Homeless across the USA is in the millions

7. 170,000 FORECLOSURES OF AMERICAN HOMES
   We have to negotiate with Black Rock, State Street, and Vanguard to help the American people. God has chosen them as leaders. You

---

[3] Arden, Lisa Lucia, MDIV God First, America our Miracle, Vote Freedom, Vote President Trump, Lisa Lucia Arden, MDIV. October 31, 2024

know how the president puts his or her hand on the Bible when she enters to take care of America? The president gives his or her life for the Covenant in Jesus Christ to take care of humanity and His land, America. See, Bibles were endorsed at the onset of the formation of our country in 1774 -1776.[4]

8. Inner Cities need to be restored

9. We have to work to restore our infrastructure

10. Emf dangerous to the Americans, killing American's cell health

11. Chemical Spray kills Americans cell health

12. The government now has the facts to support the mediation: Pharmaceutical companies that sold CCP vaccinations did not negotiate the mediation, only some statistics about giving Americans back. Billions and Billions of dollars were made by the Pharmaceuticals and 40 became billionaires the employees. This is the evil of monetization of using people's bodies for money.

13. Do not allow woke Transgender and LGBQT in children's schools when the children are too young to decide. Also, it is not the first substance of being.. It is not human to be transgender; it is a scientific object that is a secondary being.

14. Inner Cities need to be restored in Education across America. Illiteracy is predominant in many Democratic states and areas in our nation of a lower socio-economic area.

15. Small and Large Business need to be developed

16. Secrecy of Government Controls

17. Secrecy of Corporate Censorship

18. Secrecy of Governmental and Billionaires torture against the people

19. Highest inflation

---

20. Children's schooling has been worse since the CCP virus, and nothing has been mentioned since the Democratic President under Kamala did anything about it. The children are the future of our country. All schools were closed due to the lockdown, and no recovery plan exists.
21. Millions of people wounded in Business
22. The Democratic group, the Elite Communists, gives billions to anyone, even prisoners, except Americans and Inner Cities and Children and Veterans
23. The Chinese are buying up agricultural land, which is dangerous for controlling and quality food and land to hold in military systems.

There are many contraindications. Also, transportation of food and processes could be an undercover situation for the biowarfare food system, poisoning people and transporting military tools or apparatus. . You see the strategic plans of destruction across America and the world they have been planning.

We want to save our American Legacy. We do not want the geopolitical powers of China, Elite Communist, Democratic Elite Communist to control us.

I, LISA LUCIA ARDEN, HAVE SOLUTIONS

I have strategic plans and solutions to direct and empower America and the leaders. I have done this now as I have proven by the fact of my writings and Podcasts, speaking, and books, and social media responses. Yet, we first have to be justice and truth and in the Constitutional rights protecting the people.

Today, with God's power, we can save our legacy.

We, America, have God's power, happiness in our souls, and peace in our hearts, knowing we have done and do God's justice to save our legacy.

To bring "happiness" to all and our children and keep the quintessential beauties of our past. .and present and future.

The Trinity, the Holy Spirit, God Jesus Christ, King from heaven above, in whose image the Trinity formed, and with whom he is destined to live in eternal happiness, when we accept Jesus Christ as our Lord and Savior.

John 14:6 Jesus said: I am the Way, Truth, and Life. No one can come to the Father except through me. 7 If you know me, you will know my father too. From this moment, you know him and have seen him.

John 14: 16 I shall ask the Father, and he will give you another Paraclete (Holy Spirit) to be with you forever, 17 the Spirit of truth whom the world can never accept since it neither sees nor knows him; but you know him, because he is with you, he is in you. 18 I shall not leave you orphans; I shall come to you

From this very dignity and man's knowledge of it, Christ showed that men should love one another as brothers and children and live here as children of light. "It is indeed vain to expect a fulfillment of the duties of a Christian by one who does not even know them." We need to express this in what we do as believers. Such as what Pope Francis is supporting to feed the poor. "Nothing more acceptable to Jesus Christ, the Savior of souls, Who testifies of Himself through Isaias: "To bring good news to the poor he has sent me."[11]

We need to take back our America and the World Controls. We are responsible, and there is a Divine Command to care for all creation. However, to be faithful and true and not let those hurt or change God's truth.

Gen. 1:1-31 see Genesis:1:28-31

Genesis 1:27   God created man in the image of himself; in the image of God, he created him; male and female, he created them.

In Genesis 1:28, God blessed them, saying, 'Be fruitful, multiply, fill the earth and subdue it. Be masters of the fish of the sea, the birds of heaven, and all the living creatures that move on earth.' 29 God also said, 'Look, to you I give all the seed-bearing plants everywhere on the earth's surface, and all the trees with seed-bearing fruit; this will be your food. 30 And to all the wild animals, all the birds of heaven, and all the living creatures that creep along the ground, I give all the foliage of the plants as their food.' And so it was. 31 God saw all he had made; indeed, it was very good. Evening came, and morning came: the sixth day. Leviticus 25:1-7

Honor the Sabbath. Even today, we can celebrate Sunday via technology, and with prayer and reverence, we can accept God's blessings and the power of the miracles. Truly the Sabbath is everyday it is the Eucharistic life.

Arise to the power of God and look at all the things God has given us; all of creation is perfect and can heal and sustain itself. Daniel 4: The World Controls want to take everything from us. We have God's Power of His Divine Nature and Divine Law to restore and save our legacy.

MANY ARE LISTENING AND ACCEPTED JESUS CHRIST AS SAVIOR, KING, AND LORD

MANY HAVE TAKEN RESPONSIBILITY AND TAKING AMERICA BACK.

I HAVE NOW SEEN MANY PEOPLE ACROSS AMERICA AND THE WORLD HAVE AWAKENED AND ARISEN TO THE TRUTH OF GOD.

STOP NOW THE WORLD CONTROL

1. I have seen President Trump have a plan to save Americans in the power of God

2. I have seen many are STOPPING abortion GIVING VICTORY

3. I have seen many STOPPING what it means man and woman in the image of God's Creation GIVING VICTORY

4. I have seen many are STOPPING   CCP OWNING LAND GIVING VICTORY

5. I have seen many are STOPPING deforming the seed of food GIVING VICTORY

6. I have seen many are STOPPING WORLD HEALTH CONTROLS GIVING VICTORY

7. I have seen many are STOPPING THE DOWNFALL OF ECONOMY AND WE WILL RESTORE OUR ECONOMY GIVING VICTORY

8. I have seen many STOPPING WORLD HEALTH CONTROLS OF FLUORIDE WATER.
   I HAVE asked IN MY FIRST BOOK TO TAKE CARE OF OUR WATER OUR NEED TO GIVE TO THE WORLD NOW RFK UNDER THE PRESIDENT TEAM KEEP OCEANS CLEAN NO PLASTIC BAGS AND MICROPLASTICS CONTROL GIVING VICTORY

9. I have seen the SPIRIT OF THE PEOPLE AND LOVE OF AMERICANS take care of America's urgencies GIVING VICTORY

10. I have seen MANY, SUCH AS RFK AND PRESIDENT TRUMP TEAM, STOP vaccines. I have asked this also. People should have a choice. Also, vaccines are biological warfare..? Is it due to the deglobalization of people? They need enough statistics. In my other books, I said we need statistics and actual business, which

are pure substances. In prayer, in a Divine Command, I heard no vaccination.

11. I have seen Elon Musk guide and give his management and help in many aspects. I have given lists .. and all the leaders have the same direction. I am grateful. You can see it in my Podcasts and writings. God has answered my prayer .. to have others help us save America's legacy.

12. I have seen the miracle of America to save her legacy in God's Power.

Arise to the power of God in you, America… Today, all we need to restore the tragedies is the Divine Covenant of God's Power in Jesus Christ Salvation:

God sees the humanity that has been hurt and the greatest atrocities.

God asks let us all accept God's power and love for the salvation of all:

But we must be an example of Christ by taking back America and giving the needs to the poor that need to be (of God's life) protected and stop the World's Elite Communist and secret tables of evil.

The basic need to obtain justice is knowing it. This is in the Constitution: Poor in basic needs, we can give the bread for existence and home for happiness and life for the authentic personhood God created. The bread is the bread of life, Jesus Christ. We made the Covenant Prayer of the Continental Congress of 1774 with America, our Judeo-Christian Covenant … that brings justice, safety, and life. Some are poor monetarily, and some are poor that are rich monetarily. Both rich and poor could be poor in the soul. Poor in the heart. Poor life for many reasons. We need to be a powerful love of God's salvation, reflecting the tender light of Jesus Christ to soothe their need for life.. and take the veils off our eyes by the mystery of the Holy Spirit. Then, they will see in their eyes that God, their creator, is here and desires to redeem them. Yet, we, the believers, are filled with the light of God's wisdom and truth[5] .... Stop all injustices and World Powers by the Power of God upon the land and hearts of America and across the world the most treacherous atrocities against humanity. World control politics, against American Judeo-Christian covenant, and severely liberal beliefs are death to life and the greatest poverty of life; STOP THESE DEATHS UPON HUMANITY and life BRING NEW LIFE and BRING NEW LIFE to the authentic personhood of the people. WE HAVE GOD'S POWER AND COVENANT. God already knows how everything works in the Divine Nature and Divine Law.

Bring new life now: the environment, the life, the air, the water, the harvest, the computer systems, the relationships, the businesses, the health, the economy, the children's lives, the needy, the powerful, the innocent, the animal and biological harvest, the missions and dreams of each person, and the love relationships of upright truth in the hearts of the people.. Pray now: God knows what we need He created us.. and He wants to continue to live in you to make the most beauty of the greatest .. life in Him as the blood flows in your veins. You breathe the air, God in Jesus Christ .. wants you to let the life of His Eucharistic blood of Salvation flow through the veins of life.. and breathe the Messianic air of the Spirit to live a supernatural life in God's power yet; with grace and mercy enough to bring the light of God on earth in you .. and to give pouring flowing in the Holy Spirit in the Trinity to those who receive and those who accept the mustard seeds of the miracle of Jesus Christ Salvation. I have songs about the mustard seed can move a mountain. Just think when will all participate we will be able to move mountains to build justice.

Isaiah 12:2 Look, he is the God of my salvation: I shall have faith and not be afraid, for Yahweh is my strength and my song, he has been my salvation.'

---

[5] Arden, Lisa, Lucia, MDIV, God First, America our Miracle Vote Freedom Vote President Trump The United States of America, Publisher Lisa Lucia Arden, October 2024

We need first to find truth in Jesus Christ in the Trinity.

CHAPTER ONE

Karl Jasper Discussion

Discussion on the Way of Wisdom

Discussion 2009 -2010 I want to show you, readers, Americans, and the world God's work. He has been asking America… for years to proclaim and live in His, Jesus Christ's Salvation and His Truth.

Karl Jaspers (born Feb. 23, 1883, Oldenburg, Ger.—died Feb. 26, 1969, Basel, Switz.) was a German philosopher, one of the essential Existentialists in Germany, who approached the subject of man's direct concern with his existence. In his later work, as a reaction to the disruptions of Nazi rule in Germany and World War II, he searched for a new unity of thinking that he called world philosophy.[6]

We are responsible for keeping America Free and proclaiming the Salvation of Jesus Christ.

Communication is the primary aim of philosophy. Jaspers calls such ultimate situations "boundary situations" (*Grenzsituationen*). These ultimate situations, such as death, suffering, guilt, wonder, and doubt, are situations that we cannot avoid or change. We may try to avoid these

---

[6] Jaspers, Karl , https://www.britannica.com/biography/Karl-Jaspers; Way to Wisdom, https://ia800200.us.archive.org/3/items/waytowisdomintro00jasp/waytowisdomintro0 0jasp.pdf

situations in everyday life. Still, if we confront them in God's life,[7] we become truly aware of ourselves as human beings, and we become ourselves by changing our consciousness of being. The Hitlerian government controlled the Germans through threat of death. Otherwise, they would be killed. This is reflective of what they want to do today for world control; they want the death of the freedom of Americans. Today, we have a chance to communicate with justice. When we vote for freedom, vote for Americans First and President Trump.

We will not be "nothingness and acquiesced." We have to communicate that we see the issues the Communist Elite under Kamala and Biden have done and the world powers. Now we have solutions and we have justice we know the way. Ask God about your purpose in restoring America now. Yes, leadership is paramount in justice.

Democratic Elite Communist:

They did not know how to deal with it because they were controlled. The Germans had no choice; the government was in total control.

Today, we have a chance to save our America. Because "God's Power," in the Covenant, gives us power and miracles to save our legacy. Jasper wants us to recognize that there is a boundary situation the Hitlerian controls (World power and political ideologies) put up boundaries beyond human safety and integrity and justice. Also, the Hitlerian controls (world powers and political ideologies) put up a boundary not what they thought was owned by them to do a holocaust of the humanity, the Jewish people. An ethnic cleansing of the Hitlerian evil.

LET US NOW BRING THE LOVE OF GOD TO BRING A MIRACLE TO STOP Killing creation a neighbor in all parts of the world. LET US NOW PROCLAIM THE LORD'S SALVATION AND BRING THE authentic personhood in God, the most incredible beauty. LISTEN,

---

[7] Arden, Lisa Lucia, MDIV God First, America our Miracle. Published October 31, 2024

LOOK, SEE THE TRUTH.. We know that the Hitlerian controls (World power and political ideologies) are deceitful. There was no communication with the Hitlerian World powers just accepted one view. (Hitlerian) Thus, for Jaspers, the source of philosophy is found in "boundary situations" such as death, uncertainty, wonder, and doubt. However, these situations also require us to communicate with each other. Thus, for me, the ultimate source of communication of Wisdom and Justice and Love the "precepts," ethics in God, His Old Covenant in the Ten Commandments, and the New Covenant in Jesus Christ, the Holy Scriptures became flesh of our American Judeo-Christian nation in the Covenant of God of our Constitutional Rights and Declaration of Independence is the will to authentic communication. Communication is Jasper's principal aim in philosophy. And communication for me is the, how is your communication? Is it wise and faithful and loving to do the mission? Is there reconciliation?

We today cannot deny that ….. there are World Controls

God's Power can overcome all things. God loves all humanity.

In Jesus Christ's power in the Trinity, we can have Salvation.

Even with problems. in our world, we can live in God's life of the most incredible beauty and create the most astonishing beauty in the Spirit of God in us and the gifts He gives us

We, as Americans, are responsible for taking our country back NOW.

YOU HAVE THE POWER OF THE RIGHT ARM OF GOD STRENGTH AMERICA.

WE ALSO HAVE A COVENANT THAT GOD WILL PROTECT US WHEN WE SEEK HIM FIRST IN RIGHTEOUSNESS.

"And we have seen and testify that the Father has sent the Son as Savior of the world" (1 John 4:14). As Savior, Jesus is the only One Who can save us! Deliverer: "Him God has exalted to His right hand to be Prince and Savior, to give repentance to Israel and forgiveness of sins" (Acts 5:31).

I have been called for years to prepare America for the future. In 2011 and before, I wrote about the warnings of One World Controls.

Warning that we could not lose our freedoms to the Communistic World powers and Secret highest tables of evil.

Our Need To Give to the World, Heal America Love in God 2016

Arise to God's Truth, Restore and Keep America's Freedom 2020

THE WAR IS BETWEEN GOD AND EVIL

GOD'S POWER IN US WILL SAVE AMERICA

WE NEED TO SAVE THE SOULS OF THE PEOPLE AND OUR LEGACY AND AMERICA

ABORTION IS MUCH OF THE CAUSE OF THE BREAKING DOWN OF AMERICA

WE HAVE A COVENANT

We are not a pagan nation. We are a Judeo-Christian Nation that initially had a Covenant with Jesus Christ—the Prayer of the Continental Congress of 1774, the Constitution, and the Declaration of Independence.

Before 2016, I was told in a prayer that God chose President Trump to be President, and I need to promote him and keep America's freedom and restoration.

I wrote this in before warning: ..

Democratic Party Elite Communistic Obama, Biden, Kamala America they want to destroy controlled by the higher elite world powers and the secrecy of the highest evil tables. Also, the United Nations wants Agenda

21 under Obama, Bush, Clinton, Biden, and Kamala.. Taking away ownership and control by the World Health Controls and World Economic Forum. Under Biden and Kamala. Also, the CCP virus was made to kill off the people and the CCP vaccinations.

Under .. Kamala and Biden, the weather disaster destroyed North Carolina, Tennessee, and Florida. Chemical Spraying and EMFs affect the brain.

CULTURE AND RELIGION TRYING TO BREAK DOWN THE JUDEO-CHRISTIAN NATION WITH LIBERAL AND COMMUNISTIC CONTROLS : - CCP VIRUS AND CCP VACCINATION TO KILL THE PEOPLE

UNDER KAMAL & BIDEN, ALL THESE HAPPENED IN 4 YEARS.

KAMALA OPEN BORDERS USES IMMIGRANTS AS A POLITICAL IDEOLOGY TO CONTROL THE VOTE FOR THE FUTURE AND TAKE AWAY THE LIVES OF AMERICANS. SAFETY HAS BEEN DESTROYED UNDER KAMALA OPEN BORDERS. ELON MUSK ALSO HAS STATED THIS.[8]

GEOPOLITICAL POWERS NOW IN THE WORLD WE HAVE TO PROTECT OUR BORDERS

I diligently sent social media, wrote books and articles, spoke, and Podcasts and art… to many people. For years, I believed, and NOW they listened to America's Restoration EMERGENCIES and Solutions …I ask to get Elon Musk and all Democrats to come on the Republican's side to save America. I have given a list of necessary urgencies I have developed and prayed for... As we can see, RFK also speaks of all the health problems and Elon on the most urgent issues. Beautiful, brilliant fighters Tulsi, J.D, Vance, Vivek, Tucker, Rogan, Bongino, Guilian, and many others and

---

[8] Musk, Elon, X Social Media, interviewed by Tucker Carlson 2024

Americans. I have been asking and promoting for years. And now we have a miracle.

You can see my PODCAST at www.arisetogodstruth.com

GOD IS MORE POWERFUL IN YOU AMERICANS. WE HAVE VICTORY GOD THE PRIME MOVER

WORLD POWERS UNDER KAMALA AND DEMOCRATIC ELITES being and nothingness

We Americans need to RESTORE AMERICA AND PROCLAIM AND LIVE IN GOD'S COVENANT AND MIRACLES WE WILL HAVE.

Why should we make choices responsibly? As you can see, we are responsible. God's Love can overcome all things. God loves all humanity.

In Jesus Christ's power in the Trinity, we can have Salvation

Even with problems. in our world, we can live in God's life of the most remarkable beauty and create the most extraordinary beauty in the Spirit of God in us and the gifts He gives us

We, as Americans, are responsible for taking our country back NOW.

YOU HAVE THE POWER OF THE RIGHT ARM OF GOD STRENGTH AMERICA.

WE ALSO HAVE A COVENANT THAT GOD WILL PROTECT US WHEN WE SEEK HIM FIRST IN RIGHTEOUSNESS.

Prayer of the Continental Congress 1774

"And we have seen and testify that the Father has sent the Son as Savior of the world" (1 John 4:14). As Savior, Jesus is the only One Who can save us! Deliverer: "Him God has exalted to His right hand to be Prince and Savior, to give repentance to Israel and forgiveness of sins" (Acts 5:31).

I have been called for years to prepare America for the future. In 2011 and before, I wrote about the warnings of One World Controls.

GOD IS MORE POWERFUL IN YOU, AMERICANS WE HAVE VICTORY

We are responsible for voting for leaders who put the Americans first in the closest ways of the Judeo-Christian nation. We, the people, are responsible for protecting, securing, and restoring our American Judeo-Christian nation, given to us in 1776 in the New Covenant of the Prayer of Continental Congress of 1774, the Constitution, and the Declaration of Independence.[9]

New Covenant with God and America of the Prayer of Continental Congress of 1774

Also, President George Washington commanded his military to the righteousness of God.

Be Thou present, O God of wisdom, and direct the councils of this honorable assembly; enable them to settle things on the best and surest foundation. The scene of blood may be speedily closed; that order, harmony, and peace may be effectually restored, and truth and justice, religion and piety, prevail and flourish amongst the people. Preserve the health of their bodies and vigor of their minds; shower down on them, and the millions they here represent such temporal blessings as Thou sees suitable for them in this world, crowning them with everlasting glory in the world to come. We ask for all this in the name and through the merits of Jesus Christ, Thy Son, and our Savior.

---

[9] Arden, Lisa, Lucia, MDIV God First, America our Miracle. Published Lisa Lucia Arden, MDIV October 31, 2024.; www.lisaluciaarden.com; Prayer of the Continental Congress, 1774 https://chaplain.house.gov/archive/continental.html; The Constitution, https://constitutioncenter.org/the-constitution; The Declaration of Independence, https://www.britannica.com/topic/Declaration-of-Independence.

The Constitution of the United States of America

We, the People of the United States, to form a perfect Union, establish Justice, ensure domestic Tranquility, provide for the common defense, promote the general Welfare, and secure the Blessings of Liberty to ourselves and our Posterity, do ordain and establish this Constitution for the United States of America.

The Declaration of Independence:

When, in the course of human events, it becomes necessary for one people to dissolve the political bands that have connected them with another and to assume, among the powers of the earth, the separate and equal station to which the laws of nature and nature's God entitle them, a decent respect to the opinions of humanity requires that they should declare the causes which impel them to the separation.

We hold these truths to be self-evident: that all men are created equal, that they endow them with certain unalienable rights, and that among these are life, liberty, and the pursuit of happiness. . . to secure these rights, governments are instituted among men, deriving their just powers from the consent of the governed. That, whenever any form of government becomes destructive of these ends, it is the right of the people to alter or to abolish it and to institute new government, laying its foundation on such principles and organizing its powers in such form as to them shall seem most likely to affect their safety and happiness.

Do we, the people, have these rights? God gave us these rights at creation: We have been given the fullness of all the beauty of the Most Highest God so that we can live in the fullness of His love.

We have a responsibility to speak up as Christians as human beings to protect our brothers and sisters of humanity. We should have chosen this: "being" and "responsibility" instead of nothingness. This "being" is justice. Jaspers argues that the concept of human freedom without God, in which the will to make free choices is perceived as independent of God, is a concept of nothingness. If we acknowledge that we depend on God for our being and accept responsibility for making our own free choices, then our awareness of our freedom becomes an awareness of God.

We have freedom when we have God.

John 3:36 So if the Son sets you free, you will indeed be free. 37 I know that you are descended from Abraham. (See, it is God humanity of the 12 Tribes of Abraham is all humanity… His beautiful humanity is the most remarkable creation. He is calling for their Salvation)

(Jesus states): but you want to kill me (World Controls and Political Ideologies of Communistic Controls) because my word finds no place in you. 38 What I speak of is what I have seen at my Father's side, and you, too, put into action the lessons you have learned from your father.

Galatians 5:1 Christ set us free so that we should remain free. Stand firm, then, and do not let yourselves be fastened again to the yoke of slavery.

Many have "broken" the yoke of slavery, Worldly Controls, Communistic political ideologies, and the sin of death.. .. By proclaiming in the actions in their lives the greatest love of the God Most Highest in Jesus Christ. There are trials yet God in you is more powerful than the world. His grace will be sufficient.

Exodus 20:1 Then God spoke all these words. He said, 2 'I am Yahweh, your God who brought you out of Egypt, where you lived as enslaved people.

Exodus 20:3 'You shall have no other gods to rival me.'

'Master, which is the greatest commandment of the Law?' 37 Jesus told him, 'You must love the Lord your God with all your heart, soul, and mind. 38 This is the greatest and the first commandment. 39 The second resembles it: You must love your neighbor as yourself. 40 On these two commandments hang the whole Law and the Prophets.

Divine Message May 11, 2023

Questions on Water Dams and Toxin Pungent of Dairy Farms

San Francisco, California

PROTECT OUR NATION, PEOPLE, FIRST

PROTECT OUR PEOPLE FROM TOXINS

We need to ask ourselves whether other urgencies in society are tragic events that happen to communities and their people. These must be addressed wisely and justly, prioritizing the American people and their health, welfare, and living space.

Questions on Water Dams and Toxin Pungent Dairy Farms, California Exile Human treachery, and Tragic present happenings to control humans and Life.

San Francisco, Ontario, Los Ángeles, California

1. While traveling to San Francisco, my beautiful California, upon our lands of the kiss of God's Blessings, I encountered these urgencies: lands of many, and many agriculture plants and trees died, and cows in an environment that could cause cacogenic diseases to humans and animals. I was devastated to see these urgencies. While driving to gorgeous San Francisco, I saw these signs saying, *"Give us our water, Newsom."*

The paramount urgency to save our crops, farms, and agriculture is to take this action:

Dams should be built so that farmers can water their crops as needed. We can bring this to fruition and help the farmers move their produce.

I found this excellent write-up... about the dams.

"All these efforts rely upon storing water in reservoirs to meet environmental requirements. And all will struggle to adapt to rapidly changing conditions as the climate warms and droughts intensify. Reserving storage space and reservoir inflow for the environment is better than traditional regulatory approaches. And we recognize that this approach is novel — even risky —but must take some risks to manage growing threats to the health of our rivers and estuaries, the tidal mouth of a large river, where the tide meets the stream."[10]:

2. Nothing has been done to the many dead agricultural trees and plants; they are sitting there, the land is wasted, and the legacy of California farming is not protected. Let us protect the agricultural land. I never saw that.

3. **They were uprooted and still there, all dried up and dead. Moreover, no CCP owned land or Chinese. The CCP threatened to kill Chinese owned company to control them. And they could poison agriculture and use tools and transportation for warfare.**

Do not let the legacy in America be uprooted.

Exile of California

Uprooted that word gives me fear, eeriness, scary of what has happened to California, in almost every area of existence, from education and high taxes to the exile of many California, many to go for generations of life and families-built California; yet, it has been taken by many secret powerful Communistic Elite directing others in control whether they realize it or not. Terrible atrocities are the control in the social system of people, and children are ignorant and injustice; the people hired are not seasoned enough to understand the culture and justice to care for children and their families and people. Today, there needs to be ambassadors to

---

[10] https://calmatters.org/commentary/2022/08/newsoms-water-strategy-needs-to-go-a-step-further, dams

assess these systems. There is multiculturism, woke, liberalism, globalization, and even crime to control and, even without intention, make incorrect directions to our citizens.

Pharmaceuticals and Social Services

The pharmaceuticals given by professionals and social services are contingent on one another and need to be reassessed and have the natural formation of alternative methods for mental health. And also the development of the psyche and human, authentic beings. I have written about this subject and its solutions.

You should ask if they treat us with pharmaceuticals that are not excellent for our health; what do you think they would do with mental health? I have spoken to many about their experiences in mental health facilities, and it has been life-threatening and dysfunctional for healing.

Where are all the children using them for monetization?

Children at the Borders

Three hundred twenty-five thousand children are missing at the borders?

Whoever supports these vast, lucrative businesses directs it to reflect questions, and blatant crime is no question.

https://christianheritagefellowship.com/wp-content/uploads/David-Brewer.jpg?tmp=1

People know where all these children are, but they need to speak up and come to a reconciliation.

Children

We have a Divine Command to give children the freedom to be the authentic people they were created and work toward holiness, purity, and creation.

There is a Divine Command that billionaire women are supposed to help with the children.

Also, technology, systems, and entertainment need to be focused on for children's psyches to be formed into the authentic person they are created to be. Pure, holy, and developed critical thinking creation will form when the environment is pure enough. The computer systems should be minimized. There have been various discussions on children in my books.

Technology stop controls

Stop using technology to control people's minds and economic positions.

A.   Corporate Censorship

Watching the consumer and people's every action and seeking control by technology

Middle Class resurrect.

B.   Economic holocaust of the Middle Class and the people targeted that are freedom fighters. Today, the middle class has become part of the lower socio-economic levels. We need to revive America. They have used their saving because of the CCP virus and lockdowns. There is terrible inflation.. and many have lost their homes. Ask again. Why would they let all the immigrants in without negotiating funding for the immigrant countries to have commodities? There is an entire team of Democrats in power, so why was this decision made? I am asking with radiant purpose to bring the solution.

World Health has a Board of Conservative Professionals on Ethics in Governmental Decision Quality Control Ethics.

C.   Stop control of people in every way. World health needs to be conservative scientists with Judeo-Christian beliefs and parents, priests, rabbis, ministers, and practical business people who put America first, putting the people first on the World Health Association and World

Economic Forum. And if they do not agree to .. this, they need a quality control ethics person

Banking Currency and Crypto Make Bitcoin Bonds to Fix the Infrastructure and for Goods.

D.   Banking and currency forms to control all funds bring fairness to the people. I have asked not to use digital currency only. Also, to help us, since the dollar is worth much less, we can make bonds of Bitcoin. Also, Bitcoin is a trading currency for goods. Taxes also should not be increased on investments. Biden wanted to do that.

E.   We need to protect our systems in our economy. We know what to do for the people to get the vote. In 2024, President Trump won.

Today, we must remember what has happened. We need to redeem and restore all these urgencies of world control.

1. Elite Communistic Democratic Socialistic ideas conspiracy on President Trump and the Freedom Fighters.
2. CCP Virus to bring holocaust to the people.
3. Inside job in USA Fauci and Communistic Elite making the CCP Virus
4. Lockdowns and mandatory vaccinations.
5. Afghanistan's departure of failure and death of life and legacy
6. The Ukraine and Russian war was the most treacherous holocaust in technological times, and then the CCP virus.
7. Destroying the economy of the USA without using our resources appropriately.
8. Holding the money for the CCP virus that is supposed to be used by the people. Is that true?
9. Not supporting the middle class, many had to sell homes to live and then had to rent a property back.

10. Allowing crimes in the Democratic Elite Communistic in the government and more giant corporations without bringing them to federal and state courts and or removing them from office

Information about the Elite Communist

11. URGENT There is a formal group of four offices of Elite Communistic that are secret and control and direct our countries and peoples in every facet. The other two offices below these four private Elite Communist groups work to control all areas of life. These people may see death in many ways since this is the history of the time of judgment and retribution and even the truth of God's intentions. Those must decide what side they want, death and injustice or life and justice.

Transgenderism and Science

12. We need to stop supporting transgenderism against human life. Science will take advantage of the study of the human body—the same analogy to the abortion issue. Science uses babies for scientific research and to extend the longevity of the Elite Wealthy. This is why they make abortion an accessible platform for children and women to abort. We are the 3rd greatest country with the most abortions in the world after Russia second and China first. We are a Judeo-Christian nation. Thou shall not kill. We need a platform to build a better health plan for relations to have commitments and commitments never to abort and safely protected intercourse agreement never to abort a child.

13. This is only a beginning list of urgencies that need to be brought to justice with the most significant force ever in American history. We must save our legacy, freedom, present, future, children, and life in America.

Boarders by Treacherous Crime Against the American People Stop Drug Kitchens and selling humans for services.

14. The borders in California need to be protected. We are in a time of human history where many world powers will control a treacherous war on drugs, destroying American people using drugs, fear, fraudulent business, poison pharmaceuticals, ISIS entering, nuclear war tools, war tools, plans of conspiracy, and crimes. Making small drug kitchens in Texas and every state and selling people for services on the internet. Stop this…

Geopolitical Powers all safety immediately needs new strategies

15. <u>**It is a geopolitical world of powers. All safety protocols are different in every walk and way of life. New paradigms of the truth of strategic protection are necessary immediately.**</u>

Geopolitical powers will use every walk and way of life in our

America to deteriorate and destroy her beauty and justice. We have proven this.

16. Governmental spending on the protection of American's safety, life, self-sufficiency for individual's health, vocation, and freedoms to make choices of health vaccinations and education, protecting children from poverty and death and inappropriate dangers of wokeness and liberal ideologies, business self-sufficiency manufacturing and small business, children's education of basic, reading, writing, creating new ideas in always ethical delivery.

Black Life Matters and Protestors Paid to Destroy the Peace.

17. Using undercover secrecy of Communist and Black life matter fakes that are indeed paid to start division by Elite Communist power. It is known that the leaders of Black Lives Matter used the

people as a human shield to propagate their political ideology of deformity. They are set up in their million-dollar homes (Candis showed this in her videos) while they hire others to destroy business and governmental property. There needs to be new laws. Is Soros involved?

Soros has purchased many radio stations. Donated much money also to the liberals

18. WE need to becareful and rebuttal back with a new radio station because a portion of people listen to the radio while in the auto… I noticed an

19.Orpha was paid One million to interview Kamala.

Is that correct? She was paid a million dollars to interview Kamala. Is this protocol? Is this standard? Is that much money for that? Republicans told me.

Immigrant Leaders and billionaires use immigrants as a shield for monetization.

20. Allowing other country leaders of different countries to use their funds for their desire and then send their people to America and other parts of the world to seek to destroy us with their criminals and overwhelming responsibility, and many of these governmental billionaires are warlord mafia. Also, there are nine international criminal groups and billionaire secret and blatant companies that use their people and people internationally to traffic horrendous crimes against humanity and even death and other abusive, deformed atrocities.

Immigrants, let us build businesses together with the immigrants to solve the immigration catastrophe. ....

21. Let us work with these immigrant countries to build businesses and manufacturing jobs in their countries to give self-sufficiency to their citizens.

22. Please pray for America and humanity for protection, redemption, and justice

Health Questions Dairy cows:

Health is paramount in our nation; this was a past. The dairy cows' environment has a pungent smell and spraying. It must be removed from the present agricultural place, dangerously pungent with the scent. There is a disease they are carrying.. in the toxin. I noticed by the cow's movement, demeanor, and posture, and even the air seemed foggy and discolored .. .. and the sense that this is toxic for the cows and their physical bodies. Ingest the food. The mist in the air lets off a poisonous smell that goes into the bloodstream constantly.   We know there are pharmaceuticals they give the animals.

See, I want to ask you if we... are constantly exposed to the toxic smell of urine and feces that has not been moved and stays in the same place, we would become nauseated.

And even dizziness and sickness, and even weakness.

Ask why the pungent smell does not move and mix with the air. This is a serious .. issue.

It needs to be corrected now. This means the components and toxic compounds in the air are heavy and do not disperse and stay in a particular space, even if the unwholesome is a smaller capacity than the air that extends more miles than the miles or measurements of the dairy farm. I need to assess these variables belonging to Aristotle's Categories with an intricate, keen, sharp eye and contemplation of results and facts.

Spraying for Cow Smell Stop

Note that Chemical Spraying and Chemical Trails are even worse.. we need to stop this now. Anything the people breathe in that is toxic could affect their health and even an unborn child.

Since you are more acquainted with cows, it is more in our everyday life for you to see the scenario. It is difficult for people to realize the chemical spray.. when we do not see it. .they hide it from us to kill us. I have smelled chemicals in the air and seen the clouds' formations. I know that sometimes they are drones forming with the clouds. Some believe there are no chemical sprays; I'm afraid I have to disagree.

I saw this same problem in Arizona. The hotel was near a dairy farm, and they said they sprayed twice daily to remove the pungent smell…. People smelled the spray toxin, and I did, and I got dizzy and impaired my breathing.

Hence, because of the following life-threatening contraindications present and future for humanity, animals, and the environment, we should rapidly address this.

a.   Test the air for toxic substances from the urine and feces, and, of course, test the air at different times when they spray. Also, test distances and other creatures, foods, and people positions exposed to the toxins.. and a timeline

b.   STOP Toxins the cows breathe in from the urine and feces toxins for spraying they.. breathe in and pass through the blood flow.. and because the toxins are in a heavier density, they may stay in the molecular field and cause chronic air pollution of toxicants of the area sprayed regularly

c.   STOP Toxins the people get when they use dairy or meat products

d.   STOP Toxins the people breathe in from the dairy farms if they live near there

e.   STOP Toxins the people breathe in from the spray

f.   STOP Toxins the pregnant animals have in the system that may pass to the calf

g.   STOP Toxins the pregnant woman may breathe in and may pass to the baby

h.   STOP Toxins the pregnant woman may get when ingesting foods that are from these animals in invested fumes

Remember, all people are vulnerable, and their children and lands can also be exposed to the toxins they spray to keep the smell of the dairy cows down. This is also relative to agriculture spraying to keep off disease on the plants and soil. Also, we need to assess the fertilizers we use. Ask what about the workers. They will breathe in these toxins, as will all nearby people.

Moreover, we will discuss in the following paragraphs that the chemicals may not disperse in the air and stay in the area where they were sprayed, building up dangerous toxins in a mass, a capacity that could cause diseases and a carcinogenic atmosphere.

Let me interject that helicopter helicopters and small planes are spraying in other cities and areas. There are findings that spray is used as a toxic substance and is dangerous for humans.

Protect the Agriculture

While driving in the lovely land of California, I saw the perfectly manicured agriculture. I have been called to visit areas in the United States of America and the world to see, assess, and research and then determine how we can help and strategically plan action and do the movement for the betterment of humanity. However, in some regions, there is a chemical smell. And my throat became tightened and my chest heavy. This is likeness to the chemicals that stay in the air and do not immerse themselves in the vast atmosphere. They are too heavy to disperse and remain in the air near.. the area where they were sprayed. Over time, these chemicals could stay in the capacity of the air near the crops. I did not see any product spraying while driving; hence, it can be deduced that the chemicals they use for the crops stay in the air near the crops and influence human health and even animals and other crops not designated for spraying that intended area.

Do not allow Elite Powerful to purchase agriculture and animal products. They would change the process and substance to synthetic, making it toxic and changing the form of vegetables and animal products. Moreover, they could control the prices. These statements are facts, findings, and urgencies that need to be brought to the forefront of Americans' everyday lives to save America and her people now and in the future. As believers in God, we are responsible for being just and truthful.

Divine Message: On August 14, 2024, before I warned about biowarfare starting in 2018- 2019, and in the present 2024,

I am experiencing scientific testing on the body of hand-held and placed drones and machinery in the United States, as well as chemical sprays and possibly poisons. This needs to stop now. There will be restitution from God.

There is evidence of the biowarfare.

The leaders of the CCP affiliate took it over. 15-20 million was paid to the California Institute of Technology. These Colleges and others need to be assessed as stated.

I have prayed, and we need to find these companies who do this.. and also those who do chemical spray in the skies.. and destroy them.

March 12, 2019

Divine Message for the people of America

<u>**St. Bede the Venerable Catholic Church**</u>

La Canada, California

God has a gift for the people; this gift is that He stated for each to plant a "fruit tree because" this is a symbol of the fruit that we now are being blessed with because, under the leadership of President Trump and his team, we have had much fruit. We have been an instrument to save America with the commands that God has ordered President Trump, and the team has .. America.. has .. brought fruit to our country and or .. .. states, our communities, our people, our children, and each one that seeks to see the goodness of what it is to be American and respect America and its justice system.

God told us also ..to put food on our shelves.. …The shelves should be filled with food, knowing that the fruit will bring a harvest and restoration to America because of justice and work, brilliance and strategy, and dedication to upholding America. Because those whom He gave gifts of justice and righteousness have worked for wholeheartedly in the government and the people, the face of America should be children being held by the parent, the children being guided by the adult by hand. Then, children were sat down and given the BOOK OF THE BIBLE AND a book on the history of our great country. Children were allowed to live, grow, be creative, and learn aesthetic and scientific development STUDIES.

St. Bedes Church in La Canada Flintridge, I had a vision where I saw the children carrying small books with them. The children must have a book that contains biblical prayers and bible verses. They should have it with them when they go to school, and it is referenced in different classes. The phone is a personal item that most kids have today, and they use it for their daily needs. They must carry a small book with rules, regulations, and ethics about the Judeo-Christian Catholic teachings. There is a foundation, and then they will be addressed in each subject matter that can be referred to answering questions of the truth of our country's sense. Communities have become globalized and understood by different aspects of all nations, cultures, and ideologies. The children do not know what is correct for GLOBALIZATION and MULTICULTURAL ADULT LIBERAL IDEAS AND WOKE IDEAS questions and answers. Children do not have the critical ideas and thought processes to ask all the questions. Moreover, their characteristics and personalities have not developed you. See what we put in our children's environment and teach them what they will become. They needed and need to be protected.

This is why we have so much division in the country because of the leaders of the Democratic Elite Communist and the World Controls, proven by the fact of all the urgencies and .. tragic happenings. Also, the history of America should be required and discussed, as well as all the beautiful and extraordinary achievements that our country has achieved. It should be remembered and used to inspire the students regularly each year. Whether it is a Christian Catholic School or a Public School, the people in history should be recognized, understood, and developed, hooking on to their pure ideas and uplifting and developing them. When they are pure ideas, they bring forth four foundational truths: Peace, Justice, Reconciliation, and Forward Building in Love. In my book Arise To God's Truth, Restore and Keep America's Freedom.[11]

For public schools, this can help children realize a foundation of ethics on how to treat each other. [Of course, the "small book" they carry should have the foundations of ethics and proven intentional well-being. There should be a series, I will write them.] In this prayer of the Divine Message, I can recall the Spirit of the Lord telling me the book's foundations are on the four foundational truths: Peace, truth, Transformational healing, and Forward Building in Love.

Justice

---

[11] https://www.amazon.com/-/es/Ms-Lisa-Lucia-Arden/dp/0578816113, Arise to God's Truth, Restore and Keep America's Freedom

Peace
Restoration
Forward building .. in Love

In seeking the Four Foundational Truths:

They will build something that needs to be achieved using the pure substance of the idea of the first things with the technological times. However, we know that .. all things that are created to be good and withheld in society to be built in the wholeness in society that keeps the American dream is to take the tools of humanity attributes is vision, hope, faith, hard work, unity, reconciliation, and always working forward to justice, and never giving up, one aspect cannot be without the other; they are essential to work integrating .. asking does what I do, create, make, teach, work for, and live for all these aspects. Humanity needs to be kept in line with the first substance of truth, young yet ancient, contemplative yet fast as the speed of light, renewed yet forward, restored yet building. .. …

St. Andrews Church Pasadena, California

Virgin Mary... broad shoulder... she said, "Daughter, look at my shoulders. I did, and I saw this: " Her shoulders were wide and complete as excellent. While I looked at her shoulders, I saw this: carrying many, carrying many, and carrying all. She carries America upon and within her arms, and Mary carries America in your soul and heart. Mary has guided the son of God to truth, and she can guide America to truth. Seek her and ask her how to live. She also said God has given you great shoulders to bring the message of victory.

In Prayers I have been told and shown the solutions. .to give solutions for America and Nations to help humanity in God's justice and to proclaim His Salvation.

Also, guidance, direction, and empowerment of others for the solutions in their lives in Jesus Christ and to proclaim Salvation to Jesus Christ.

41

CHAPTER TWO

Political Urgencies

March 17, 2024

Brief Notes on Political Urgencies

I will be your professor, the Lord stated. Psalm 91

Psalms 91:1   You who live in the secret place of Elyon, spend your nights in the shelter of Shaddai, 2 saying to Yahweh, 'My refuge, my fortress, my God in whom I trust!'

Aristotle Politics

Politics 1 III. 11-13 pg.38- 41

"In Politics, Aristotle focuses on an aspect of practical wisdom which

is much less prominent in Nicomachean Ethics. The difference is instructive.

In Politics, Aristotle focuses on what we might call the universalist

side of practical wisdom, on its role in designing constitutions

23. See 1 309'14-26, 1 3 09h18-35, 1 3 1 0'2-12, 1 3 1 5•40-hl . and developing universal laws appropriate to them or to existing ones. He claims the laws should be as complete and detailed as possible and leave as little to "as unreliable a standard as human.

Wish" (1 272bS-7).25 In the Nicomachean Ethics, conversely, the particularist side of practical wisdom is more in focus."[12]

Please see the book written before this one, embarking on the continuous Mission to save America, our Judeo-Christian Nation.[13]

My Response:

See in deep prayer of contemplation and listening and logic of experience and study.. what America… needs today.. is ethics and justice and truth, and God's love in the people.. with a blessing of forgiveness of each other, is paramount. It is logical because ethics is truth. Ethics are the Ten Commandments. Our Constitution is based on the 10 Commandments. The Declaration of Independence declares the highest justice, echoing the Holy Scriptures. Yet, forgiveness is not allowing the abuse or injustices or treachery to carryon .. IT NEEDS TO BE STOPPED. Otherwise they even try to use the innocent, ask discussed.

America, we NEED TO STOP THE DEMOCRATIC COMMUNIST ELITE AND WORLD CONTROLS IN the USA.

America, we have a Responsibility

America, we have God-given Rights to have Justice and Liberty for all

America, we need to save our Legacy

America, we need to save our children's future

Ethics

Ethics are the truth and actions that allow whatever is being addressed to be placed in a position of the most incredible justice and life without

[12] Reeves, C.D.C, Aristotle Politics Translated, with Introduction and Notes, Published by Hackett Publishing Company

[13] Arden, Lisa, Lucia, MDIV God First, America our Miracle, Published Lisa Lucia Arden, October 31, 2024

boundaries of life. They express proof and truth that it brings life and restoration for the present, past, and future and proves that it is best on all sides. God's truth of Divine Nature brings God's love to the people. Did you know there is a Covenant between Americans and God? shown.

Did you know ethics is safety? Safety is the highest justice and the highest truth. Ethics are actions in preparation to eliminate .. dangers, less-than-life actions, and injustices and to have the fullness in life of a conservative beauty that makes beauty

The Prayer of the Continental Congress, 1774, the Constitution, the Declaration of Independence, and laws are also included.

"Here, the emphasis is on deciding what it is best to do in a particular case in which laws give, at best, fairly minimal guidance. We are forcefully reminded, therefore, of the limited utility of laws and principles: "Questions about actions and expediency, like questions about health, have no fixed answers. And when our universal account is like that, the account of particular cases is all the more inexact" (1 1 04'3-7; also 1 094b 14-22, Rh. 1 374' 1 8 -b23).

24. 1324h22-1325'14 i s particularly worth reading i n this regard."

The explanation of this difference of focus is plain enough: private individuals within a city-state are given by the constitution itself the laws that must guide their decisions; they do not have to devise them for themselves. Therefore, the primary task they face is determining what to do in these circumstances, considering the laws. The statesman, by contrast, is charged with the business of developing laws in the first place or of modifying existing ones. Hence, the universalist side of his wisdom comes to the forefront.

However, even politicians will often have to be particularists to deal effectively with problems that outstrip the letter of the law. In any case, if we are to understand practical wisdom or statesmanship correctly, we need to see both sides and study both Ethics and Politics.26 Introduction xliii

I opened this page …. Of " The Art of Exchange."

My response:

See "Exchange on these lines, therefore, is not contrary to nature, nor is it any branch of the art of wealth-getting, for it existed to replenish the natural self-sufficiency.(pg.14)"

See, self-sufficiency is "the nature" of life. Anything less is not empowering the people.

Bartering "existed for the replenishment of natural self-sufficiency."

This is why.

1. We need to empower the people and not control and return them properly for the work they do. In the 1970s, they did not increase the wages of the regular classes, and inflation went up. What their daily wage did not pay enough for their daily expenses. Hence, they needed to use credit cards, and the 1 and 3 percent kept all the funds of the GPD … This has happened today with the transfer of wealth from the middle class to the rich. When we empower the people we can . restore and resurrection the economy for more to live a more wholesome thriving life.
2. We need to realize that the barters of things have specific ways of using the "natural order of things.. because men had more than enough of some things and less than enough of others. …"
3. We need to realize that all things do not have limitations; yet, they have specific peculiar usages, one specifically uses and others not specifically usages.
4. See, this is why ethics are paramount. Even Aristotle speaks of "health. " What is ethical? We know the law they tried to make

mandatory would not and would not and will not be justice and suffice to fulfill justice and the truth for humanity.

5. To have ethics, you need truth; to have the highest truth, you need wisdom. To have wisdom, you need to have those 10 Commandments in your seeking working order, which is the flowing life of the Constitutional. Then, it would help if you had the justice of action to have that life of ethics. Consequently, we see today that some wounds need to be healed. We can heal the Wounds of America with God's Power to save our legacy.

God will heal the wound upon USA ethics in the Wisdom of God's power

God will heal the wound upon USA truth in the life Divine Spirit of God's Covenant

God will heal the wound upon USA   justice in the Divine Spirit in the People.

God will heal the wound upon the USA and have our promise of the Covenant.

Of our Constitutional Rights .. of the Covenant Prayer of Continental of 1774

God will heal the wounds upon the USA with the Covenant of the Declaration of Independence when .. we .. bring liberty to the Present Government under Biden and Kamala and the Democratic Elite communists.

America, we NEED TO STOP THE DEMOCRATIC COMMUNIST ELITE AND WORLD CONTROLS IN THE USA AND BE PROTECTORS OF HUMANITY ACROSS THE WORLD.

God has given us power when we have righteousness. And he sees what people do.. ;hence, we cannot be judged if things seemingly unexpected .. when we seek His righteousness He will redeem us. He knows what the secret stealthy treaherious Elite Communist and the workers have done to America and individuals that fight for freedom of God's purpose.

He has and will continue to deliver us; His grace is sufficient..

America, we have a Responsibility.
America, we have God-given Rights to justice and Liberty for all
America, we need to save our Legacy
America, we need to save our children's future
Please see my book, Published October 2024, God First, America Our Miracle by Lisa Lucia Arden, on Amazon .. other sites proclaim all the emergencies.. www.lisaluciaarden.com

We know what emergencies are. I have been asking and pleading and advocating for years. It has been proven by my work. They justice to me off Linkedin this week and even tictok .. because of speaking about Political urgencies. And, promoting President Trump and promoting my books.

See, We Have God's Power to Save America's Legacy.

We can work with the World Powers and even Political Ideologies to bring peace and planning to restore our nation because, as stated in many of my works and Podcasts. I believe we can do this.. Because some of the World Powers are conservative and want freedom for America .. And there is a new enemy the have now and the world.. The Geopolitical Powers of China and Iran .. and other secret friends.

There is a more immense evil than the World Powers that control internationally with the United States of America .. there are .. evils .. of Iran, Isis, Hamas, and secret ..allies of Iran. Is it true that the people of the world control Iranian and Persian peoples? Yet, I have heard that they start wars when they want.. and start viruses, weathering controls, chemical trail sprays, EMFs, and many other controls when they want? **But I do not believe all leaders in the USA and these countries are involved in these**

Yet, I still believe there is a hierarchy that still has tension between them. See when they deal with evil. Evil cannot ever be trusted and is the greatest deceiver and greatest deception, to kill, to steal, and to destroy… Hence, this is why the powers fight against each other internationally and at the highest tables of World Control and evil.

Before 2007 and earlier. I advocated, warned, educated, and spoke about "One World Government."

"One World Government," "World Control," I studied in my Bachelors .. and began to make others realize the urgencies in the.. before 2007 in the United States of America. Before 2007, I launched my canvas bag and GoDaddy website to educate people about oceans, seas, and rivers, killing fish and birds choked by microplastics and destroying our waters and human health. We consume and eat fish in the seas, which are invested in microplastics, poverty, and other urgencies. The recycling waste must be addressed, with plastic bags choking sea animals. I saw people with low incomes at the Flower Mart. I would get flowers and business for events: gorgeous places.. with flowers from all over the world and all types. Yet, a few blocks down, there were homeless people. The Lord told me that the poor must be helped in Los Angeles; otherwise, it will become a disaster. I asked and helped.. in my internships .. and volunteering, but that was not enough.

I asked to make recycling plants to give the poor jobs.. and set up housing that needed to be taken to build. There was this powerful minister named Andy. He loved people and had the greatest gift of God's authority to help the poor. His skin was suntan because I think he was outside many hours helping the poor, and you could see the glow of the dripping of the mystery of God's love on him. His clear blue eyes shined like God's Ocean with the sun's love.. and his hair was blonde.. like an Angel you see or see in the drawings. He.. helped much of the Los Angeles poverty that I worked with in Pasadena, California, at a transitional home. His work moved to Los Angeles to alleviate the poverty there. And the Catholic Church .. Big Brothers, and Catholic Charities have helped the poor endlessly. Yet, they have been up against the world's control of evils and the hidden secrets of the billionaire cartels. Things are different now. Even when I enter certain places, I can smell poisonous sprays in other areas. And I react on my skin and body. They have used chemical sprays to poison, but we need to be careful. Because they know God's power is in the people to bring justice. I have many stories and facts of events that have been life-threatening; God has given me grace and mercy and new life and abundance. Others have also seen His love and justice because of these experiences.

Today, the Elite Communist use Technology, severe drugs, geopolitical powers, globalization, government tension, laws, and regulations are not sufficient for technology and information systems and globalization.

Even the Elite Communist will control the financial situation .. and where you will live and trade business.

I have promoted President Trump for years, and America regarding the restoration. I consulted on Podcast, writing, speaking, singing, book signing. Specialist on consulting health, no vaccinations early on couple weeks after the CCP came existence, prior warning about a virus year prior, 2007 microplastics, 2007 foods health, toxins chemical spray, self sufficient economy 2016, geopolitical 2016,20200 China geopolitical powers, there will be a division black or white to chose God, electrotherapy softer than a heart mermor, America First Book, 2011 Article on Holocaust of America Biowarfare cell change makeup, economic holocaust and morality and immortality war against America,

We know President Trump won. I knew he was going to win. I wrote it prior. I had this book done for a while, the outline and the information. They(I do not know who it was) did everything to stop

me from writing. They took my computers and held them. And they have done much biowarfare on me. I am alive. Many times they have broken my laptop.. and taken it. See, the lovely insurance company will not insure me anymore for my computer because I have so many claims.

Question: Do you think Kamala, Mayorkas, Biden, Pelosi, and others were paid or had a plan on the side to let all the immigrants in .. or had a criminal plan? We still need to be careful about the future.

They do not speak of the contraindications of crimes.. regarding the borders and other urgencies.

What do you think?: Kamala and Biden and the Democratic Elite Communist are not speaking of this, you know why, because they are a part of these World Powers starting wars, World economic.. and World health controls.. .. open borders to destroy safety and our legacy and our freedom and using the immigrants a shield of evil for their political ideologies…. And allowing the Pharmaceuticals to get away with the Vaccinations of death. The Federal government did not take them to mediation or litigation as Plaintiffs to protect the American people.

Today, I weep in my heart. I know that this has happened. Many have become sick and lost members to the CCP and the CCP vaccinations.

To save your legacy, let us restore our country and all the poverty worldwide today with other leaders of God's goodwill and power.

Dr. Beck's Protocol Electrotherapy softer than a heart murmur and Gerson's Method

2014, I wrote a book on "Electro-Therapy" and Dr. Beck's Protocol Method. … He. Dr. Beck was a physis .. from The University of Southern California. Dr. Beck was thought to have been killed by the pharmaceutical companies because he had an invention and treatment to cure diseases .. with non "chemical" substances of pharmaceuticals. Also, simultaneously with Dr. Beck's Protocol, I studied and wrote about Dr. Gerson's nutrition method and how foods could heal diseases. I wrote the book for a man representing a German Electrotherapy company. When I called him to promote, he said, know. It is dangerous.

First, we need to take care of our bodies to prevent sickness. The body heals itself with its energies and natural sources, such as excellent, wholesome, "nontoxic" foods.

Listen, Plant-based Meat and Products:

It costs more monetarily and people's health to have Plant plant-based meat.. and synthetic vegetables. This is just one aspect of emergencies. We must build quality, not quantity, for our human consumption and life .. of existence. And in the long run we will have better success and better outcomes. Our bodies will be healthier and we will have better production. Forgive, me to say this .. but this is what many world powers are doing they want to weaken us. I could never fathom that; but, it is true. See they do not realize the more injustice that is done the less they receive their gifts from God.

In prayer, there is a Divine Command in 2024. Billionaires and builders must build for quality for the best of the majority and not quantity to monetize. Monetizing is excellent, yet only when balanced with actions and the "Aristotle Categories" can it bring the highest justice, happiness, liberty, and justice for all.

Divine Command 2024: All people pray first to God and ask for direction. They look at all the contraindications and successes of the Aristotle Categories. They ask for the highest wisdom of God, now even to restore.

Quality asks God not Quantity only Quantity with Quality

Build Structures that have a future.

We have the greatest information systems and technology and workforce to be the most highly efficient in our restoration and new projects international. We ask though .. how can we use the product that cannot be in use .. how can we recycle it for energy and usage?

I will never forget ..of great magnificent told me ..from Europe, he was a major .. or governor.. and he told me building those high risers, skyscrapers will be outdated .. and we do not need .. those offices .. Just the cost to keep them clean and in working order is enough. The building should be considered more efficient.. in quality and not waste... not the quantity of garbage. We must put our humanity first and treat our people with incredible justice and love.

Today, we need a process for recycling buildings or restoring them. Children and college students could study this. There is a significant need for tires, all in India, in a junkyard tire place where fumes and thick chemicals are in the air. We have many jobs for restoration.

Vaping causes death and marijuana smoke to cells and brain

Just like I have begged, no vaping kills the people. Also, marijuana smoke kills brain cells. Many things I have promoted .. it is not in this book.

Stop using humans for science and world controls

Today, we cannot accept the building of human usages, whether ABORTION or controlling OUR CHILDREN AND THEIR EDUCATION and DANGEROUS CHEMICALS PEOPLE ARE EXPOSE TO: it reminds us ALL of the TRUTH .. AND SAYS TODAY .. PROTECT THE families and the CHILDREN of GOD'S PEOPLE.[14]

CHEMICAL: chemical spray TRAILS, TOXIC FOODS, PHARMACEUTICALS, TECHNOLOGY OF CENSORSHIP, WEATHER CONTROLS TO DESTROY LAND, AGRICULTURE

---

[14] Emmanuel, Mari, Mari https://www.youtube.com/watch?v=7eOEf_Rbe18

control, ECONOMIC CONTROLS, etc. HUMAN TRAFFICKING, OPEN BORDERS, GOVERNMENTAL CENSORSHIP, AND ECT. EMF.(ELECTRIC WAVES WEAKENING THE PEOPLE. Electromagnetic fields), MANUFACTURING OF TOXIC ITEMS HUMANS USE, TAKING AWAY OWNERSHIP OF PROPERTY AND LAND.

I think President Trump and the team have to hire investigators, and we need to close up and de stroy all these types of businesses that are criminal and dangerous to humans and even land and harvest and even creatures in the ocean. I am speaking very simply here to open your mind.

Ask if it is the best for you under the present Elite Communist Controls. At present, Kamala and Biden:

What is it? FOR HUMAN'S FOR AMERICANS

Let's begin with a few… emergency issues

I wanted to prove the point about the plant-based meat costing more because I heard many billionaires purchased land to make this type of meat and that it would cost more to show them. It is a process that needs energy to produce .. and traditional meat is generated. It does not need

First notes only: Process to make the Plant-Based Meat Does the .. Plant-Based

1. Prior research and business plan to develop cost
2. New land to plant-based meat cost
3. New land structure preparation of the soil cost
4. Research to make the Plant- Based .. Meat cost
5. Finally, the substance used to make the Plant- Based Meat cost
6. Continuous. A new team to oversee the project cost
7. New manufacturing machines of the plant-based .. meat COST

8. Note that it takes more energy for people to digest synthetic meat and toxic foods. Also, synthetics may stay in the body if they do not have organic substances. All foods should be natural. People will get less nutrition, put out more energy, and have severe contraindications to using synthetic elements in food.

9. Hence, the monetary outcome results in less production and waste. Therefore, not only is the cost more for the company to make …, but in the long run, it also brings more detrimental costs that do not supply nutrition to the person who digests it.

If the Plant-Based substance meat is made, it will be by the fact a secondary being substance that is unnaturally made and against Divine Creation and Divine Nature and have a substance that will be "less than life and .. only "generated," by the force of extra components of energies regularly because it cannot regenerate itself to the most effectiveness as compared to the "ungenerated," cow or chicken AND THIS IS ALSO RELATIVE TO NATURAL FOODS AND VEGETABLES.

Containers and synthetics of plant-based meats .. Smaller in circumference, more apt to promote disease and or sickness or development of new

Smaller space to form plant-based beef after it is taken from harvest.

Compared to the traditional format of processing natural Foods.

Are unlimited divine. Foods have a divine nature; cell makeup is connected to the environment to grow and be healthy for human consumption.

There is enough food and all the tools humans need to exist; it needs to be adequately dispersed and shared, not just for the 3 percent.

AMERICA WE ARE RESPONSIBLE

THERE IS AN EMERGENCY.

I saw it in the sky. It looked like they were spraying the clouds. STOP CHEMICAL SPRAYING, KILLING THE PEOPLE, PLANTS, ANIMALS, HARVEST, AND EVEN THE BABIES IN THE MOTHER'S WOMB COULD BREATHE IT. I HOPE THE UMBLICAL CORD FILTERS OUT THE TOXINS.

ALSO, ALL Biological life cycle of Zoology.. needs to be protected and magnified for new populations.

Ocean and Seas and Water and Rivers and Water Filtration and Basins

In 2007, I pleaded to address the microplastics in water.. and water and water basins filtration..

THE OCEAN AND SEAS AND RIVERS. AND ALL THE WATERS TAKEN CARE OF

THIS IS MOST IMPORTANT .. WE ARE MADE OF 60 PERCENT WATER.

I warned about this in my book Our Need to Give to the World, Heal America Love in God.

Today, we must install water filter systems in all children's schools and homes, protect water systems, and clean the oceans, lakes, and rivers.

Weather Controls for Monetization is this a conspiracy?

North Carolina

All of Nature is unlimited and divinely created perfectly for humans. It is a treacherous evil to destroy a nation for money and control .. controlling the weather of North Carolina for the ..lithium .. mines and Tennessee and Florida.. for control. Is this a conspiracy? Remember, there are prophetic warnings that we will have much destruction, and we have the .. imbalance of the eco-systems... Why did they mention Black Rock wants to get the

Lithium mines? Lithium.. is the most valuable mineral for microchips .. and is hard to find.

Maui Burning Malfeasance or Mercy to save the peoples land[15]

What about Maui.. also .. it is known that there is a scientific technology company adjacent to the destruction and burning of the Maui area, Lahaina; the destruction before the burning, all city peoples evacuated.. children were told not to go to school, and other prior strategies. There were large sounds that were not natural, and the burning and destruction were from inside trees, autos, and buildings. And the specific color of blue objects was not burned. This was a scientific experiment for controls for specific reasons.

For many years, we went to the University of Southern California Medical Convention in Kapalua, near Maui. Lahaina is a precious historical place that has a spirit of the island gorgeousness of Hawaii and cultural love music mixed with American music, Hawaiian hula, delicious food, historical artifacts, the loveliest fragrance of the flowers and coconut oil upon the skin, and people of peace. You can see the shimmering sand lighting in their eyes of the ancient beauty of the Maui serene ocean shores.

Let us always be transparent about the motive if there are questions about what is wanted to build the economy or what desires. There can be negotiations.. We cannot destroy the culture and beauty of lands and peoples of America.

Was there a disease, and they wanted to burn there, or did they just want to rebuild the area .. or even do a scientific.. experiment?

America, we have a responsibility to bring justice.

---

[15] https://www.npr.org/2023/09/28/1202110410/how-rumors-and-conspiracy-theories-got-in-the-way-of-mauis-fire-recovery, Maui Fire

America: God gave us our America. We need to protect her.

America, we know we have the power, strength, and wisdom to save it with the Covenant of God, as proven in the Constitution, Declaration of Independence, and our laws.

And also the .. the Prayer of Continental of Congress of 1774

Aristotle continues about Politics:

"Of all beings naturally composed, some are ingenerated and imperishable all of eternity, whereas others are subject to coming-to-be and perishing.

The former possess value- indeed divinity- but we can study them less because both the starting points of the inquiry and the things we want to know about present extremely few appearances to sense perception.

We are better equipped to acquire knowledge about the perishable plants and animals because they grow beside us, and much can be learned about each existing kind if one is willing to take sufficient pains.

Both studies have their attractions. Although we grasp only a little of the former, yet because of the value of what we learn, we get more pleasure from it than from all the things around us, just as a small and random glimpse of those we love pleases us more than an exact view of other things, no matter how numerous or significant they are. But because our information about the things around us is better and more plentiful, our knowledge of them has an advantage over the other. And because they are closer to us and more akin to our nature, they have their compensations in comparison with the philosophy concerned with divine things. . . . Even in the study of animals to the senses, the nature that fashioned them likewise offers immeasurable pleasures to those who are naturally philosophical and can learn the causal explanations of things. (PA 644b22-645"10) introduction Politics xliv.

Natural energy opposed to Synthetic needs energy

See foods. Unlimited divine does not need to change to synthetic processes to find the answers for a process. Using synthetic processes is more costly even for the most powerful, even in the lesser of what we .. developed using them. Sometimes, there are bacteria and viruses, yet we can protect them adequately.

Of all beings naturally composed, some are ingenerated and imperishable for eternity.

Wow, look, listen, see, here. "Ingenerated," they do not need energy; they are energy and never die; they have life. And even after life, they do not die; they have eternity.

Other perishing .. that is the "Plant-based, Meat," it needs .. energy generation to ... exist, and it is perishable if it is not generated by .. energy.. see .and it doe perish.. .. after you produce it and it is harvesting people.. still. Eat it. .and the harvest may still be there. However, at the onset of development, much energy and generation was imperishable from waste. It did perish since it could only exist by the induction of a substance to sustain its original components.. and even if a new . . secondary substance is produced that is the specific particular created and composed by God. when the human.. ingests, it has a secondary substance entering the body that .. . is foreign to the original way a human was given to consume food by the given creation of all creation God gave.. at Creation. And remember. Another point needs to be made. I just had it. Help Jesus, and God is the Prime Mover. And he knows best, not man. Oh, there is another point.

Also, remember that there may still be other generated purposes that need to be used to uphold "Plant-based meat." Obviously, by finance, time, and logic, there will be, at the onset and sometimes even with the maintenance of a new system.

A cow, chicken, fish, and vegetables are already "be," and they are.

See, look, "Plant-based meat." we need more energy and cost to make it even among investors .

See, it is relative to creation. God has a purpose for all things. In my other writings, I speak of this. The Spirit of God said, "Cities, communities, and individuals and all things have a certain purpose at creation, and even cities have a certain purpose... And all countries have commodities to help sustain them."

Note that many secrets and information control our world and other worlds.

Even when President Trump gets in, and the four years after him, we need to continue to restore our country.

What we do for Justice we do for our Children's future and our country.

Yet, we need to set our minds on God First and purpose, and He will give us power, grace, mercy, and wisdom.. to carry on.. in a society that has dichotomies of injustice and justice.

Dichotomies of the

DEMOCRATIC ELITE COMMUNIST

KILLING CHILDREN.. PERSONA AND LIFE FUTURE ..

BECAUSE OF THE OPEN BORDERS.

Foster Parent Interviews

FIRST, LISTEN, CHILDREN ARE INNOCENT: 300,000- TO 500,000 FROM THE USA AND UKRAINE ARE DISPLACED, AND THE FOSTER PARENTS HAVE NOT BEEN INTERVIEWED.

And World Controls

Also, crimes and wrong GOVERNMENTAL ACTIONS such as open borders.

Explain about contraindications: here

<u>I WILL REPORT AGAIN EMERGENCIES OF PROOF OF THE MOTIVE OF KAMALA</u>

<u>BOARDER TREASON TO THE AMERICAN PEOPLE AND THE IMMIGRANTS.</u>

<u>LISTEN, KAMALA USED THE IMMIGRANTS AS A HUMAN SHIELD FOR HER POLITICAL IDEOLOGY AND WORLD CONTROL. SHE WANTS TO BRING THEM IN TO GET THE VOTE FOR NOW AND THE FUTURE..</u>

<u>LISTEN, IMMIGRANTS, DOES SHE EVEN MENTION A SOLUTION SHE IS USING YOU? There is increased crime and human trafficking .. in America. President Trump has reminded us many times that all immigrants are from all over the world.. and many countries have emptied their prisons.. to let them pass through the borders.</u>

<u>Question: Do you think this is what a governmental official would do to care for the American people and their safety?</u>

<u>Immigrant's Countries have Commodities they can help pay USA</u>

<u>IMMIGRANT COUNTRIES NEED TO NEGOTIATE THEIR COMMODITIES TO HELP THE .. IMMIGRANTS ..</u>

<u>THE CRIMINALS ARE NEED TO BE ASSESSED</u>

<u>KAMALA IS USING THE IMMIGRANTS AS A HUMAN SHIELD TO PLAN A COMMUNIST WORLD CONTROL OF THE USA ..</u> <u>AND THE IMMIGRANTS. USING THEM FOR HER AND DEMOCRATIC SILENT ELITE COMMUNIST GROUPS.</u>

JUST LIKE HAMAS .. USED THE PALESTINIANS AS A HUMAN SHIELD TO TRY TO TAKE OVER THE TERRITORY AND KILL THE JEWS TRYING TO MAKE A HOLOCAUST

THIS IS THE SAME AS KAMALA IS TRYING TO MAKE A HOLOCAUST TO STOP THE FREEDOMS OF THE AMERICAN LEGACY.

HERE, SPEECHES ARE JUST WORDS OF RHETORIC PEOPLE WRITE THOSE SPEECHES.

AND SHE and the Elite Communist DO NOT WANT TO GIVE AMERICA FREEDOM SHOWN By THE FACT OF THE OPEN BOARDERS NORTH CAROLINA, TENNESSEE, FLORIDA, SECRET DESTRUCTION OF WEATHERING CONTROL. TO GET THE LITHIUM MINES AND OTHER CONTROLS.

LIST OF EMERGENCIES YOU WILL SEE IN THIS BOOK AND MY OTHER BOOKS

NEWEST BOOK "God First, America Our Miracle." Vote Freedom Vote President Trump

IF THE GOVERNMENT IS ALLOWING IMMIGRANTS TO STAY .. WE NEED TO NEGOTIATE THE COMMODITY OF THE IMMIGRANT COUNTRIES

Woke Transgender and LGBQT

1. SINCE KAMALA AND BIDEN AND THE REGIME OF THE DEMOCRATIC LIBERAL NON-CONSTITUTIONAL COMMUNITIES ARE TRYING TO CONTROL CHILDREN IN A WOKE SYSTEM. Children cannot be brainwashed and obstructed of their true selves by a woke system of scientific sex changes and emotional instability of gender. Their critical and emotional welfare needs to be protected. They do not have the

capacity to differentiate facts, emotional positions, and contraindications.

2. We need to give children education that relies on critical thinking and with absolutes. Please, see my lists of solutions in this book and my books.Abortion, Warren Buffett, Stop... .. LISTEN OUR CHILDREN ARE OUR FUTURE.. WHAT THEIR EDUCATION IS AND COMMUNITY AND HOME LIFE WILL BE OUR FUTURE. LBGQT AND TRANSGENDER PEOPLE ARE NOT IN SCHOOLS; THEY ARE TOO YOUNG TO DECIDE ... DECIDE AS ADULTS.

Abortion Warren Buffet Stop

3.Please SEE notes: Promote and educate the women and children.. give scholarships or have schools in communities to enhance women instead of killing life. Using abortion as birth control and being afraid of the financial cost and acceptance of these girls and ladies to have their children are some of the boundaries they are set up against. The abortion clinics make it easy to abort. They even have sites set up in residential areas to kill the babies for scientific testing.

4.Because of our Covenant with Jesus Christ with America we have become like pagans killing human flesh.

WE ARE NOT A PAGAN NATION. SEE, IT IS LOGICAL NOT TO KILL A BABY IN MOMMIE WOMB, YET THE GIRLS ARE TAUGHT IT IS OK BECAUSE THEY USE IT FOR SCIENTIFIC RESEARCH. MANY OF THE GIRLS WHO ABORT ARE IN THE LOWER ECONOMIC .. LEVEL AND HAVE NOT HAD THE OPPORTUNITY TO CONSIDER A GREATER EDUCATION AND SELF-DEVELOPMENT SO THAT THEY GET INVOLVED WITH MEN.. THAT IS A

NATURAL .. INSTINCT, YET MANY DO NOT WANT TO KEEP THE BABY FOR MANY REASONS, AND THE MAIN ONE IS THE AVAILABILITY OF FUNDS AND HELP, AND ACCEPTANCE. HENCE, WE NEED TO TEACH THE GIRLS SELF-DEVELOPMENT IN SCHOOLS WITHOUT EVEN MENTIONING ABORTION. WE CAN BE SURE THEY ARE OCCUPIED AND RESPONSIBLE FOR FORMING TRADE REQUIRED AND ETHICS IN EACH CLASS AND ASSIGNMENTS THAT GIVE IMMEDIATE MERIT BASED.. I BELIEVE MANY BILLIONAIRES WILL HELP WITH THIS. WARREN BUFFET NEEDS TO DO THIS INSTEAD OF GIVING MONEY FOR ABORTION. SEE, THAT IS JUST SMOTHERING THE KILLING OF THE PROBLEM, NOT TAKING CONTROL OF IT, AND FINDING THE PROBLEM'S ROOT. PLEASE, WARREN BUFFET .. DIVINE COMMAND NOT FROM ME FROM DIVINE NATURE. IT IS NOT THE CASE THAT WE ARE TRYING TO CONTROL THE GIRL'S BODY TO VOTE IN NO ABORTION .. IT IS THAT WE DO NOT WANT THE GIRL TO KILL HER FAMILY AND FLESH AND BLOOD AND A LIVING BEING. AND THAT TO USE ABORTION AS BIRTH CONTROL. CHEMICAL ABORTION ALSO DESTROYS CELLS AND .. ORGANS OF WOMEN

5. Did you think that aborting an actual human is a foreshadowing or symbolism of aborting HUMAN LIFE AND KILLING IT. AND LIFE ON EARTH AND FOR ETERNITY..indeed what it means to be human and to live in abundance and justice without World Controls in Science?

See it is a high amount of babies being kill. We are the highest in the world to kill babies third after China and Russia.

I do not believe in abortion. However, we have facts that the argument is that . there is a large mass of abortions .. for a domestic country. Also, it is easy to access. However, if the laws will not consider stronger laws against abortion.. I believe the time factor for aborting a baby months and months into the pregnancy needs to be addressed. Also, incest, rape, mental health needs to be addressed. Yet, we know there are exceptions

6. Ethics needs to be at the highest leve and security for in vitro fertization to protect the baby also the mother that will hold it in her womb. High safety of scientific research should be.. addressed .. What would they do if the eggs and sperm was used to implant into another system that is other than a woman, female.[16]

7.https://www.mayoclinic.org/tests-procedures/in-vitro-fertilization/about/pac-20384716

Pray now for those who want to abort.

8.GOD WANTS TO GIVE YOU LOVE SO YOU DO NOT ABORT GO TO HIM IN PRAYER NOW. STOP ABORTION; THEY USE THE BABIES FOR SCIENTIFIC RESEARCH.

Chemical Abortion of pill sending in the mail stop

9.ABORTION IS KILLING YOUR FAMILY AND YOUR FLESH. STOP ABORTION PILLS THROUGH THE MAIL COULD HAVE TERRIBLE CONTRAINDICATIONS, AND THE GIRL STILL HAS TO GO TO TWO CHECKUPS.

Divine Vision Aborted Babies in Heaven

.. I asked the Spirit of the Lord. What do you do with all the babies when they die? The vision was given to me. I saw many baby faces

---

[16] https://www.mayoclinic.org/tests-procedures/in-vitro-fertilization/about/pac-20384716, In-vitro-fertilzation

beautiful in the light white with a pink hue. The babies were smiling…many altogether looking at me as if they were waiting to meet their families and parents.. and happy to be in the heavenly with Jesus Christ.

Pharmaceutical Companies

10. Reassess all pharmaceutical companies entering mediation and negotiation to give the people back funding for vaccination acceptance in the medical business. Stop all vaccinations of children and people. All pharmaceuticals must be reassessed, and the known deaths and contraindications must be examined.
Most pharmaceuticals have contamination and contraindications, especially over a more extended period, the patient becomes immune to it.

Cancer Research

11. Cancer treatment must be reassessed of radiation treatments. It is known that there are severe discrepancies in the cure of cancer under radiation treatment. In my books, I speak about this .. most people die from and alternative medicines must be used with treatments and accepted by insurance companies.

Vaccinations

12. Using vaccinations.. should be obsolete. Alternative medicine only. See, they want to monetize. There were not enough statistics for the authorization to use the vaccinations.

Chemical Spraying

13. I have spoken about this many times before. Divine Command: stop Chemical Spraying. It would not be difficult to find these companies

Emf stop the Electric force against the people.

14. I have spoken about this many times before. Divine Command stops EMF's

Utilities costs and upgrades to the technology

15. Check the financials and bills for the utilities. They did find corruption in certain states

Fusion energy and nuclear

16. There are new ways to make nuclear energy production of lower energy levels.. of nuclear. It is meager cost to produce. .My nephew told me that Nuclear energy is excellent if used properly. He is a Nuclear Scientist Internationally. Fusion Energy is another form of energy that is less costly and toxic.. that the say

Vaping is a new product of scientifically proven deathly health problems to humans and Marijuana.

17. No marijuana smoking or vaping in restaurants or places of business.
18. No smoking, marijuana, or vaping in schools or Universities
19. New law: no smoking marijuana or vaping in public spaces or schools .. Marijuana was made in nature to eat or chew, not to smoke.

World Health Controls

20. World Health Controls uses ideas from a board of people who know little or nothing about medicine and identify with pharmaceutical medicines. Also, there is no ethics or free choice.

Geopolitics

21. Allowing others to gain geopolitical access to other countries and our own when it does would bring the USA into a more dangerous and vulnerable position. I have spoken about the geopolitical positions of countries that have changed all things.

I have been a Geopolitical specialist for a while now. I have a podcast, social media presence, and writing regarding this subject. Geopolitical powers now. And China is in the center.

China Brief notes;

BRICS[17]

---

[17] BRICS is an intergovernmental organization comprising Brazil, Russia, India, China, South Africa, Iran, Egypt, Ethiopia, and the United Arab Emirates.
S was originally identified to highlight investment opportunities.[3] The grouping evolved into a geopolitical bloc, with their governments meeting annually at formal summits and coordinating multilateral policies since 2009. Relations among BRICS are conducted mainly based on non-interference, equality, and mutual benefit.[4]
The founding countries of Brazil, Russia, India, and China held the first leaders summit in Russia in 2009 under the name BRIC. Following a renaming of the organization, South Africa attended its first summit as a member in 2011 after joining the group in 2010.[5][6] Iran, Egypt, Ethiopia, and the United Arab Emirates attended their first summit as member states at the 2024 summit in Russia. Saudi Arabia has not yet responded to an invitation received on January 1, 2024 to join BRICS, and it is still under consideration.[7][8][9][3]
Combined, the BRICS members encompass about 30% of the world's land surface and 45% of world population.[10] South Africa has the largest economy in Africa whereas Brazil, India, and China are among the world's ten largest countries by population, area, and gross domestic product (GDP) nominal and by purchasing power parity of which Russia emerged as Europe's largest economy in the latest financial year.[11] All five initial member states are members of the G20, with a **combined** nominal GDP of US$28 trillion (about 27% of the gross world product), a total GDP (PPP) of around US$65 trillion (35% of global GDP PPP), and an estimated US$5.2 trillion in combined foreign reserves (as of 2024).[12][13]

The Group of Seven (G7) is an informal forum of seven of the world's most advanced economies and their heads of state and government:

Canada, France, Germany, Italy, Japan, the United Kingdom, and the United States. The Brics now has approximately 50 plus countries joining It to Build a multiply-order world order.[18]

BRICS an <u>intergovernmental</u>

<u>organization</u> comprising <u>Brazil</u>, <u>Russia</u>, <u>India</u>, <u>China</u>, <u>South Africa</u>, <u>Iran</u>, <u>Egypt</u>, <u>Ethiopia</u>, and the <u>United Arab Emirates</u>. BRICS was initially identified to highlight investment opportunities.[19]

Not Saudi Arabia. See, when I found out about this, I pleaded to have them not go in. I don't think they are part of Bric's. I am studying the Brics' understanding ahead with Jim Rickard Paradigm Press.

G7

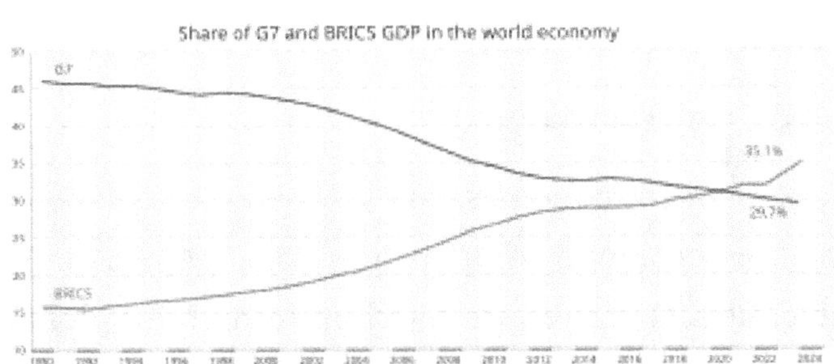

Share of G7 and BRICS GDP (PPP) in the world[14]
The BRICS countries are consider

---

[18] https://www.youtube.com/watch?v=jH-dcOXiHs4, BRICS New Members: 50+ Countries to Join BRICS, BRICS grows, adding 13 new 'partner countries' at historic summit in Russia

[19] https://en.wikipedia.org/wiki/BRICS#:~:text=BRICS%20is%20an%20intergovernmental%20organization,joining%20the%20group%20in%202010., Brics; https://www.youtube.com/watch?v=wUdlzmk73Ns, BRICS grows, adding 13 new 'partner countries' at historic summit in Russia

North America, Europe, Japan

29 GDP

Brics

50 countries

35 GDP, and all countries have not entered yet

See, trading economy and geopolitics are all factors to our country's power, safety, and geopolitical powers and safety.

Even if we loose business with the Brics we can regain with be a self sufficient nation .. and enter into fair contracts.. with all countries.

International Contracts

22.We will gain international contracts and build relationships with other countries.

Liquid Gas

23.Our liquid oil is the most significant commodity we can sell to other nations. We need the vessels and transportation portals to transport it to be made

Commodities Internationally and Nationally

24. We must assess all our commodities and address our contracts strategically when exporting and importing goods and services. Determine if the contracts are relevant and up-to-date for global geopolitical interactions and powerhouses. Look competitively and not just at short-term contracts. '" spontaneously look at all contraindications. ' Please see my brief explanation in this **book.**

Big Corporate and Brics and International Diplomacy

25.And big corporate businesses need to be careful because of geopolitical powers.. will get the business's first exchange shown and reflected in the "BRICS" .. .. in 10-30 years if we do not exchange international company and work to protect our borders and international diplomacy we can lose much. Also, the protection of information systems is mandatory. We need to become a more self-sufficient nation.. for newer exports .. and manufacturing .. not just a country of business...[20] Our liquid oil can subsidized the brics.

26. Since oil and big business are not traded in U.S. Dollars, they will mostly be traded with the brics group and specific countries.[21]

27. Look at the imports and exports in terms of timing, of course, over some time, the costs, and how can there be deliberations

Safety of Imports

28. Use imports from other countries at a minimum; check the toxins and liability controls for safety, technological controls, war tools, and toxins.

China was the top supplier of goods to the United States, accounting for 16.5 percent of total goods imports. The top five suppliers of U.S. goods imports in 2022 were China ($536.3 billion), Mexico ($454.8 billion), Canada ($436.6 billion), Japan ($148.1 billion), and Germany ($146.6 billion).[22]

29. .. Companies are importing and not setting enough tariffs or any at all. Most importantly, we need to give our country a chance to

---

[20] US companies in China struggle with raids, slow deal approvals, anti-espionage law https://www.reuters.com/business/raids-exit-bans-us-companies-face-growing-hurdles-china-2023-08-29/;https://www.youtube.com/watch?v=jH-dcOXiHs4

[21] The Difficult Realities of the BRICS' De dollarization Efforts—and the Renminbi's Role https://carnegieendowment.org/research/2023/12/the-difficult-realities-of-the-brics-dedollarization-effortsand-the-renminbis-role?lang=en

[22] https://ustr.gov/countries-regions, The Offices of The United States Trade Representative

develop and promote small and large businesses with benefits that are competitive with imports.

30. Enter each state .. and resurrect the companies that closed

31. See what adjacent states can offer each other .. so the transportation is not expensive.

Nuclear energy and fusion energy have begun to develop.

32. Begin now studying and working on nuclear .. energy and fusion

Liquid Gas and Energy

33. The liquid gas we need to build the new transportation .. vessels to sell the product to Europe and the world.

Small Oil Well companies

34. They can reopen many stop drilling when Biden and Kamala went in. See if they can get a forbearance of benefit for reopening because it is costly to reopen oil wells.

Trucking Business

35. The trucking business must be reviewed to see what is being delivered, especially for Chinese and other connected companies. Are there any tips or questions that need to be explained? This would also be detailed.

North Port on Russia to Canada and China access to the North

36. There is a port north of Russia that goes to Canada. What is being delivered? I envisioned delivering cargo trucking to China, and something in the trucks was illegal and dangerous.

Canada Biowarfare tool with China?

37. Canada is the make a biowarfare tool with China

Canada's border with the USA needs to be watched. China can enter through that passage.

Honduras is right below .. Mexico and China have business there.

38. See, those borders have to be watched. Why can we not access the contracts? We should get a better deal since we are close and do not have to pay for transport goods.

Russia, why in Cuba so long

39.Re-assess undercover why Russia stayed so long and what they set up. We know they did practice runs, yet they still have access and look. Cuba needs new leadership.. they were like the USA in the '50s; many Cubans are distraught and deeply hurt by their country's destruction

Haiti New Leadership

40.Make America under President Trump and Freedom Fighters .. a paradigm to this war-torn country

Nuclear setup

41.Safety of Nuclear warfare and nuclear new laws

Military tools of China in Las Vegas

42.Is it true there are military tools in La Vegas in a storeroom

Econ System.

Torture and Scientific Research and Oppression and Suppression stop.

43.Put out a reward for anyone knowing that is torturing people and torturing people in science or animals and ecosystems or malpractice or abuse.

44. And any other practices . of business reward for turning people in,
    and if they are part of the crime.. they will get less time
    See, that is where the problem is: Is the crime committed
    knowingly or unknowingly? The person seeks to make a good
    business; a crime could be committed knowingly or unknowingly.

Eco System notebooks and Restoration of Infrastructure and Periodically Table elements

Children's education projects on what needs to be corrected in society, including reports on infrastructure, as discussed before. Each has a notebook on ecosystems. Recycling of products and structures not used.. speaking, all have a trade out of high school—extra reading and writing courses. Using the private school paradigm, children are thriving.

Children's Vocabulary notebooks and handwriting

45. Journal handwritten vocabulary words .. written part of speech, a
    derivative of the word, definition, and .. put in a sentence
    Then, use it in a story.
    Also, they should write in another language not just English.

Children's Bible Reading and handwritten assignments

46. Write about their thoughts about the story's characters and subject
    and what they learned.

Restoration of older buildings and infrastructure Discuss review.

Children's science projects recycling solutions.

47. Find the process for what to do with old buildings: keeping them or
    restoring them for manufacturing.
    a. Teach children studying and universities how to restore the older
    buildings to recycle .. or them instead of putting all the rubbish in
    the junkyard.
    b. Each area or state could have recycling .. companies.

We should also teach children to study infrastructure and how to correct it with a notebook because we know the problems.

Periodical Table Study required

c. If they study the periodic table, they will know the elements. Then, they will see the substance, the component of the fracture that needs to be built or restored, and they can see how we can recycle it to be used.

Recycle the Solar Screens and Tires and Scrap Metal and Structures buildings.

What can we do .. for this? Of course, investigate, begin testing.., and plan ideas to prove that it is not costly and not toxic to recyle the solar screens and our tires .. and old scrap metal.

Drones made and found and Surveillance.

1. Drones and technological apparatus are in our skies, and they can affect our people and be used for crimes. New laws need to be made about their usage and the actions that are done with them. For example, China makes drones that look like birds.
2. However, I believe there are handheld.. drones and drones and apparatus that have the military power to torture and try to hurt and even kill people. These companies that make them.. who purchased this apparatus? Find them? These apparatuses should not be available to the public.
3. Mass surveillance needs to be adequately assessed. And if they do mass surveillance, it should not be torturous or affect them in any way, health, emotional, personal, or financial.
4. Do not use people with gifts for scientific testing .. at any time of billionaire peoples, military, or government.

4. Section 702 violates our constitutional rights, but the courts have failed to intervene.

The Fourth Amendment guarantees the right to be free from unreasonable searches and seizures. Government agents must obtain a warrant to access our emails, online messages, and chats. Large-scale, warrantless surveillance of Americans' private communications contradicts this fundamental constitutional principle.

Section 702 also violates the Constitution by inhibiting freedom of speech and association. The reasonable fear that the U.S. government is spying on communications may deter journalists, lawyers, activists, and others from communicating freely on the Internet. We all have a right to exchange messages with our friends, family, colleagues, and clients abroad without worrying that the government is reading over our shoulders.[23]

Export and Import and Services more explanation

48. Because of technology, geopolitics, and developments in sciences and manufacturing, many products and services have become obsolete or need to be reassessed for more efficient quality, cost, and delivery control.

49. Compare the costs of the imports and exports. Expenses of the costs.. and is it fair business

50. Office of the government Reiterating that I was told that .. every office needs to be checked and reviewed in the .. government .. costs.

    a. Costs of spending and what is the spending on. Is it necessarily is it outdated, or is it an obsolete process, yet still keeps the project or action

---

[23] https://www.aclu.org/news/national-security/five-things-to-know-about-nsa-mass-surveillance-and-the-coming-fight-in-congress, **News & Commentary**
Five Things to Know About NSA Mass Surveillance and the Coming Fight in Congress

b. What has been the history of the .. costs and actions? Has there been any extraordinary changes?

c. What would it cost .. to outsource the jobs to the regular Americans and not a full-time government employee?

d. What services should we provide in the government? Do we need them? Are they paramount? Are they woke? Are they outdated?

Do they benefit the American people immediately?

Export and Import

51. More questions about export and import discuss

List the USA and Country type

Compare and contrast will need to be done in another piece of writing. These are just brief notes.

The United States is the world's second-largest trading nation, behind only China, with over $7.0 trillion in exports and imports of goods and services in 2022. The U.S. has trade relations with more than 200 countries, territories, and regional associations worldwide.

a. What can we export to the other countries that they need

b. What can we make ourselves that we are importing that is more profitable?

c. For example, REPEATING the recycling. Logically, this can be

d. How will we support our citizens when there is a need for jobs, and they have enough education to do these jobs

e. , We discussed the solutions in this book. Please see Lisa Lucia Arden, MDIV.[24]

---

[24] Arden Lisa, Lucia, MDIV, Our Need to Give to the World, Heal America and Love in God, Published Lisa Lucia Arden, 2016Our Need to Give to the World: America Love in God,

f.   If we keep the immigrants in America, how will we supply them with jobs?

As discussed, negotiate commodities of other countries to be given to support the immigrants.

New businesses are built with many ideas, commodities, agriculture, and recycling.

Business is built between countries.

g.   Look at all the financials. They are straightforward to access, especially for the government, when exporting and importing goods and services. You will see. There are discrepancies and outdated projects.

h.   Yet independent companies need to stay apprised of the changes. Several companies closed this year because of the Chinese raiding of information. [25]

Heal America- Kindle edition by Arden, Lisa Lucia. Politics & Social Sciences Kindle eBooks @ Amazon.com., Arden, Lisa Lucia, MDIV www.lisaluciaarden.com; www.arisetogodstruth.com

Arden, Lisa, Lucia MDIV, Arise to God's Truth, Restore and Keep America's Freedom, Lisa Lucia Arden, December 2020, geopolitics https://www.amazon.com/ARISE-GODS-TRUTH-LUCIA-ARDEN-ebook/dp/B08T8LJ8TR/ref=sr_1_3?crid=6SLHFQ1ND2FV&dib=eyJ2IjoiMSJ9.xtnuqkBr2J VwfsZJzfYFXvR9uvMZNWtuV_HxjEuwOvfGjHj071QN20LucGBJIEps.BdlOV17fMuCB5UaG KHXzRVhCRaXwjn1uxaR_D-OW1R4&dib_tag=se&keywords=lisa+lucia+arden&qid=1731487580&sprefix=%2Caps% 2C213&sr=8-3, Arden Lisa Lucia, MDIV, www.lisaluciaarden.com; www.arisetogodstruth,com

Arden, Lisa, Lucia, MDIV, God First, America our Miracle Vote Freedom Vote President Trump The United States of America, Publisher Lisa Lucia Arden, October 2024GOD first, America Our Miracle: Vote Freedom, Vote President Trump: Arden MDIV, Lisa Lucia: 9798345121887: Amazon.com: Books, Arden, Lisa Lucia, MDIV www.lisaluciaarden.com ; www.arisetogodstruth.com

[25] https://www.reuters.com/business/raids-exit-bans-us-companies-face-growing-hurdles-china-2023-08-29/

Goods Exports

The United States is the 2nd largest goods exporter in the world, behind only China. U.S. goods exports totaled $2.1 trillion in 2022, up 17.5 percent ($307.3 billion) from 2021. Canada was the largest purchaser of U.S. goods exports in 2022, accounting for 17.3 percent of total U.S. goods exports. The top five purchasers of U.S. goods exports in 2022 were Canada ($356.5 billion), Mexico ($324.3 billion), China ($150.4 billion), Japan ($80.2 billion), and the United Kingdom ($76.2 billion). U.S. goods exports to the European Union 27 were $350.8 billion.

52. Goods Imports

The United States is the largest importer of goods in the world. U.S. goods imports totaled $3.2 trillion in 2022, up 14.6 percent ($413.7 billion) from 2021. China was the top supplier of goods to the United States, accounting for 16.5 percent of total goods imports. The top five suppliers of U.S. goods imports in 2022 were China ($536.3 billion), Mexico ($454.8 billion), Canada ($436.6 billion), Japan ($148.1 billion), and Germany ($146.6 billion). U.S. goods imports from the European Union 27 were $553.3 billion.

Goods

GOODS	USA IMPORT	USA EXPORT
TOTALS	3.2 TRILLION	2.01 TRILLION
CHINA	414 BILLION	150 TRILLION
MEXICO	455 BILLION	324 BILLION
CANADA	436 BILLION	365 BILLION
JAPAN	148 BILLION	80 BILLION
GERMANY	146 BILLION	73 BILLION
EUROPEAN UNION	553 BILLION	350 BILLION

27 COUNTRIES

UK   64 BILLION   76 BILLION

The solution is seen when importing 3.2 trillion and Exporting 2.01 Trillion; if they are correct, these values were in 2022. See, it can be subsidized by drilling oil and liquid oil and intricately combing through the hair of each trade to ensure it is current to the prices in brilliance.

Furthermore, we can develop more of our self-sufficient country, the USA. Note: Mexico is making autos now, but we need to first manufacture them in our country.

Also, the Brics wants peace not wars.. ; and they want global .. intersection with many countries 50 total some waiting.. on a wait list. .They said they want give the opportunity to smaller countries to trade.

Is the EU the largest trading partner of the US?

The United States is the European Union's largest trade partner, accounting for a fifth of EU exports in 2023, and remains its largest investment destination, accounting for 55 percent of total investment into the United States.

Is the EU the largest trading partner of the US?

The United States is the European Union's largest trade partner, accounting for a fifth of EU exports in 2023, and remains its largest investment destination, accounting for 55 percent of total investment into the United States.

a. Are we trying to ensure we get the tariffs? Be careful how much you ask. Then, they might increase the price. Also, the price will be higher if the product becomes difficult to get.

b. **We have imported from** many of these businesses for a more extended period. Is the quality appropriate? Is it safe? Are there toxins or dangers for humans? Are all the contracts fair

c. business?

d. c. Are they hiding crimes or trafficking other components or items through the original business transaction? For example, I consulted to look through all of China's manufacturing that could have dangers when used or other contraindications, and we saw they have apparatus made controlling all the cranes at the delivery ports.

e. Organize each export .. and review it from its country.

   Hire a trusted person for a report investigation. Use these questions and statements as a beginning.

f. Compare and contrast. Why do we import and export to different countries? Have we looked at better deals?

g. I know I am just starting a new subject, but it relates. I saw the title Harvesting of Organs of China in the Epoch News Paper... I need to read it. I will look into it again. I have talked about organ harvesting for years now and want to stop it and any crimes that occur.[26]

h. See, we are humanitarians. We are called to protect humanity. We need to use this as leverage (they can be penalized if they do crimes like this). There should be new laws and peace treaties that protect humans from this.

i. Governments should be penalized for using people for scientific research or abuse and testing. New laws are needed.

There are facts in my history of biowarfare and controls of computer systems

---

[26] Arden, Lisa, Lucia, Arden, www.lisaluciaarden.com

j.   I believe many governmental agencies in science new laws and reassessed. Companies need to give reports.

k.   and social welfare with children.. need to be reassessed. Many of the .. social workers do not understand the human psyche and cultural relations between families.

l.   Are these countries doing trafficking of young workers or employee abuse? Humanitarian safety.

m.   How does it affect one country from another when we export and import?

n.   Use the Aristotle categories for each process.. because so many variables have changed technology and geopolitical powers .. we need to look at all contraindications

o.   Repeating resurrecting the state's manufacturing, see what has been shut down and lost.. see if it can be restored. Also, the buildings involved can be restored ..if not .. do they need to be taken down.. have the universities and children study dismantling structures that are destroyed or in dangerous conditions that cannot be restored for recycling?

How can these buildings be used properly? For example, the tires in India need to be framed. I asked and consulted about this because the air is very toxic. [27]

p.   Infrastructure we spoke about before each community develop. The trade schools, health, nutrition, small markets, jobs, school non woke, new paradigm of school, and manufacturing set up there ..a

q.   Form Bitcoin Bonds to sell to the government and communities for investors.. to use to fix infrastructure.

---

[27] https://www.dw.com/en/how-india-is-making-new-roads-from-recycled-old-tires/video-68857469,How India is making new roads from recycled old tires

r.   Make sure the funds are going to the correct project for peoples. What funds are best used appropriately to bring the safety, health, and wholesome life of humanity.

s.   It is stated that we owe 800 billion to China. We are paying interest only.. .. and our taxes go to that. How can we leverage a penalty for fentanyl in our country? How can we negotiate this balance we owe?

t.   Drones and military systems are made in the USA .. watch where they are sent to and who purchased them

Services Exports

The United States is the most significant services exporter in the world. In 2022, U.S. services exports were $926.0 billion, up 16.4 percent ($130.7 billion) from 2021. U.S. services exports account for 30.7 percent of overall U.S. exports in 2022. Ireland was the largest purchaser of U.S. services exports in 2022 accounting for 9 percent of total U.S. services exports. The top five purchasers of U.S. services exports in 2022 were: Ireland ($83.1 billion), the United Kingdom ($80.9 billion), Canada ($69.5 billion), Switzerland ($52.4 billion), and China ($42.2 billion). U.S. services exports to the European Union 27 were $238.6 billion.

As a result, the US dollar became the primary currency for international trade, with other countries holding US dollars as reserves. This allowed the US to finance its trade deficit by printing more dollars, as other countries needed them to purchase oil and other commodities.

1.   **Consider the Brics now has formed 2024 and many countries will not be trading their commodities with .. the American dollar; hence, we will not make those funds..**

2.   **Yet the USA does get money for tariffs is essential.**

<u>**This is why we need to make sure that other countries are fair with tariffs .. such as the auto AND ANY OTHER PRODUCTS SUCH AS PRESIDENT TRUMP SAID. now will be making in Mexico. There needs to be Tariffs on them..**</u>

3. <u>**When we begin to drill and export this will balance the Brics that others are not trading with the dollar**</u>

4. <u>**When we get our liquid oil in a production this can also get our export services higher that will help us balance our import spending .**</u>

a. China 400 billion more we import .. and we only export 42

Services Imports

The United States is the most significant services importer in the world. In 2022, U.S. imports of services were $680.3 billion, up 23.7 percent ($130.3 billion) from 2021. U.S. imports of services account for 17.2 percent of overall U.S. imports in 2022. The United Kingdom was the largest supplier of services, accounting for 10.4 percent of total U.S. service imports in 2022. The top five suppliers of U.S. services imports in 2022 were: the United Kingdom ($70.8 billion), Germany ($42.0 billion), Canada ($40.6 billion), Japan ($38.5 billion), and Mexico ($37.3 billion). U.S. services imports from the European Union 27 were $166.7 billion.[28]

SERVICE	USA IMPORT	USA EXPORT
TOTAL	680 BILLION	926 BILLION
UK	71 BILLION	80.9 Billion
GERMANY	42 BILLION	BILLION
CANADA	41 BILLION	70 Billion
JAPAN	39 BILLION	
MEXICO	37 BILLION	
EUROPEAN UNION	167 BILLION	239 BILLION

---

[28] https://ustr.gov/countries-regions

IRELAND	83.1 BILLION
CHINA	42 BILLION
SWITZERLAND	55 BILLION

Note that we are not speaking largely about the economic issues in this .. book. I have interjected the Paradigms of Power Article. Here, you will see the monetary systems of income and statistics and that America is still at the top in many ways. God wants us to regain what we have lost. An emergency in China's army and Russia together is massive. Even though we are at the top in many areas of life in the truth of justice, God's Judeo-Christitan principles of wisdom and justice are paramount. Did you see Russia attempting to bring items through the airports? Also, they set up missiles to make in South Africa. And we recently visited Cuba.. warning us to stop attacking them with USA missiles.

I have spoken a lot about my Podcast and writings and interjection of social media communication.

In restoring America: WE NEED A BUSINESS and a TEAM OF PEOPLE WITH JUDEO-CHRISTIAN SOLUTIONS OF ECONOMY, CULTURE, SAFETY, HEALTH, EDUCATION, AND RESTORATION.

WE HAVE IT UNDER PRESIDENT TRUMP and the TEAM

We need to live with God's higher intention and have greater wisdom to make us live a more quintessential life.

As this passage shows, the best things to study are ingenerated and imperishable for eternity. Among these, the very best is God himsel£. Hence, the very best theoretical activity consists in studying God: theology. That is why only the study of theology fully expresses wisdom (NE 1 1 412"1 6-20 with APo. 87"3 1-37).

NOTE GIVE THE SENTENCE ABOVE TO THE PEOPLE THAT ARISTOTLE SAID IF THEY DO NOT BELIEVE OR RESPECT THEIR FOREFATHERS

HIGHEST WISDOM IS GOD .. AND UNDERSTANDING INGENERATED SYSTEMS

One reason Aristotle holds this view about theology is this. 27 The

Aristotelian cosmos consists of a series of concentric spheres, with the earth at its center. God is the eternal First Mover, Prime Mover, or first cause of motion in the universe. But he does not act on the universe to cause it to move.

He is not its efficient cause. He moves it so that an object of love causes motion in the things that love or desire it (DA 4 1 5"26-b7). He is love.

27. The other reasons are these: God is the best or most estimable thing there is, so that theology, the science that studies him, is the most estimable (Metaph. 983'5-7, 1074h34, 1075'1 1-12). He is also the most intelligible or most amenable to study of all things because he is pure (Metaph. 1026'1 0-32). Introduction xliv Introduction

My Response:

We must prove that which is what Jesus Christ in the Spirit always does for me. He proves it because He is the truth. See, when He tells me something, He is proving it because all of Him is truth, and proof is the truth of the substance and wisdom He has given us.

As Aristotle said, certain things have specific usages; some are explicitly used for the purpose, and others are not. This is relative to the choices that are made when a person chooses less than what is not the purpose.

It is often and rightly said that Aristotle's philosophical method is dialectical. Here is his description of it:

As in all other cases, we must identify the phenomena and go through the problems first. In this way, we must prove the Mendoza. . . ideally all the Mendoza, but if not all, then most of them and the most compelling. If the problems are solved and the *endoxa* are left, it will be adequate proof. (NE 1 1 4Sh2-7) Introduction xix

Aristotle says dialectic is proper to philosophy "because the ability to go through the problems on both sides of a subject makes it easier to see what is true and what is false" (Top. 1 0 1 •24-26).

If he is a competent dialectician, he can follow the consequences of supposing it and believing it is not. He will be able to see what problems these consequences face, and he will be able to go through these and determine which can be solved and which cannot. Introduction XX

In the end, he will have concluded that we may suppose that one person rule is better, provided that the person himself is outstandingly virtuous (1288• 1 5-29). However, in reaching that conclusion, some of the Mendoza on both sides will almost certainly have been modified or clarified, partly accepted and partly rejected (Top. 1 64h6-7). Others will have been decisively rejected as false. But the philosopher will need to explain away: "For when we have a clear and good account of why a false view appears true, that makes us more confident of the true view" (NE 1 1 54•24-25). In other words, some beliefs that seemed Mendoza and deeply unproblematic will have fallen from grace. However, if most of them and the most compelling are still in place, that will be adequate proof of the philosopher's conclusion since there will be every reason to accept it and no reason not to. Introduction xx

My Response:

Proof will show whether one thing is better than the other, yet one has to begin with God's highest purpose, regardless of the situation, or that what is focusing or proofing is its real specific purpose at creation.

See when we distort or deform or integrate lessor values we. Undermined our existence. .. of what our purpose is. .. And we even begin to deteriorate what's around us; those in power use their power in a lesser way that is not specified.

Declaration of Independence

When, in the course of human events, it becomes necessary for one people to dissolve the political bands that have connected them with another and to assume, among the powers of the earth, the separate and equal station to which the laws of nature and nature's God entitle them, a decent respect to the opinions of humanity requires that they should declare the causes which impel them to the separation.

In our covenant with God in the Prayer of the Continental Congress of 1774 and the Constitution, we realized that only in the Wisdom and love and Trinity's power and grace and mercy.. of God could we overcome all trials and make unity and humanity liberty and justice for all.

Be Thou present, O God of wisdom, and direct the councils of this honorable assembly; enable them to settle things on the best and surest foundation. The scene of blood may be speedily closed; order, harmony, and peace may be effectually restored, and truth, justice, religion, and righteousness prevail and flourish amongst the people. Preserve the health of their bodies and vigor of their minds; shower down on them, and the millions they here represent such temporal blessings as Thou seest expedient for them in this world, crowning them with everlasting glory in the world to come. We ask for all this in the name and through the merits of Jesus Christ, Thy Son, and our Savior.

Amen.

Reverend Jacob Duché, Rector of Christ Church of Philadelphia, Pennsylvania
September 7, 1774, 9 a.m.[29]

"Jesus Christ is the way, the truth, and the life, and no one comes to the Father, accepted by Him."

Knowing the truth, the truth of the God of Abraham, Judeo-Christian percepts, and defining the opposing side will strengthen the truth of God's side.

We must realize we must be united to identify the truth, and then we can achieve peace, justice, and love. Our America was built on Judeo-Christian ethics .. a capitalistic nation of helping those in need and empowering them with some social services.

Yet today, we need to return to America's authentic foundation, the Judeo-Christian nation, empowering the individual to become what we work together to be: excellent citizens with a genuine purpose in life.

And even with time, time will show the changes and the seemingly better choices—for example, the Democratic Elite Rule. We had Clinton and Obama's two presidential terms, Biden, and many democratic people. Our country has gone down in many ways.

Yet, the morale of the present government under Kamala and Biden and the nonnegotiable diplomacy internationally (or do they want the war to make money on military tools)? Reiterating: There are three companies, as RFK told us, that are making military tools and the money we spent on Ukraine. We could have paid for all the homeless housing in the USA).[30] Under Kamala and Biden, Economically and even Culturally .. America.. under this political ideology of World Powers, Economics, and Health,

---

[29] www.lisaluciaarden.com; Prayer of the Continental Congress, 1774, https://chaplain.house.gov/archive/continental.html;
[30] Senator Robert Francis Kennedy,
https://en.wikipedia.org/wiki/Robert_F._Kennedy_Jr.

and now they want to control our children's lives, indoctrinating liberal ideas .. and turning away from the Covenant that we have with Jesus Christ of the God Highest.

We, the people, have God's love first and have the power of God's strength to save our legacy.

We, the people, have God's Power and Salvation to have the peace fighter's strength, wisdom, and heart to pour the flow of living waters upon America, her people, and even the nations among us.

We now need to choose the light of God, the Highest, the God of Abraham, or darkness.

I pray that many come to the Salvation in Jesus Christ.

People now see that as the reason for the tension. We can work together for peace when we vote for leaders who respect the Judeo-Christian nation and give our lives to Christ Jesus.

Again, I will repeat that the Judeo-Christian nation contains all the most significant truths and wisdom from every culture because it is based on the Biblical history of the Torah and the Holy Scriptures. This is God's experience with humanity in the Western Hemisphere and worldwide. It has the highest ethics and wisdom in any book on earth...

However, today, geopolitical powers across our nations need to be addressed. This is why many aspects of government need to be checked and intricately reviewed. Please see my coin ideas of Paradigms of Power. You will see the topic in this book. It is a divine command that all government and military offices be reviewed to uphold justice in our USA. One out of every 100 (the amount you think) of the military needs to be checked. Any questions about military personnel need to be checked. You will find espionage, other.. crimes, and even unfair business connected to the people against the

U.S.A. Also, unfair injustices in the military hierarchy have not been addressed.

NOTE: There needs to be training simultaneously in regular exercise for the prevention of suicide. I have begun a research study on this .. and one of the points is that the military forces individuals feel uncomfortable going to the same army personnel for questioning. See, then they feel awkward and know their most intimate thoughts. Perhaps, for mental health, an excellent physician and counselor can listen to them outside the regular military personnel.

Also, as stated before, communities with cities of specific cultures where they know they sell drugs.. need to be checked. Chinese Fentalyn, we need to track that; where do they deliver it? Where are the companies? Demand negotiation peace treaty to stop the companies in China; otherwise, there will be penalties. New humanitarian laws. In reiterating the 'Paradigms of Power" have caused the

Black Rock, State Street, and Vanguard, we need to negotiate. We know they own most of the Real Estate in the U.S.A. and internationally. By 2030, they are supposed to own .. the most in percent. Hence, we need to negotiate the loans and the positions of safety.

The World Health Controls and World Economic Controls are doing specific severe crimes against individuals and groups—billionaire communists.

    a. Individual torture scientific testing

    b. Controls of income of jobs. Certain powers pinpoint, oppress, and suppress people who are freedom fighters and thinkers and have solutions and people's trust. This is challenging to prove. Only the person they commit the crimes against could show you the pattern. Yet, we need to put a word out again:

anybody knowing they are suppressing and oppressing certain people should be a witness, and if they are involved, give them a lesser charge.

c. **Banks and more significant Corporate businesses, where are the funds that the criminals of Fentanyl work with? They should be penalized.**

Please think and listen: This is why borders should not be open and why World Controls and Government Control should be maintained, even if the World Controls have enemies as large as themselves or bigger.

Today, there are nine Criminal Billionaires. We know some of their business are good and other parts are crime. America is infested in a war with the Chinese Cartels.. of drugs.. the top cartel of billionaires. It is as if we have a separate war with the Chinese Cartel. How can we enter into .. a more just business with these .. Criminals and stop their drug cartels. .. these criminals in the United States of America bring many drugs. And mostly all the drugs and crimes... We need to consider how we can stop this and make it obsolete. Otherwise, it will grow more extensive, and the longer a person has the drug availability, the longer there is .. dysfunction and drug addiction and .. .. poison to a country .. that is the death .. losing part of life and life around those involved.. and even the use the funds for other .. .. . . death and even. "

In my book, I discuss China and the geopolitical powers as experts.

Arise to God's Truth, Restore and Keep America's freedom.[31]

Think, listen, look, and compare.

---

[31] Arden, Lisa, Lucia, MDIV Arise to God's Truth, Restore and Keep America's Freedom, Lisa Lucia Arden Published United States of America, December 2020 www.lisaluciaarden.com

NOTE THAT STEVEN BANNON IS A HERO FOR HELPING US AND PROTECTING US FROM CHINA UNDER TRUMP AND HIS DAILY WORK.

China's Geopolitical plan stops their take over only notes for your thoughts to spark warnings:

1. We owe 800 billion in debt to China. We pay the interest only from the taxes of our country, and China gives the money to themselves to make the largest Army in the world, the Red Army
2. We have our manufacturing from them
3. They have brought fentanyl in to kill our people.
4. Socio-logical entered into universities and promoting their ideas .. donating funds, and hiring professors they control
5. Stealing business ideas of big business
6. CCP VIRUS killed the people and destroyed people's lives across the world.
7. Secret police and offices set up controlling computer system
8. Want to take over Taiwan.
9. Want to do war.. directly from seeking to take items and faulty business
10. Censorship in computer systems and CCP peoples in the USA.
11. It was said two years ago that in Ten years, they want to control. USA
12. They have entered geopolitically into many countries to gain power and control.
13. Under Kamala and Biden, many governmental-controlled loans to China made making military tools
14. BIDEN WAS INVOLVED IN CHINA TREASON USA.
15. Gates is an advisor to the leaders of China
16. Is Black Rock indeed loans China to make military tools?

17. Secret CCP business set up laboratories and businesses next to Military stations. And in each state .. censorship of our American

18. Threatening our energy and computer system

19. These are just some ideas of urgency. There are many more.

20. I started and consulted to look at all overseas military tools, and they found the apparatus of China.. technology

21. I also started and consulted to look at all the manufacturing we get from China. Items that affect the significant daily lives of humans are found in Cranes, where they deliver food. Technology controls all crane apparatus from China, which can be controlled virtually by Wi-Fi.

22. I also stated that if you looked at all government offices, you would find Communist people selling information to China, and they did.

23. There are drones made by China in our skies that appear to be birds and other drones.

24. China has developed the largest marijuana plant in Northern California, illegally, running it and even trafficking they have taken over 90 percent of the marijuana business illegally. Other scientists and I have found that marijuana smoke kills brain cells and other contra-indication. Is it true that they are building a large dispensary for marijuana in California?

25. Did you know China has also developed invisible war tools that can be used?

26. These are just a few points. We know there are many, and they are severe. Also, I have discussed China's entry with other nations in my arguments on social media and Podcasts.

We need to take EMERGENCY heed, and when President Trump and the Team enter, we need to oversee and investigate all areas of business and manufacturing.

I pray that the leader believes in Jesus Christ as their Lord and Savior since we are a Judeo-Christian nation.

The leader must be that person who believes and acts upon the .. "ingenerated and imperishable the original creation of what was intended for humans at creation." .. Ingenerated is that being can exist in the way it was intended by its first substance of being ingenerated .. existed by the whole .. int eternity of the time of creation.

The person has to see the sides of each action's contraindication.

2 Chronicles 9:7 IIow fortunatc your people are! How blessed your courtiers, who are continually in attendance to you and listening to your wisdom! 8 Blessed be Yahweh, your God. Because your God loved Israel and meant to keep it secure forever, he has made you its king to administer law and justice.'

Ingenerated before perishable

Of all beings naturally composed, some are ingenerated and imperishable for eternity, whereas others are subject to coming-to-be and perishing.

Ethics before Politics

We need to have excellent ethics before politics. If we would have assessed "*endoxia*," Dialectic is helpful to philosophy, Aristotle says, "because the ability to go through the problems on both sides of a subject makes it easier to see what is true and what is false" (Top. 1 0 1 •24-26).

Aristotle says debate is helpful in philosophy "because the ability to go through the problems on both sides of a subject makes it easier to see what is true and what is false" (Top. 1 0 1 •24-26).

CHILD AND FAMILIES MOST IMPORTANT

My response:

Who is running and looking to protect the United States of America when Biden seems to have health issues, and Kamala is running for office?

Families need protection and empowerment.

Today, more than ever, we need to support our families first. Our America is a country of people and families that need support and empowerment, and many need vocational skills that could bring revenue, housing, and restoration from the many trials they have been exposed to.

Just recently, many families and children were lost in the Weathering controls of North Carolina, and 83 billion dollars in damages, mainly housing, were caused in Tennessee and Florida. [32]And what about Maui?

Today, the consensus is that millions of Americans expect to lose their homes.

Where is our government, Biden and Kamala.. did they help

The wars, what are both sides..?

Home Foreclosures 170,000

Today, the consensus is that tens of millions of Americans expect to lose 170,000 homes in foreclosure.

Today, there are 84.33 MILLION FAMILIES IN AMERICA

FOR IMMEDIATE RELEASE

As the US grapples with Coronavirus's human and financial fallout, a new study reveals a deep undercurrent of housing insecurity.

---

[32] Hurricane Helene storm [2024] https://www.britannica.com/event/Hurricane-Helene

- Fear of eviction and a lack of financial resources are the top reasons X
- The coronavirus outbreak will likely push more families into insecurity and may tip vulnerable populations over the edge unless urgent actions are taken.

As the pandemic adds further financial strain to families across the US, a new study finds that 34 million people living in America—13 percent of the adult population—expect they will lose the ability to continue living in their homes over the next five years. The first-of-its-kind poll, taken before the virus outbreak, likely underrepresents current housing insecurity exacerbated by the worsening economy.[33]

Why did they not take care of the homes first…

Billionaire Cartels and Open Boarders

The open borders and the Cartels and immigrants of crimes?

Fentanyl and open boarders

Fentanyl, did they think it was death for the people?

What about the immigrants being used for human trafficking?

Also, not caring for our disasters, homeless, veterans, and tribulations.

See, we are not taking into consideration the "Cartels," and many billionaires and even politicians use America as a place to send their citizens .. planning many deceptions against America. What do you think?

Afghanistan and casualties

---

[33] Tens of millions of Americans expect to lose their homes,
https://www.prindex.net/news-and-stories/press-release-tens-millions-americans-expect-lose-their-homes/

Afghanistan the way they left.. and many deaths and billions of military tools.

I believe we can negotiate with these men. Of Isis, some want peace. It is God's nature to pinpoint leaders to help.

We can enter a peace treaty to help the children and women.

Is it true that we are paying 40,000 million a week to the Taliban for war negotiations? Perhaps we can use this as a tool?

At this time, when this happened to Afghanistan, many children, women, and even men.. became in the 'evil' custody of the Taliban. My heart is still wounded from this. I pleaded they get an ambassador there .. to help the Taliban.. this is part of their culture and belief system; they are treacherous and injustice to the entire personhood of an innocent child. Eight years old to be .. controlled by an abusive criminal man .. entering a marriage. God help us.

AND THE JEWISH CHILDREN AND PALESTIAN CHILDREN. NOW LET US HELP THEM.

WHY DID THEY NOT TAKE OUT ALL THE PALESTIAN CHILDREN LIKE THEY DID WITH THE UKRAINE WAR?

These children are innocent and too young for that level of relationship.

In Afghanistan:

Ask: since Biden is a Democratic Elite Communist and Kamala

Why are wars, World Health and World Economic Controls, Boarders safety, Children Trafficking, and Children bringing danger to immigrants and America?

Do you think .. looking and contemplating, this was all a strategy to take down America under the freedom of President Trump and the American freedom fighters.?

I also believe Kamala did not disclose all her motives, fabrications, treason, and open borders and that her campaign is a "Money Scheme."

That is what others have said. She and Biden happen to be involved. The Democratic Elite Communists have not taken care of our children.. or country.

Many lives were lost.. in that situation .. of leaving Afghanistan .. even the American.. military.. who protected that area for years.

Think, contemplate.. it is our country's heart upon that land .. and then.. we have a governmental leader of the USA .. choosing to leave .. Afghanistan .. in the way of destruction.

Stop Muslim Leaders entering into marriage of girls 8 years old

Give women and girls integrity and safety

Mostly rapidly... I beg the Muslim leaders to help these children .. who are forced into relationships at the age of 8 or younger. And help educate the Taliban to evolve into god-like Christians. Nothing is impossible with the Lord.

This is reflective and analogous to the children on the borders, which are controlled by many we do not know. Also, the World and even government controls are trying to bring a woke system and not helping the people who lost their homes in the weathering and treachery control in North Carolina. They are threatening to take their children away because they do not have adequate housing. They need city governmental documents to build rapid housing.

I believe there is a secret society of higher evil tables, a society that is not secret in America.

Now that the American people see the truth, we can have redemption.

God will help us, show us and guide us, and give us His Power to

In God's Power, America Save our Legacy

Brotherhood Muslim Extremist Jihad stop

They are blatant, saying they want to kill … and take over. 'Brotherhood,' of Muslim extreme Jihad .. professes they wish to bring a holocaust to believers and Jews, that is, Hamas, Isis, and Iran. This is the extremist.

Muslims in America and across the world see the truth and try to bring peace. Did 50 to 60 countries come together to ask to bring peace to the war.. in the Middle East?

They are not the loving Muslims of peace.

We need to pray without stopping and seek negotiations.

Even though we know many of these happenings are prophetic,

Let us ask God to protect all the people.

We know the wars and see them. I also have spoken on Netanyahu and his position to protect Israel and even the Palestinians, who are used as a human shield... Also**, Netanyahu has safeguarded the areas of Europe and even the USA.. from the war against America. And Netanyahu has saved much part of the world.**

Oxford letter

Today, in a globalized world of geopolitical powers, it is paramount to understand the multi-cultural beliefs and working acceptance, respect, and negotiation of work to fulfill all missions and protect the life of humanity and all life. Understanding and entering into the culture and the complexities of Islamic life and life of other dominant cultures and even third world countries is the pinnacle of delivering peace and liberty and evolution of well-being and safety and empowerment of humanity. Knowing and planning intercultural communities of relationships at professional levels promotes the highest movement of life to allow what is formed in a culture already and will enable it to evolve to the best for humanity and the ecosystem. Because of the World Forums and Elite powers of many World Controls, it is essential to integrate, assess, and develop relationships that serve its culture with the utmost justice and peace and protect the people first and children at the most urgent work.

There needs to be relationships and work and successes that have peace treaties to protect humanity at all levels, nuclear, economically, culturally, individually, communities, safety, conservative values protecting children and family, empowering life self sufficiency in each country; hence, scholars and leaders alike need to be negotiable and compassionate with wise and knowledge understanding to deliver accountability to bring truth for each country's culture yet live in diversity of peace a the highest level of justice.

Paper for Oxford University Lisa Lucia Arden, MDIV

Many see that higher powers within our own country and internationally have set up the mass destruction and control of the people worldwide. Immediately, we need to protect our children across the world. See, by human nature, humans were created to be free and live with the purpose of self-development, to develop children, and to share with family and community, all in a relationship with God. God made humans with a specific intention of a first substance of being, and when it is less, Divine Nature strikes. God demands justice.

Of course, you know China and Russia are not the only diabolic Globalists and geopolitical Powers.

Geopolitical economic controls use technology to seek world control. There are even higher powers that seek to control the world and humanity.

There has been no time in history that we have all these horrendous powers, horrifying powers of

'Hitlerian diabolism,' of all aspects of life seeking a 'holocaust' and deforming all elements of

Immediately, we need to begin at the table of life in the home, the community, and the church. To stop communistic controls, wokeness, transgender, and injustice against children, families, and marriage.

The JUST AND TRUE powerful billionaires empower the people and invest in conservative leaders in the community, states, and the nation. They are protecting all classes.

STOP THE Hitlerian diabolism. Communistic leaders have been planning to destroy the freedom of humanity, proven by deliberate crimes of and to name a few:

1. Human trafficking, abortion, wokeness, transgender
2. Deforming children's life and education
3. Open borders of hardcore criminals and drugs
4. Corporate Censorship
5. Fraudulence Vote USA 2020 President Trump won 2020
   They wanted to take President Trump down.
6. Conspiracies and crimes against all humanity

7. Afghanistan exit crime against humanity, allowing ISIS's power and control, perhaps to soothe them to stop their violence and give billions of dollars of war tools

8. Ukraine-Russian War a holocaust of Humanity

9. CCP Virus holocaust against humanity and Lockdowns Wanted to destroy humanity, the elderly and humans and all life existence

10. CCP Mandatory Vaccinations deaths, diseases, infertility

Stealthy evils of attempting to bring the USA and control of other economies in the world down by the acts of the economy and trade and obliterating culture and the crimes against individuals' life family, and what it means to be human and even marriage

11. Pharmaceuticals and Foods control World Health Controls

12. Stop CCP Buying agricultural lands for control

13. Threatening the Economic controls of the digital currency

14. Rich takes most of the funds and needs fairness in the distribution of funds.

15. Stagnation of the development of human authentic being

16. Empower the people in justice and truth in the life of compassion. God's Divine Sovereignty overpowers Hitlerian diabolism

Saint Faustina Divine Mercy

17. The holy righteous nun, Saint Faustina, told us to pray for God's Divine Mercy for the world.

18. Pray in righteousness. Divine Mercy God has given us across the world. He gives us

19. Pray in righteousness. Divine Mercy God has given us across the world. He gives us God never forsakes His people.

20. The holy righteous nun, Saint Faustina, told us to pray for God's Divine Mercy for the world. They want to control the world .. and human beings.[34]

WAR BRINGS DEATH IN THE LIFE OF THE NATIONS

BRING A PEACE TREATY

I HAVE PLEADED WITH MUSLIM LEADERS TO ENTER A MEETING .. YET NO SOLUTIONS HAVE BEEN MADE .. PLEASE, I PLEAD TO BRING NEGOTIATIONS

Russia and Ukraine negotiate the land commodities.

ALSO FOR RUSSIA AND UKRAINE. GIVE A GIFT TO STOP THE WAR. NOW SAVE THE LEGACY

FIRST, TRY TO NEGOTIATE THE .. WITH LANDAND SHARE COMMODITIES NATIONAL BUSINESS COMMODITIES. ALSO, ASK OTHER COUNTRIES TO INTEGRATE INTO THE PEACE TREATY WITH A BUSINESS INCENTIVE, PLEASE, NOW. SEE THAT .. WHAT THE WAR CAUSES JUST BEGINNING NOTES war lost PEOPLES, CHILDREN LIFE, LAND INFRASTRUCTURE, monies .. what you could have built if you were not at war.. ALSO PRESENT WAR LOST.

What war does:

1. BEGINNING LEGACY LOST
2. PAST LEGACY LOST.
3. PRESENT LEGACY LOST
4. FUTURE LEGACY LOST.
5. VERY DISTANCE FUTURE LEGACY LOSS (FOR restoration of International Business ..... and Diplomacy division

---

[34] https://www.thedivinemercy.org/message/stfaustina, Saint Faustina **Saint Maria Faustina Kowalska: The Humble Instrument**

6. Loss of Business EXCEPT BUSINESSES THAT MAKE THE TOOLS FOR THE WAR.
7. Loss of FRIENDSHIPS WITH OTHER COUNTRIES

EVEN IF THE COUNTRIES BELIEVE THEY MAKE MONEY.. AS USA HAS THREE COMPANIES MAKING MILITARY TOOLS. AND UKRAINE IS NOW KNOWN TO HAVE COMMODIES OF HARVEST.. .. WE WILL HAVE OUR HANDS ON THE BLOOD OF THE NATION. RFL TELLS US THE MONEY WE SPENT ON THE WAR WITH ..UKRAINE COULD HAVE PAID FOR ALL THE … HOMES FOR THE HOMELESS. I ASKED PUTIN TO NEGOTIATE HE WANTED TO IN 2022. I asked them to exchange gifts.

Wars Money and Malevolence

RFK .. LISTEN .. TOLD US. The government under Biden and Kamala wanted the war to stay and make military tools so the three companies in the USA and Ukraine could pay with their commodities.

THESE WARS ARE STARTED BY WORLD POWER LEADERS OF EVIL CONTROL. FOR THE DESTRUCTION OF THEIR IDEAS. POWER OF THE HUMAN DARKNESS, WHAT SHOULD UKRAINE DO .. SINCE THEY HAVE FEWER TOOLS? This is just the beginning. ALSO, STRATEGICALLY SET UP THE ENTRY OF THE AMUNITION WITH A BETTER TARGET SO YOU CAN CONTROL MORE ACCURATE SHOTS. AND ALSO GET A .. TOOL THAT HAS MORE ENERGY OR POWER THAT CAN MAKE AN ACCURATE SHOT TO STOP THE ENEMY. FIND OUT WHERE RUSSIA IS SHOOTING AND TRY TO TARGET THE AMMUNITION. AND DIRECTLY BEFORE IT GOES OFF. DRONES?[35]

---

[35] www.lisaluciaarden.com   https://www.msn.com/en-us/news/world/france-hands-ukraine-massive-arms-boost/vi-BB1kSYfp?ocid=msedgntp&pc=U531&cvid=9683b87b83014c13ac010a904fb2287b&ei=3 2WAR BRINGS DEATH IN THE LIFE OF THE NATIONS AR POINTS

Large Submarines and small submarines

I also asked them to make small submarines to watch the waterways and fix our giant submarine to keep all the submarines updated. They have done this. They now used the small submarines now for the war of Russia and Ukraine.

Dome the Iron Dome

https://www.politifact.com/article/2023/oct/13/us-may-not-have-iron-dome-but-military/

Also, President Trump has invested in the military to make a "dome" to protect any force coming in from all sides. I drew a " dome " to cover the entire United States of America. I formed and designed a beginning drawing to draw an architectural picture. My dome is different to place .. drones and when .. you know there are military war urgencies. And also to protect the skies all the time .. You can have the drones constantly in positions across America, and then when they see the enemy coming from aerial view, the drone can activate the iron dome to proceed to block the incoming arsenal .. [36]

https://www.politifact.com/article/2023/oct/13/us-may-not-have-iron-dome-but-military/he

Also, I have spoken about positions, other areas, points, and urgencies of war.

The most important are prayer, peace treaties, negotiation, and preparation to show strength. We also need to prepare all the high-tech military tools used by other countries so that our forces can protect ourselves. Moreover, undercover persons should understand the complexities of different

---

[36] https://www.politifact.com/article/2023/oct/13/us-may-not-have-iron-dome-but-military/, Iron Dome

countries. And, of course, build friends and... countries we can rely on... together.

Note: I am explaining these few concepts because it is paramount that we have a leader who understands war yet has the highest level of negotiation and is respected in international diplomacy.

Even though I do not believe in war, I think in hindsight and minimum or no violence. Use tools to show your opposing side you have the tools to protect yourself. Of course, do not tell them everything you have. Peace treaties can solve many wars because monetary components and commodities are easily in place. Usually, countries start a war because they want money, power or cultural beliefs to protect themselves. And we know there are other reasons: geopolitical power, friends, and allies.

Instead of paying all that money for the war, we could have given Putin a little liquid gas. Yet, they want to make money on war tools. Also, as stated, we could have given Putin a gift from Ukraine. This is what I asked.

We see the countries as Israel has also been in an unnegotiable position.. and one country after the other .. . fighting Hamas, Hezbollah, and Iran.

Psalms 62:11 Once God has spoken, twice have I heard this: Strength belongs to God, **12** to you, Lord, faithful love.

Wars can be brought to Peace and Treaty

They can enter different contracts with all the money the military business spends on war tools. There can be negotiations. War is unnecessary; there is much to trade, and tools and other tactics could be used.

I think war is a time of technology and globalization, and geopolitical powers are massive tools that could be used for a great victory: transportation, computer systems, technology, new commodities, and land and restoration and contracts of services. 'There are levels of powers that control the global network .. originates from ancient Iranian blood land, which was investigated by tribes. Junagranier4@ instagra.

CHAPTER THREE

Emergencies America
Save Our Legacy

Controls in the Communist arms

Agenda 21

Eliminating the Middle Class

http://www.renewamerica.com/columns/cobb/130219

By <u>Don Cobb</u>

www.freedom21santacruz.net

Discussion of the information of Agenda 21:

1. United Nations organizations will implement The Sustainable Development Agenda 21 Comprehension plan globally, nationally, and locally.
2. This is the agenda 21 century. Living for a brave world that you cherish and love will no longer exist.
3. It elevates nature above man, and it is called a precautionary principle: you are guilty before you are proven innocent.
4. Philosophy to bring human beings throughout the world under the control of the Elite.
5. Global movement coordinate action plan

a. End of national sovereignty

b. Abolition of private property

c. Restructure of the family unit

d. Increasing limitations of mobility and individuals' opportunity

6. Abandonment of the Constitution Rights

7. 'It is the sacred principles [injustice and slavery] enshrined in the United Nations Charter to which the American people henceforth pledge their allegiance.'

8. Human beings stack and pack the people in the apartment, controlling where we live

9. Bush and Clinton. Obama supported Sustainable development

10. New World Order using the taxes of men to build the New World order

11. Children cared for by the state .. taking children away from families

12. Steal a generational of children and teach them to--Education loyalty of the government instead of the family

13. Teaching children objective reality is not knowable.

14. They learn that mathematics is artificial and arbitrary, and reasonable solutions are arrived at by consensus among those who are considered experts.

15. Generally, more highly educated people with higher incomes consume more resources than poorly educated people, who tend to have lower incomes. In this case, more education increases the threat to sustainability.

THE NEW AMERICA: Agenda 21 and the U.N. One World Government Plan

Press release: Tens of millions of Americans expect to lose their homes[37]

Agenda 21 is being implemented across America, and many Americans have never heard of it. A list of mayors who have signed on to support it

---

[37]https://www.prindex.net/news-and-stories/press-release-tens-millions-americans-expect-lose-their-homes/Tens of millions of Americans expect to lose their homes

is on the ICLEI website. It is a list of Progressive politicians, including mayors of nearly every major American city. (See diagram above.) What this means, interestingly, is that when polled. At the same time, Progressives make up less than 20% of the political landscape in America; they've made an awe-inspiring nationalized effort to put themselves into leadership in many of America's largest cities! Bravo to the Progressives, but aren't you curious how they managed that?

So, the media has been almost silent about this, but has nearly every large city in America signed on to support Agenda 21? Should you or I be concerned about this? I am concerned, and I'll tell you why: The only civilized nation without officially signing onto the One World Government plan is the good ole USA. President George H. Bush, President Clinton, President George W. Bush, and even President Obama signed on in 2011. Still, there has been no formal public announcement of this plan to hand America over to the OWG folks, virtually no media attention, and most importantly, no buy-in from We, the People! Can a U.S. president legally commit to handing the governing authority of The United States of America over to the United Nations? Not according to our Constitution AGENDA 21.

DOES KAMALA WANT AGENDA 21? IT LOOKS LIKE IT LOOK WHAT SHE DID TO THE BORDERS, NOT PROTECTING AMERICANS.

Today, the consensus is that tens of millions of Americans expect to lose their homes.

IT DOES NOT MAKE SENSE WHY SHE OPENED THE BORDERS TO PRISONERS ALL OVER THE WORLD. AND KNEW OUR COUNTRY AND OUR FAMILIES ARE

EXPECTED THE CONSENSUS OF TENS OF MILLIONS OF AMERICANS TO LOSE THEIR HOMES.

USING THE IMMIGRANTS AS A POLITICAL IDEOLOGY TO TRY TO KEEP DEMOCRATS IN.

WHY DID THEY LET ALL THE IMMIGRANTS AND PRISONERS FROM ALL OVER THE WORLD WHEN THEY HAD TO PRINT ALL THE MONEY MORE THAN ANY TIME IN THE HISTORY OF ANY NATION? IT WAS ALSO BROUGHT ON BY THE LOCKDOWN SURPLUS CHECKS. AND BAD BUSINESS FOR THE OIL WELLS

ALSO, WE HAVE THE MOST DEBT .... EVER IN THE USA AND ANY OTHER COUNTRY. PLEASE SEE MY PODCASTS AND SOCIAL MEDIA. [38]

Biden took from President Trump's reserves and also spent more.

Hence, Biden's debt is more.

Over Trump's entire term, including the 2020 spate of emergency COVID spending, the debt increased by $7.7 trillion—a staggering total, to be sure.

However, about 15% of the $1 trillion of that debt resulted from the Treasury's choice to keep additional cash on hand during the pandemic. Former Treasury Secretary Steve Mnuchin, unsure how much tax revenue would be collected, borrowed well over $1 trillion—but kept it in reserve without ever spending it.

However, Biden spent that reserve and borrowed another $7 trillion on top of it.>

Instead of allowing that one-time emergency COVID spending to expire, Biden and the Democratic Congress continued spending at that same COVID-era level, thus institutionalizing multitrillion-dollar deficits.

---

[38]https://www.heritage.org/debt/commentary/the-lefts-7-trillion-lie-biden-far-outpaces-trump-racking-the-national-debtThe Left's $7 Trillion Lie: Biden Far Outpaces Trump in Racking Up the National Debt Jul 2, 2024 4 min read Commentary By Senior Visiting Fellow, Economics Research Fellow, Grover M. Hermann Center

Accounting for the changes in Treasury cash balances, the debt rose $6.5 trillion during Trump's entire term and is up $7.9 trillion in less than four years of Biden's tenure.

Worse, the Treasury has announced that it anticipates needing to borrow another $800 billion from July through September of this year, followed by hundreds of billions more from October to December as federal finances further deteriorate.

All told, Biden will likely oversee a net increase in the debt of more than $9 trillion in a single term—a new record.

>>> How Bidenomics Is Crushing Generation Z

Biden wanted to spend $2 trillion more in the last year and a half, but conservatives in the House blocked the added bloat.

You can bet the farm that if the radical left wins the White House and Congress in 2024, that $2 trillion outlay will be first on their legislative agenda.

Biden's other big lie, backed by the CRFB analysis, is that extending Trump's tax reform will drown the economy in debt.

Yet federal tax revenues have increased since that tax reform was enacted—and federal revenues as a share of GDP have not fallen.

Today's debt increases due to both parties' massive, out-of-control federal spending.

However, with a debt headed to $50 trillion if reelected and a political agenda that stifles economic growth, Biden has set America on an unsustainable fiscal path that will lead to financial oblivion.

This piece originally appeared in the New York Post

Former Treasury Secretary Steve Mnuchin, unsure how much tax revenue would be collected, borrowed well over $1 trillion—but kept it in reserve without ever spending it.

Biden, however, spent that reserve (THE RESERVE OF PRESIDENT TRUMP'S 1 TRILLION) and then borrowed another $7 trillion on top of it.

Instead of allowing that one-time emergency COVID spending to expire, Biden and the Democratic Congress continued spending at that same COVID-era level, thus institutionalizing multitrillion-dollar deficits.

Accounting for the changes in Treasury cash balances, the debt rose $6.5 trillion during Trump's entire term and is up $7.9 trillion in less than four years of Biden's tenure.

Worse, the Treasury has announced that it anticipates needing to borrow another $800 billion from July through September of this year, followed by hundreds of billions more from October to December as federal finances further deteriorate.

All told, Biden will likely oversee a net increase in the debt of more than $9 trillion in a single term—a new record.

>>> How Bidenomics Is Crushing Generation Z

Biden wanted to spend $2 trillion more in the last year and a half, but conservatives in the House blocked the added bloat.

You can bet the farm that if the radical left wins the White House and Congress in 2024, that $2 trillion outlay will be first on their legislative agenda.

Biden's other big lie, backed by the CRFB analysis, is that extending Trump's tax reform will drown the economy in debt.

Yet federal tax revenues have increased since that tax reform was enacted—and federal revenues as a share of GDP have not fallen.

Today's debt increases due to both parties' massive, out-of-control federal spending.

However, with a debt headed to $50 trillion if reelected and a political agenda that stifles economic growth, Biden has set America on an unsustainable fiscal path that will lead to financial oblivion.

This piece originally appeared in the New York Post

Former Treasury Secretary Steve Mnuchin, unsure how much tax revenue would be collected, borrowed well over $1 trillion—but kept it in reserve without ever spending it.

However, Biden spent that reserve and borrowed another $7 trillion on top of it.[39]

DEMOCRATIC POLITICAL IDEOLOGY COMMUNIST.

PLEASE SEE IN MY OTHER BOOK DISCUSSION OF THIS COMMUNIST[40] SLAVERY OF AMERICANS TO THESE PEOPLE **WORLD AND GOVERNMENT CONTROLS SECRET SOCIETIES AND SECRET PLANS AGENDA 21**

CLINTON
OBAMA two Presidency
BIDEN
THE USA HAS LOST MANY AMERICAN FREEDOMS AND FUNDS TO RICH COMPANIES FOR MANY YEARS. AMERICA HAS

---

[39] The Left's $7 Trillion Lie: Biden Far Outpaces Trump in Racking Up the National Debt Jul 2, 2024 4 min read Commentary By Senior Visiting Fellow, Economics Research Fellow, Grover M. Hermann Center https://www.heritage.org/debt/commentary/the-lefts-7-trillion-lie-biden-far-outpaces-trump-racking-the-national-debt

[40] Arden, Lisa Lucia MDIV, www.lisaluciaarden.com www.arisetogodstruth.com

NEVER BEEN IN A WORSE POSITION WITH ALL THE TRAGIC HAPPENINGS.

AND WITH MUCH WORLD CONTROL, THEY HAVE BEEN PLANNING THIS

THIS IS WHY THEY DID NOT WANT PRESIDENT TRUMP IN THE SECOND TERM. THEY STOLE THE VOTE

IS THAT TRUE PELOSI. IS THE ONE THAT CAUSED THE JANUARY 6TH.. 2024? THE PRISONERS. NEED TO BE RELEASED.

JESUS CHRIST OVERCAME THE MARK OF THE BEAST SATAN

Only IN THE POWER OF GOD CAN WE BRING JUSTICE TO OUR NATION AND SALVATION TO OUR PEOPLE AND FAMILIES

Revelations 20:2 He overpowered the dragon, that ancient serpent which is the devil and Satan, and chained him up for a thousand years. 3 He hurled him into the Abyss, shut the entrance, and sealed it over him to ensure he would not lead the nations astray again until the thousand years had passed. He must be released at the end of that time, but only for a short while.

Revelation 20:4 Then I saw thrones, where they took their seats, and the power to give judgment was conferred on them. I saw the souls of all who had been beheaded for having witnessed for Jesus and for having preached God's word, and those who refused to worship the beast or his statue and would not accept the brand mark on their foreheads or hands; they came to life and reigned with Christ for a thousand years. 5 The rest of the dead did not come to life until the thousand years were over; this is the first resurrection. 6 Blessed and holy are those who share in the first resurrection; the second death has no power over them, but they will be priests of God and Christ and reign with him for a thousand years.

See, God gave us America and the Nations we need to protect our countries and proclaim the Salvation of God in our lives and actions and our brave and bold reconciliation to save our countries in the power and covenant in God in the hearts and lives of the people

37 Jesus told him, 'You must love the Lord your God with all your heart, soul, and mind. 38 This is the greatest and the first commandment. 39 The second resembles it: You must love your neighbor as yourself. 40 On these two commandments hang the whole Law and the Prophets.

1 Timothy 2:4 wants everyone to be saved and fully know the truth. 5 For there is only one God, and there is only one mediator between God and humanity, himself a human being, Christ Jesus, six who offered himself as a ransom for all. This was the witness given at the appointed time,

This is a brief note to bring a BRILLANT LIGHT OF GOD UPON THE PEOPLE of urgency for humanity to

First Commandment

Love God with all your heart and soul and put no other God before the

John 14:6 Jesus said: I am the Way, Truth, and Life. No one can come to the Father except through me. 7 If you know me, you will know my Father too. From this moment, you know him and have seen him.

Remember, there is not a sin that is too bad that God cannot forgive.

Isaiah 1:18 'Come, let us talk this over,' says Yahweh. 'Though your sins are like scarlet, they shall be white as snow; though they are red as crimson, they shall be like wool. 19 If you are willing to obey, you shall eat the good things of the earth. 20 But if you refuse and rebel, the sword shall eat you instead— for Yahweh's mouth has spoken.'

Pray for those who follow the "Beast."

2Corinthians 5:20 So we are ambassadors for Christ; it is as though God were urging you through us, and in the name of Christ we appeal to you to be reconciled to God. 21 For our sake he made the sinless one a victim for sin so that in him we might become the uprightness of God.

The Beast comes in different forms and different definitions.

This is just a brief note on the Beast.

Rev. 12:9 The great dragon, the ancient serpent, known as the devil or Satan, who had led all the world astray, was hurled down to the earth. His angels were hurled down with him. 10 Then I heard a voice shout from heaven, 'Salvation and power and empire forever have been won by our God, and all authority for his Christ, now that the accuser, who accused our brothers day and night before our God, has been brought down. 11 They have triumphed over him by the blood of the Lamb and by the word to which they bore witness because even in the face of death they did not cling to life. 12 So let the heavens rejoice and all who live there; but for you, earth and sea, disaster is coming— because the devil has gone down to you in a rage, knowing he has little time left.'

The Beast is in different forms

1. Forms of evil
2. Individual
3. Community
4. Nation
5. Cults
6. Government
7. Businesses
8. Secret Society
9. Churches
10. Cartels
11. Associations

See, God .. loves them and wants them in their life to be His children in His SACRED

1 Timothy 2:4 wants everyone to be saved and fully know the truth. 5 For there is only one God, and there is only one mediator between God and humanity, himself a human being, Christ Jesus, six who offered himself as a ransom for all. This was the witness given at the appointed time,

It is our responsibility as believers to proclaim the Salvation of the Lord

America, we have a Covenant with Jesus Christ. We have a Formal Prayer

"Prayer of the Continental Congress of 1774"

Divine Message 3.16.23

Save our Legacy of America

Experience is sometimes hidden from the eyes of the successful monetarily. Experience is also defined as a passion for truth that makes and creates the first substance of justice and life. It cannot be purchased, and it cannot be measured monetarily. Much of the time, since it is the first substance of truth, many think they should have the information freely without paying the person who has delivered the experience of justice and truth that is the highest meaning of human life.

See, experience is allowed by life's existence. Sometimes force, sometimes freely given, is sought for; however, it becomes history, time, place, attitude, and measurement: The Aristotle Categories. It is shared with life, testing good or bad, integrating into all life, and allowed by the Divine Nature of life. However, beauty and the highest life are achieved with justice and the Preeminence (God) of love.

Please, listen this is for individuals that have information that are in view.. and the people take them the powerful and use them. Whether it is someone writing a script, writing on political solutions, or an employee working in a corporation. This is a most wholehearted, saddest story .. a young girl wrote the script for the Barbie movie. She worked and was affiliated with the people who made the movie. They stole her ideas and never paid her. I tried to help her, but she was very upset about her life work. ..stolen. I hope she will continue to try to bring justice.. if it has not already been done.

Yet, there is also a larger point here.. All the legacy that America has worked blood, sweat, and tears, the Elite Communist and some Democrat, and also geopolitical powers want to take it from the people.

See, experience is allowed by life's existence. Sometimes force, sometimes freely given, is sought for; however, it becomes history, time, place, attitude, and measurcment: The Aristotle Categories. It is shared with life, testing good or bad, integrating into all life, and allowed by the Divine Nature of life. However, beauty and the highest life are achieved with justice and the Preeminence (God) of love.

October 22, 2024

Do not give our America to the Democratic Elite Communist

Our American legacy has been given freely to all the Americans of each generation to have liberty, freedom, justice, happiness, and safety from generation to generation in the Covenant of the God of Abraham, the Highest under the Judeo-Christian Nation.

Let us save our legacy so our children can be that authentic being God created.

Let us save the legacy of all generations, our years of blood, sweat, and tears. [41]

Since the Covenant of Prayer of Continental Congress 1774

---

[41] First Prayer of the Continental Congress 1774 https://www.history.com/this-day-in-history/congress-creates-the-continental-association

First Prayer of the Continental Congress 1774

O Lord our Heavenly Father, high and mighty King of kings, and Lord of lords, who dost from thy throne behold all the dwellers on earth and reigns with power supreme and uncontrolled over all the Kingdoms, Empires, and Governments; look down in mercy, we beseech Thee, on these our American States, who have fled to Thee from the rod of the oppressor and thrown themselves on Thy gracious protection, desiring to be henceforth dependent only on Thee. To Thee have they appealed for the righteousness of their cause; to Thee do they now look up for that countenance and support, which Thou alone canst give. Take them, therefore, Heavenly Father, under Thy nurturing care; provide them with wisdom in Council and courage in the field; defeat the malicious designs of our cruel adversaries; convince them of the unrighteousness of their Cause and if they persist in their sanguinary purposes, of own unerring justice, sounding in their hearts, constrain them to drop the weapons of war from their unnerved hands in the day of battle!

Be Thou present, O God of wisdom, and direct the councils of this honorable assembly; enable them to settle things on the best and surest foundation. The scene of blood may be speedily closed; that order, harmony, and peace may be effectually restored, and truth and justice, religion and piety, prevail and flourish amongst the people. Preserve the health of their bodies and vigor of their minds; shower down on them and the millions they represent such temporal blessings as Thou sees suitable for them in this world and crown them with everlasting glory in the world to come. **We ask for all this in the name and through the merits of Jesus Christ, Thy Son, and our Savior.**

Amen.

Reverend Jacob Duché, Rector of Christ Church of Philadelphia, Pennsylvania, September 7, 1774, 9 a.m.

The Reverend Dr. Margaret Grun Kibben, Chaplain, U.S. House of Representatives U.S. Capitol, Room HB25, Washington, DC 20515-6655

2 Chronicles 9:7 How fortunate your people are! How fortunate your courtiers are, continually in attendance to you and listening to your wisdom! 8 Blessed be Yahweh your God. Because your God loved Israel and meant to keep it secure forever, he has made you its king to administer law and justice

We want government officials, leaders, and organizers to have the "highest wisdom of God Truth, the God of Abraham. It is part of our heritage.

"The Declaration of Independence."

"The Constitution"

Contemplate: For example, our most beloved Crown Saudi Prince, Mohammed bin Salman Al Saud (Arabic: محمد بن سلمان آل سعود**), is a worshipper of God, and that is what his country is built on. He does not allow other cultural beliefs to take over the God of Abraham's country's belief systems and the entire nation.[42] Even though I believe and ask him to give women rights and protect young girls in marriage at 8 years old, please, my brother.Crown Prince. These are old practices of tradition that are lesser than life. You are my brother, and I am supposed to tell you. See, some cultures do have areas that need deep healing, and there can be a miracle.**

Contemplate: For example, our most beloved Prime Minister of Israel, Benjamin Netanyahu, נולד ב ;- בתשרי כ"ח ה'תש"י) הוא פוליטיקאי ישראלי

Israel has been a leader of the nation of the God of Abraham since ancient times. Netanyahu does not allow his country to be taken by

---

the evil brotherhood of death and secret hierarchies and world powers in corners of the Jihad.[43] Furthermore, Netanyahu is a leader God has chosen to protect Jews and believers across the world. Also, hidden cultural traditions are less than life and need to be redeemed. Please, my brother, you know the God of Abraham is asking to bring justice to the God of Abraham. All nations have areas that need redemption. Ask in God's power to redeem the legacy and bring a miracle.

This is our same Covenant with God, in Jesus Christ America.

Even in whom we choose to lead our country and communities, we need to select people who believe in the God Highest of Abraham. We are a Judeo-Christian nation. See, that is justice. It is not a religion of "God Most High". It is the highest truth and is the foundation of our Constitution and Declaration of Independence. I say this because we need a solid foundation, which was the foundation on which America was built. It serves the people first, not the political ideology of the foundation of the artificial ideas of Political Regimes, to control the people under a foundation of communistic rule. And our America never had that foundation; hence, this is why Americans now see the truth is revealed: the Democratic Elite Communists are not for America's legacy and life and freedom. "Constitution real truth, moral principles of the natural law." Hillsdale College Excellent. Schools should follow these programs.[44]

I think it is the Democratic Elite Communists who are trying to make a new Constitution, not our original, and wiping out all we worked for World Controls and taking all ownership of life, legacy, personhood, and children.

---

[43] https://en.wikipedia.org/wiki/Benjamin_Netanyahu Prime Minister of Israel, Benjamin Netanyahu, ⓘⓘב נולד ;-21 באוקטובר 1949, ה'תש"י כ"ח בתשרי) הוא פוליטיקאי ישראלי

[44] Hillsdale College - Developing Minds. Improving Hearts.;Start Your Free Online Course Today | Hillsdale College Online Courses

The fact proves this.
Of the Covenant of Prayer of Continental Congress 1774
Constitution
Declaration of Independence
Many other documents – Look them up[45]
And our American law
And our Biblical Traditions

Philippians 2:12 So, my dear friends, you have always been obedient; your obedience must not be limited to when I am present. Now that I am absent, it must be more evidence, so work out your salvation in fear and trembling. 13 It is God who gives you the intention and the powers to act for his own generous purpose.

There is the sanctification of His blood .. that .. can and does redeem them .. See .. he has created the image of Him in them .. and he will allow certain things to happen to make them realize that their actions are evil and not of the Trinity. Remember, God gives us free will to choose …

They are His most beautiful creations. THERE WILL BE A MIRACLE

GOD FIRST, AMERICA, OUR MIRACLE, their bodies, hearts, and their soul BE REDEEMED SAVED IN JESUS CHRIST

See, God has brought me to these places not only on land but put on proclamation in speaking, writing, and singing to plant seeds of HIS MIRACLES to get the powers of principalities to the cross of Jesus Christ, SAVED by JESUS CHRIST.

Listen, please. Whether you know it or not, your works of sound and life are in God's eyes and even hands. He gave you what you have and all that you do. We have a Covenant with Jesus Christ, America; you could never break that. We are

---

[45] Ibid, Hillsdale College

(32) WHO ARE THE EMPIRES THAT WILL RULE THE WORLD AS REVEALED IN DANIEL AND THE BOOK OF REVELATION - YouTube[46] July 4th 2023

Rulers of the World that are Beast Definition

There are different levels and places that need to be redeemed.

In the places, the Spirit of the Lord tells me.

Just like they mutilate the cities and starve the people and make trickery and even seek to feed them sickness. -

There is a group of people now who are religious, and they call themselves. Many of them have been assimilated from both tables. The church uses masonry. I am not sure about all aspects of their lives, but I know they are doing witchcraft, and many have been exposed.

This is the same analogy as our American government seeking to change our tradition under the Democratic Elite Communist, woke world controls, secrecy, and trying to take away ownership.

We need to make a miracle of redemption of this .. in the prayer to save them. Now.

They are our brothers and sisters

At this very moment, I ask for a miracle. . . .

The parents need to teach the children the correct things. When the children see what has happened, it will affect them. Their actions are

---

[46] WHO ARE THE EMPIRES THAT WILL RULE THE WORLD AS REVEALED IN DANIEL AND IN THE BOOK OF REVELATION(32) WHO ARE THE EMPIRES THAT WILL RULE THE WORLD AS REVEALED IN DANIEL AND IN THE BOOK OF REVELATION - YouTube

negative and toxic; the children will see this and the toxic actions of injustice.

Children are insightful.. and they will learn incorrect and cultural practices that are not of God or our country. We want our children to be pure and Holy.

We want our people to seek purity, holiness, and righteousness.

I believe Americans are righteous and want a Country of Judeo-Christian Belief.

Americans want God to be their leader, not the ideas of men.

When we put God first in our lives, we can experience miracles of redemption and restoration.

Mat. 19:26 Jesus gazed at them. 'By human resources,' he told them, 'this is impossible; for God, everything is possible.'

Discussion on Topics

Brief notes on China

Communistic and Socialistic Elite

Please note that I discuss China in my book Arise to God's Truth, Restore and Keep America's Freedom.[47]

To:luciarden@hotmail.com

Here are just brief statements

Wed 9/7/2022 8:23 AM

Divine Discussion for the Peoples for Freedom June 5, 2022 We as a people need to realize that the Communistic and Socialistic Elite powers in the fast-paced life of technology moving at the line of speed of light have a direct relationship to the effects it puts on the human life; Listen and the justice and peace and truth under our Constitution and God-given rights under the Law of the land and even the Divine nature of life and all creation, humans, animals, nature, eco-systems, and all of the human developments and evolution is in the war with "Communistic Evils of World Controls."

First, we must realize the Communistic and Socialistic global powers are vast and treacherous and do not serve the people first. These global powers serve their artificial ideologies blinded like the cold, stagnant, diseased river standings still in every nation where communism and socialism are rampant recipes. They are interjected into the countries of human life. See, Communism and Socialism(rampant) do not empower the people. They find the people's strengths and gifts and build them up; then, when the treacherous leaders find the gifts of the people, they use them for their purpose and enslave the people. And they, the Communist leaders, remove

---

47 Arden Lisa Lucia, MIDV "Arise to God's Truth," Restore and Keep America's Freedom. www.lisaluciaarden.com

the ownership of land, remove self-development, bring the death of the seed of life(abortion), and even suffocate the life of the authentic being of the person to create.

The Communists and Socialists have had a plan for years for a "one-world government." Even under Reagan, he speaks of the "evil" of the Communists, and under all circumstances, we need to keep peace and keep America free from Communistic ideologies.

History repeats itself; From the days of Moses and the Israelites, he is the person God chose to lead the people out of "Slavery" from the Pharaoh (the Communist), and it was done.. after all the plagues.

And realize we are the USA birthed in the foundation of Judeo-Christian ethics, yet a guardian of all nations and all peoples to build and live in freedom and justice and have a home to be a people of truth and respect, empowering each other to be human and live in peace and happiness. Remember when the settlers ran and chose their land? Today, the land is taken by the Elite influential and communist leaders. Also, ownership and control of people and their lives today are controlled by the government and even elite leaders with no experience in specific issues that must bring justice to the people first.

Prior, the funds were unequally distributed, and now it is the most detrimental ever in history; since the phases, the evilest atrocities against humanity across the world have taken place; hence, many Americans and people around the world have become victims and are controlled by the communists in power.

There is a division in our country between the Democratic Communistic Leaders, Democratic peoples of liberty, and the Republicans that desire freedom and justice for America and humanity. And in all this is the global powers of the Elite controlling these Democratic leaders and, in some cases, the Republican leaders.

These Elite, influential Communist leaders, Communist countries, and USA politicians have become a thick, diseased, stagnant river with a toxic life of the evilest ever in the existence of humanity. Today, we have all we need to bring life across every nation: well-being, justice, and authentic personhood concerning the community and country to life as human beings.

See, the urgency is that if we wait year after year, we will have our freedoms taken away step by step and in the evilest strategic process of the global Communist.

Please, let me show you.

The One World Government Elites have been trying to control America and even the world for years.

China has become a mighty nation, and Russia has integrated into the world powers.

During World War II, America could have taken over the East and West; instead, it empowered them and helped them reach their feet.

America is a country given to people who will respect her and live in justice and peace, abiding by the Constitution and living in truth. America is like no other country in the world. She is the mother of all Nations in God to bring peace and justice at home and in the world.

Now, the Communist leaders and Socialist leaders globally today have shown their purpose to take UNDER THE DEMOCRATIC ELITE COMMUNIST.

They thought they would continue to accept their injustices.

ALL THE FREEDOMS AWAY FROM AMERICANS, proven by the fact of these actions taking place.

1. Under Obama, his desire and the Elite in control wanted America to become Socialist through his actions, which made America weaker at all levels. Please see the books *"The Amature"* and *"Our Need to Give to the World, Heal America Love in God."*

2. Even under Clinton, many detrimental actions destroyed our production, housing, banking system, mortgages, and economy.

3. The Democratic leaders of the Communistic Elites were shocked when President Trump got in. This shows that the people of America wanted a change and realized the urgency to protect our freedoms, our children's lives, and the blood, sweat, and tears our people have endured to keep America strong and free.

4. President Bush, Iraqi war and 911 and Agenda 21

5. When President Trump was President, the Democratic Elites of Communist ideologies conspired to make a strategic process to take down his work and his team. Despite all that, President Trump and his team were able to put Americans first and build the military, the economy, and human dignity, protect the seed of life, and have countless other successes.

6. Then the CCP virus was made in the laboratory to do the evilest violence in human history, destroying the lives of all humanity across the world, the human holocaust. Also, killing the elderly weakens the people and decreases the population.

7. More than at any time in human history, Americans have not had crimes against them regarding our justice system. When the vote for the 2020 Presidential Election was counted fraudulently, vast crimes occurred. President Trump won the presidential election in 2020.

8. The failure to exit Afghanistan strategically was also one of the most terrible wounds in American history in the hearts of people across the nations when the USA had the strongest and most

strategic military in the world. The Taliban owns Afghanistan now, and many Americans today are still there as prisoners, and the women, children, and men are abused; many have lost their homes, all their life work, and the years and billions of dollars America put into Afghanistan to protect her. Billions of dollars of the USA's military tools were left there in Afghanistan. Do the Taliban now have these war tools powerfully stolen from the USA? Remember, the Taliban's business is to sell war tools internationally. This is a holocaust to humanity's freedom and the holocaust to the history of life in justice attempting to bring the life of humanity to death. Our American borders are open? The Taliban We are in the most dangerous position ever in human history for America.

9. The failure to protect Ukraine strategically was also one of the most significant wounds in American history in the hearts of people across the nations when the USA had the strongest and most strategic military in the world. The failure to rapidly and strategically aid and protect Ukraine was also one of the most significant wounds in American history in the hearts of people across the nations when the USA had the strongest and most strategic military in the world. This is a holocaust to humanity's freedom and the holocaust to humanity to death. Even though we stay there at the onset. We gave our tools in a manner of hopefulness, not strategically. Emergency that needs to be reiterated: And now we are in a war where we have spent billions that could have given homes to all people experiencing homelessness across America .. See, they want to make military tools, and they know that Ukraine has commodities.

10. China's geopolitical power is vast across the globe.

The hands of these evilest deformities of the most treacherous atrocities in history are the hands of death upon our nation. And today, we need to bring a miracle of God's power to our country.

God help us; God protect us from the evil Communists and Socialists; God shows us the way.

I pray the United States of America and its people will be saved and our freedoms redeemed.

I pray for the world that the Communist and Social torture and abuse, taking away ownership, and human trafficking WILL STOP.

CHAPTER FOUR

Ethics and Liberalism

Topics of Urgency

Brief notes

Divine Message: April 15, 2023 Ethics and liberalism: what should we do?

1. I have told you all I can now, daughter.
2. You continue what I have told you to do.
3. See, they have taken a conspiracy of freedom fighters like yourself and committed crimes, causing them to look like criminals or in the wrong or cannot have or complete.
4. Nothing goes from my eyes, daughter. I see them in everything they do. I know the violence they have done and what they are preparing to do. And I see across the nations and universe.
5. They must pray continuously daily and ask Me to guide them and help them seek righteousness.
6. They need to pay back those they took from intentionally or did not deliberately take from * As soon as possible. I do not know when My Father will strike.
7. They need to help and empower people experiencing homelessness, including women, widows, and men.

See How can we improve?

1. The Spirit of the Lord states: It begins molecular daughter. The molecular is the spiritual daughter. It causes comments, attacks, and attacks and creates and enters an environment that makes changes. .and depending on what the molecules are in .. and how they respond and their intention. .will cause a reaction and form and create and dissipate using energy to develop and create different forms. See molecules that are closer to God's truth.. always want to love because it is preeminent, and preeminent is God's love. This is why God uses His people to help those who need help.

   ["It is God's fight," we are His people of righteousness. Jesus Christ already overcame death by His Resurrection.]

2. The Spirit of the Lord states, "Not always do I stop evil or injustices. It is the free will of the people to choose." I ensure they have been warned; however, they choose differently.
3. {This is why ethics is essential to God's ethics … and ethics comes from the Ten Commandments.}
4. This is why it is essential to fund the police now with ethical training and the schools and people with ethics.. because today, we have a globalization of different measurements of the powerful controller's truth that is not the best truth. It is not God's truth}. My thoughts {} []
5. All ethics are within the Ten Commandments.
6. Comment: See[LA1], then I thought about something that happened that I made a mistake… yet it was caused and provoked by their sin and their conspiracy .. then the Spirit of God gave me a way to show the truth and protect myself. Hence, this indicates that God will get you out of the clutches of unrighteousness and criminals if you seek

righteousness; yet, sometimes, we go through trials, and there are living Jobs. And there needs to be someone to be a reflection where there needs to be God's truth and love.

7. {Rules are as important as ethics; rules are within ethics, and ethics are within regulations. Ethics connect to the human psyche, which consists of the soul, brain, spirit, and physical movement. Because ethics are infinite of God's precepts

8. This is why we need to return to the basic ethics of wholesome ethics: family values and protecting children first.

9. Comment: I have discussed this prior. Many causes of societal deformities have come from modernity, post-modernity, and the present technology life that do not correspond or naturally mix with the human being. For example, liberalism has many characteristics of entering into the lesser truth and deformity of aspects of all ways of life that do not protect children, innocent family values, and our Constitutional rights. We need pure ethics, justice, protection of family and children's values, and even a basic way of life to choose the authentic being and make decisions of clear betterment for themselves, their families, friends, and the community to be self-sufficient and healthy and develop their authentic being. This comment is just a general statement. See, our country needs to allow the creative flow of the children in a wholesome environment of pureness and justice. We have the lowest development of the creation of ideas compared to all the countries that have a good standing for their people. We must return to the pure right to protect the children's families and people. Constitutional rights and ethics and making our decisions for our health.}

10. Comment: {Since the powerful controllers of Elite Communists have done the most treacherous atrocities bringing death upon human life….. The powerful controllers of Elite communists have not

brought justice and not truth to the people. They have brought death to the lives of our nations. There have been documented facts against the people.

11. Comment. Therefore, we have the right to choose freedoms, justice, and liberty, not to be controlled. Hence, in a pleading conclusion of the most significant warning, VOTE TO SAVE USA AND HUMANITY}

VOTE PRESIDENT TRUMP AND THE FREEDOM WARRIORS OF PEACE AND JUSTICE AND TRUTH

Divine Message April 15, 2023

The Spirit of the Lord told me to rest and pray.

I did and prayed, I slept, and then I pleaded. What liberal ideas do you want me to say are incorrect?

I was begging. Something was trying to hold me back from the information. Remember, these are prayers, and timing and position are paramount. God, it is in His control.

Liberal and Democratic Elite Communistic Ideas

Whatever it takes to bring Peace, we need to bring peace. Reagan

Note: I have already discussed these points in different aspects and order. However, we need to pin them down to help the people see.

1. Abortions are a liberal idea promoted and Comment
   a. **Thou should not kill**
   b. **See when schools concentrate on developing the individual student to participate in society justly and flourishing with tools to be a person of life and success and diligence, integrity, dedication to trade and job and position a mission to be that person that is evolving. Yet,**

the curriculum, circumstances, and environment must be pure, just, and conservative in children's upbringing in America. Otherwise, there are more legalities of selfhood and even world controls, such as entertainment and technology mind controls.

See, the higher abortion rate is more on the lower economic level for younger girls. Hence, let our public schools follow the paradigms of successful schools. This has been discussed in my writings and Podcasts.

c. See, abortions are not the natural way intended at the creation of humans.

d. Science of deformed and deranged minds of man's ideas has developed it to use as birth control, not just an emergency if the woman or child is in danger of death and medical problems.

e. Science then has become so big. This Science then has become a way to control and monopolize these innocent girls and women to abort their babies so they can use them for scientific laboratory tests and even use them as substances to intake for humans as a youth medicine.

f. Chemical abortion is dangerous and causes and changes organ deformity.

g. Also, there is a monetary variable here. Those who oversee the aborted babies get funds. See, these people are using their bodies and great gifts. A human can have a child and innocent babies that cannot protect themselves from the woman and the girls and the man and the boys involved.

h. Note: There should be education that the parents deliver. NOT SCHOOLS. Many churches and groups and local parent groups can now discuss this to tell their children no sex out of marriage; even if they may not do that .. because of the culture, they should still teach it. So their children see that sexual encounters are a most beautiful human expression of love and a gifted honor of giving oneself to each other and exchanging intimacy. See, when one has sex, they become flesh. Then they take on each other's self. We know humans build relationships sometimes and many times, especially when we have sexual relationships. See, when the man or woman or girl or boy does not want to keep the baby, then it stimulates the girl or woman to have an abortion also since they love the boy and man and wish not to lose him.   And even for the protection of sex of committed relationships, not to have abortions and marriage

i. There is a psyche deep in the soul that has a wound when there are abortions when a woman or man comes.. to the realization that babies after conception are the breath of God and human life. It takes healing and forgiveness.

j. Since marriage has decreased and sexual encounters are still occurring, this also increases abortion if there is no protected sex. Because there is no commitment to having a family or children. This may seem small, but every life of a baby is life and should be saved. You would think the pharmacies would have them on every front lane in the store. Where do they keep them in the store?

k. The minds of men have ideas that do not benefit the human being. Abortion is the taking of human life from the gift from the creator to have and enjoy and make life

l. The woman and girl do not know what is best and are forced and misguided.

m. What are the responses of a girl or woman who is contemplating abortion? She feels hopeless because of the responsibility of the baby; the man does not want the baby, and she is hiding it from her family and community for various reasons. In this paper, we will not discuss all the variables. However, we do know that finances are a more significant part of the decision and support of the family and friends and shame. Let us create an environment for girls and women to keep their babies.

n. What does it mean to be human in note is not to be killed or murdered at any stage after conception .it means the freedom not to abuse or kill or use the intended purpose of a natural human being, especially when they are innocent and cannot protect themselves

2. World health controls

3. Boarders and safety

a. It is most important for our military protection to protect the lives of all the people. Not to use technological controls that will bring torture or financial oppression.

b. We protect the entry of suite cases and airlines.. security. Yet, we leave open

4. Business and Dispersion of funds: most wealthly is owned only by 1 percent of all people. Today God is asking to give..in His power leaders now, Daniel 4 read.

5. Education .. and preparation of self-sufficiency..

6. Social Media and Music Entertainment

a. Not reality for all people because

7. Transgender is a secondary being.. and the extremely liberal and scientific secret powers want to do scientific testing on humans. Moreover, these scientific people and people who want to be

transgender are searching for true life.. because they have not accepted God in a way they were created as a perfect human being in His sight. God is compassionate and forgives and seeks to enter into a humble and repentant relationship.

In praying received this thought.

See just as we as believers and hopeful those who seek justice in God's truth.

We hear, we are guided, we are commanded, we are called, we are strengthened, we are filled with the Holy Spirit, we are directed to bring God's glory, we are redeemed, and we bring God's victory.

However, there is another side that is not of God that uses life for human ideas, and there are different levels of human actions that are criminal and confuse truth with lies. See people who do not believe in God and conservative ideas and perceptions to bring life and protection of children and all peoples to be that.

Words of salience War of Hamas and Israel .. Iran

Never again shall there be a holocaust of the Jews? Never shall there be a killing of six million Jews. Yet, today, there is a "holocaust," catastrophe," treacherous evil upon the people of the world. The World Controls

What does *Shoah* mean in English?

CATASTROPHE

Shoah is the Hebrew word for "catastrophe." This term means explicitly the killing of nearly six million Jews in Europe by Nazi Germany and its collaborators during the Second World War. English-speaking countries more commonly use the word Holocaust, which is Greek for "sacrifice by fire." [48]

I must tell you my first book, *Our Need to Give to the World, Heal America Love in God.*

Pontifical Saint Thomas Aquinas University in Rome, Italy

When I went to Pontifical Saint Thomas Aquinas University in Rome, Italy, I was called there to Get a portion of information from the book to show.

When I went to the Dean's office, he ran down the hall after he accepted me into the school, and I ran after him. He caught his robe on the Fire Hydrant, and he was shocked. I will never believe that we have to put the fire out of injustice. And proclaim God's Salvation.

See, there has been an evil fire of a plan to take and destroy the Jews, Christians, believers, and those who want freedom.

Not only to we have a great atrocity of the present

VENGEANCE

Punishment as retribution for harm against persons. It seems quite clear that the OT endorses the notion of both human and divine vengeance (from Heb. nqm) at least under certain circumstances. The OT records specific

---

[48]https://www.google.com/search?q=holocaust+definition+stanford+university+definiti on&rlz=1C1CHZN_enIT1045IT1045&oq=&gs_lcrp=EgZjaHJvbWUqCQgAECMYJxjqAjIJCA AQIxgnGOoCMg8IARAuGCcYxwEY6gIY0QMyCQgCECMYJxjqAjIJCAMQIxgnGOoCMgkIBB AjGCcY6gIyCQgFECMYJxjqAjIJCAYQIxgnGOoCMgkIBxAjGCcY6gLSAQkxMTQxajBqMTWoA giwAgE&sourceid=chrome&ie=UTF-8Shoah is the Hebrew word for "catastrophe".

instances where God declares war against an enemy of the Israelites as an act of vengeance for a previous atrocity (Num. 31; Deut. 25:17-19). In fact, at least one prophet apparently considered vengeance to be an attribute of God (Nah. 1:2). A similar view of God can be found in the NT (Rom. 12:19; 2 Thess. 1:5-10).

The question of human vengeance is somewhat more complicated. The OT does recognize the right of relatives of an accidental homicide victim to take direct vengeance against the perpetrator. However, the OT also seeks to limit this right by allowing the perpetrator to flee to one of the cities of refuge (Exod. 21:13; Num. 35; Deut. 19:1-13). While some biblical characters do take vengeance (1 Kgs. 2:5-9), it is also true that the OT condemns vengeance when it is directed at another Israelite (Lev. 19:18). This attempt to discourage human vengeance becomes an important part of Jesus' message (Matt. 5:38-48).

Matt. 5:38 You have heard that it hath been said: An eye for an eye, and a tooth for a tooth. 39 But I say to you not to resist evil: but if one strike thee on thy right cheek, turn to him also the other: 40 And if a man will contend with thee in judgment, and take away thy coat, let go thy cloak also unto him. 41 And whosoever will force thee one mile, go with him other two. 42 Give to him that asketh of thee, and from him that would borrow of thee turn not away. 43 You have heard that it hath been said, Thou shalt love thy neighbor, and hate thy enemy. 44 But I say to you, Love your enemies: do good to them that hate you: and pray for them that persecute and calumniate you: 45 That you may be the children of your Father who is in heaven, who maketh his sun to rise upon the good, and bad, and raineth upon the just and the unjust. 46 For if you love them that love you, what reward shall you have? do not even the publicans this? 47 And if you salute your brethren only, what do you more? do not also the heathens this? 48 Be you therefore perfect, as also your heavenly Father is perfect.

John1: 7 He came as a witness, to bear witness to the light, so that everyone might believe through him. **8** He was not the light, he was to bear witness to the light.

The witness of the light protects humanity and justice.First, reconcile, and ask and ask in the community and ask in government. If they do not reconcile, we still need to protect the "light of God" upon His humanity of life.

CHAPTER FIVE

Brief Notes on the Eucharist

Blood of Jesus Salvation of the Word

Eucharist May 1, 2015. Written… He told me .. April 30

Pray for God's Will Brief Notes: You ask also

My Lord my God in Christ Jesus Help to do your will

I know many things you have shown me and made me aware. Help me to do all and each and everything every moment in your purpose and your glory in these later days. O Almighty Father in Heaven, Alpha, and Omega help me to do your will. I am asking what I should do to help America and the world.

Jesus told me in these last days two days ago at the Church that these are the last days the Eucharist table.. we be used for all our food… all our purpose…. Everything we do we should do in the body of Christ with Christ for Christ in Christ in the strength and power of Christ .. not for our self's, even for our development as a beautiful human but for the beauty of His purpose… to bring in those lost sheep.. to bring in those.. people across the earth.. into His Kingdom.. .. to protect the ones in the Church now.. now that are at His heart..

145

John 6: 51 I am the living bread which has come down from heaven. Anyone who eats this bread will live for ever; and the bread that I shall give is my flesh, for the life of the world.'

Brief Notes: to Bring and Joy that Passes all Understanding and a Peace to know we can have life on earth abundantly in God's love.. giving His life to us so we will be worthy to be in a right relationship with Him when we humble ourselves and ask to forgive our sins.. and seek to sin no more..

The Eucharistic meal is in memory of the Cross of Christ.. and Resurrection and Sending the Holy Spirit in the Trinity as an Advocated to live in and with and through us..

ARTICLE 3: THE SACRAMENT OF THE EUCHARIST

1322   The holy Eucharist completes Christian initiation. Those who have been raised to the dignity of the royal priesthood by Baptism and configured more deeply to Christ by Confirmation participate with the whole community in the Lord's own sacrifice by means of the Eucharist.

1323   "At the Last Supper, on the night he was betrayed, our Savior instituted the Eucharistic sacrifice of his Body and Blood. This he did in order to perpetuate the sacrifice of the cross throughout the ages until he should come again, and so to entrust to his beloved Spouse, the Church, a memorial of his death and resurrection: a sacrament of love, a sign of unity, a bond of charity, a Paschal banquet 'in which Christ is consumed, the mind is filled with grace, and a pledge of future glory is given to us.'"135

I. THE EUCHARIST – SOURCE AND SUMMIT OF ECCLESIAL LIFE

1324   The Eucharist is "the source and summit of the Christian life."136 "The other sacraments, and indeed all ecclesiastical ministries and works of the apostolate, are bound up with the Eucharist and are oriented toward it. For in the blessed Eucharist is contained the whole spiritual good of the Church, namely Christ himself, our Pasch."137

1325   "The Eucharist is the efficacious sign and sublime cause of that communion in the divine life and that unity of the People of God by which the Church is kept in being. It is the culmination both of God's action sanctifying the world in Christ and of the worship men offer to Christ and through him to the Father in the Holy Spirit."138

1326   Finally, by the Eucharistic celebration we already unite ourselves with the heavenly liturgy and anticipate eternal life, when God will be all in all.

1327   In brief, the Eucharist is the sum and summary of our faith: "Our way of thinking is attuned to the Eucharist, and the Eucharist in turn confirms our way of thinking."140

See

II. WHAT IS THIS SACRAMENT CALLED?

1328   The inexhaustible richness of this sacrament is expressed in the different names we give it. Each name evokes certain aspects of it. It is called:

Eucharist, because it is an action of thanksgiving to God. The Greek words eucharistein141 and eulogein142 recall the Jewish blessings that proclaim — especially during a meal — God's works: creation, redemption, and sanctification.

1329   The Lord's Supper, because of its connection with the supper which the Lord took with his disciples on the eve of his Passion and because it anticipates the wedding feast of the Lamb in the heavenly Jerusalem.143

The *Breaking of Bread,* because Jesus used this rite, part of a Jewish meat when as master of the table he blessed and distributed the bread,144 above all at the Last Supper.145 It is by this action that his disciples will recognize him after his Resurrection,146 and it is this expression that the first Christians will use to designate their Eucharistic assemblies;147 by doing so they signified that all who eat the one broken bread, Christ, enter into communion with him and form but one body in him.148

The Eucharistic assembly (synaxis), because the Eucharist is celebrated amid the assembly of the faithful, the visible expression of the Church.149

1330   The memorial of the Lord's Passion and Resurrection.

The *Holy Sacrifice because it presents* the one sacrifice of Christ the Savior and includes the Church's offering. The terms *holy sacrifice of the Mass, "sacrifice of praise," spiritual sacrifice, pure and holy sacrifice* are also used,150 since it completes and surpasses all the sacrifices of the Old Covenant.

The *Holy and Divine Liturgy,* because the Church's whole liturgy finds its center and most intense expression in the celebration of this sacrament; in the same sense we also call its celebration the *Sacred Mysteries.* We speak of the *Most Blessed Sacrament* because it is the Sacrament of sacraments. The Eucharistic species reserved in the tabernacle are designated by this same name.

1331   Holy Communion, because by this sacrament we unite ourselves to Christ, who makes us sharers in his Body and Blood to form a single body.151 We also call it: the holy things (ta hagia; sancta)152 — the first meaning of the phrase "communion of saints" in the Apostles' Creed — the bread of angels, bread from heaven, medicine of immortality,153 viaticum. . . .

1332   Holy Mass (Missa), because the liturgy in which the mystery of salvation is accomplished concludes with the sending forth (missio) of the faithful, so that they may fulfill God's will in their daily lives.

III. THE EUCHARIST IN THE ECONOMY OF SALVATION

The signs of bread and wine

1333   At the heart of the Eucharistic celebration are the bread and wine that, by the words of Christ and the invocation of the Holy Spirit, become Christ's Body and Blood. Faithful to the Lord's command the Church continues to do, in his memory and until his glorious return, what he did on the eve of his Passion: "He took bread. . . ." "He took the cup filled with wine. . . ." The signs of bread and wine become, in a way surpassing understanding, the Body and Blood of Christ; they continue also to signify the goodness of creation. Thus in the Offertory we give thanks to the Creator for bread and wine,154 fruit of the "work of human hands," but above all as "fruit of the earth" and "of the vine" — gifts of the Creator. The Church sees in the gesture of the king-priest Melchizedek, who "brought out bread and wine," a prefiguring of her offering.155

1334   In the Old Covenant, bread and wine were offered in sacrifice among the first fruits of the earth as a sign of grateful acknowledgment to the Creator. But they also received a new significance in the context of the Exodus: the unleavened bread that Israel eats every year at Passover commemorates the haste of the departure that liberated them from Egypt; the remembrance of the manna in the desert will always recall Israel that it lives by the bread of the Word of God;156 their daily bread is the fruit of the promised land, the pledge of God's faithfulness to his promises. The "cup of blessing"157 at the end of the Jewish Passover meal adds to the festive joy of wine an eschatological dimension: the messianic expectation of rebuilding Jerusalem. When Jesus instituted the Eucharist, he gave a new and definitive meaning to the blessing of the bread and the cup.

1335   The miracles of the multiplication of the loaves, when the Lord says the blessing, breaks and distributes the loaves through his disciples to feed the multitude, prefigure the superabundance of this unique bread of his Eucharist.158 The sign of water turned into wine at Cana already announces the Hour of Jesus' glorification. It makes manifest the fulfillment of the wedding feast in the Father's kingdom, where the faithful will drink the new wine that has become the Blood of Christ.159

1336 The first announcement of the Eucharist divided the disciples, just as the announcement of the Passion scandalized them: "This is a hard saying; who can listen to it?"160 The Eucharist and the Cross are stumbling blocks. It is the same mystery and it never ceases to be an occasion of division. "Will you also go away?":161 the Lord's question echoes through the ages, as a loving invitation to discover that only he has "the words of eternal life"162 and that to receive in faith the gift of his Eucharist is to receive the Lord himself.[49]

John 6:51 I am the living bread which has come down from heaven. Anyone who eats this bread will live forever, and the bread that I shall give is my flesh, for the life of the world.'

I want to say . that I believe in the Eucharistic meal taking the Eucharist .. going to the Church directly..

I have not been able to get to Church every Sunday.

And actually, it has been difficult. I believe Jesus Christ in the Spirit of the Trinity in the Holy Spirit.. is in unity with the Eucharistic meal.. in heaven and earth.

In all we do, we are living and being and participating in the Eucharistic meal. We see we are part of the Body of Christ, the Body of Believers in the Church of God. We have an intimate personal relationship with God in all we do, and we accept that He gave His life for us.

---

[49] CATHOLIC CATECHISM (ENGLISH) The Catechism of the Catholic Church (English) (C. Catechism-E)©1997 Libreria Editrice Vatican, Vatican City Used by permission of Amministrazione del Patrimonio Della Sede Apostlica, Vatican City Electronic text hypertexted and prepared by OakTree Software, Inc.Version 1.5,Eucharist,

I have had many spiritual experiences at the Eucharist in the Church. It has been God's honor and spiritual gift to me to experience His healing Eucharist.

Divine Message February 19, 2023

Church Mass .. Divine Vision and Divine Message of the Eucharist

I saw a vision of blue and aqua … blue and light rim… The border of the robe… is white…….. and the cross on the left shoulder light… yellow-white and a little orange …

Hand and on the right, Carrying the light… the people… and holding the candle pol... the writing the Bible words… there were … in Greek… Hebrew… Latin, and maybe other languages... they were holding the candles polls and then a light… a flame large and thick… and strong.

We carry the cross for specific purposes they were small crosses and the people were together.. I asked what are they going toward. The thought came to my heart toward the Resurrection.. toward heaven, toward God, Toward truth, Toward Jesus

Eucharist…

The Eucharist is the body and blood (Gave is life sacrifice to cleanse us from our sins) of Christ, but it is the Trinity. It is the Trinity, the Holy Spirit, the advocate; Jesus Christ said He is going to send down God of Abraham, who sent Jesus the King from heaven to be our Savior, the Eucharistic Body, and it is in the Trinity. And we celebrate the Eucharistic body in all that we do we are supposed to have … in Jesus not only in the Sacrament of the Church in all our work and who we are and what we hope for and what we live for and all your table and the table the Eucharistic table is the plan that God has actually for what He wants in our life it is a table a plan eating together of the Trinity and all the Saints and Angels of God and all the prophets and all the minor prophets and those believers that's the table around the table with Mary that is God wants us to do. Wants us to continue around the table the promises and on the table we are fed, we are fed with the Eucharistic body.. ; but, we also have sacraments and the Holy Scriptures and the teaching of the Saints and all the prophets, and it shines the light shines on the Eucharistic table in the world we will shine the light of God shines in us shines upon the people of God and in and with and through them and so the, world will see that we are a reflection of God's love as we are suppose to be Through Jesus we live and have life Amen. Priest represented of Jesus and He ordained and is blessed even though he is human and anointed by the mystery of the Trinity promise and God's promise to the every lasting covenant not only the old covenant but now the new covenant Jesus Christ and the Priest is the mediator between Jesus and the people but we also go hand and hand with the priest and side by side and the people are the saints and the saints and the ones at the table of God that believe and even those whom are seeking to believe; because they eat at the table we feed them the love of God in us not of us the Spirit of God and the mystery of God in us; so hence all we do we need to live in the Eucharistic Body and truth and redemption of humanity.

I wanted to say this is so beautiful Dr. Scholer a professor from Fuller Theological School [50]... Told me the most wonderful and magnificent truths about Jesus Christ.. and Theology.

He passed, and I attended his service at a Christian Church on Marengo Street in Pasadena. The Church was just around the corner from Fuller Theological Seminary. Even though I am Catholic, I also studied under Protestant Exegesis.

You know … how the Protestants believe in the Resurrection so faithful.

While His wife was speaking, I saw a vision of blood on the Cross. I was praying at a high level. It was so magnificent. It showed that Jesus Christ

---

[50] https://eewc.com/david-scholer-memoriam/Dr. Scholer, Fuller Theological Seminary

gave Professor Scholer eternal life through the blood of the lamb, and he, I believe, was resurrected with Christ Jesus.

His wife—I loved her. She did not know me, but she was amazing. She could memorize all the Bible verses, so magnificent.

All of us believers need to love each other, just like Mari, Mari, and Emmanuel said.

Then, the world would be more interested in Jesus Christ's Salvation.

Ephesians 1:3 Blessed be God the Father of our Lord Jesus Christ, who has blessed us with all the spiritual blessings of heaven in Christ. 4 Thus he chose us in Christ before the world was made to be holy and faultless before him in love, 5 marking us out for himself beforehand, to be adopted sons, through Jesus Christ. Such was his purpose and good pleasure, 6 to the praise of the glory of his grace, his gift to us in the Beloved, 7 in whom, through his blood, we gain our freedom, the forgiveness of our sins. Such is the richness of the grace 8 which he has showered on us in all wisdom and insight. 9 He has let us know the mystery of his purpose, according to his good pleasure which he determined beforehand in Christ, 10 for him to act upon when the times had run their course: that he would bring everything together under Christ, as head, everything in the heavens and everything on earth.

Do you know in the Eucharist and all we do every day when we give our life to God in all we do we find who we are.

Eucharist. 11.8.17

Jesus told me this in the Adoration.

Eucharist work

Eucharist body

Eucharist Holy Spirit

Eucharist ... Grace...

Verse what can many boast... We are not saved by works but by grace... '
See, when we take the Eucharistic mass, it gives us grace so that our works
are works of Christ in God in the power of the Holy Spirit. We become
grace for others. Carrying and sanctifying through the mystery of the Holy
Spirit with all different gifts so that the people have well-being and
wholesomeness to be the authentic human God created just as a plant and
flower needs to water regularly with good soil

When we take the Eucharist, we become Grace... of God in Christ because
we become the body and in the anointing of the Holy Spirit within the
Eucharist, which gives nourishment and sanctification in the Body of
Christ and the Holy Spirit and in God in the workings of a redeeming and
unity of life of the Trinity in the believer on earth. The Eucharistic mass
is from heaven and Brought down to earth.

Through God's Grace, we are saved. Ephesians 2:8 says, "Because it is by
grace that you have been saved, through faith, not by anything of your
own, but by a gift from God; 9 not by anything that you have done so that
nobody can claim the credit."

In all our work and life, we should apply the Blood of Jesus Christ …

When we apply the blood of the lamb Jesus Christ.

At the Eucharist meal, we enter a relationship with Him, and He blesses
us with the Glory of His purpose, which is what we were created for.

And we are then living a supernatural life in Jesus Christ.

Satan does not want this. That is what Satan tries to take the relationship
of Jesus Christ and all humanity.

Jesus Christ has already overcome satan by His Resurrection after He shed
His blood for the sins of the world.

In Ex 24:6, Moses holds the blood of victims in אַגָּנֹת. He dips a bunch of *hyssop* into the blood to sprinkle the people. In Isa 22:24 אֲגָנֹות, are common household vessels that can be hung on nails. The word appears in Assyrian *agan*(n)u "bowl" and Ugaritic (A. H. Honeyman, "The Pottery Vessels of the Old Testament," Palestine Exploration Fund, 1939, pp. 78–79).

This is the .. for telling of Jesus Christ .. crucified "nails," the blood of Christ Jesus .. and the "Bowls."

The food of life is Jesus Christ. In Revelation, the Bowls say that Jesus Christ will overcome the beast in the end times.

Revelation 16:1   Then I heard a loud voice from the sanctuary calling to the seven angels, 'Go, and empty the seven bowls of God's anger over the earth.' Jesus Christ has overcome Satan by His Cross and the Resurrection

Our Lady of Mount Carmel, December 27, 2017

December 28, 2017 Written

Adoration called for the people of the Church, America, and the World.

I was lifted in the rooms of God's purpose in the love of humanity. He has interwoven the eternal love of humanity in every aspect of His creation on Earth, in the heavens, and in the universe.

I. Look

Jesus said, "Look."

Jesus said the following, pleading in love.

1. "I am looking this way."
2. "You are looking that way.
3. "Look at Me, seek My face."
4. "Pray more than you have been praying."

5. " Come into the Sanctuary more than you have been; pray to see My Face." [Though Jesus Christ told me I had to change something up. I could not say. Before and at the present prayer. This is why I did not come to the sanctuary. Now I know what He wants at the moment.]

6. "Seeking My face is the "food of life." [I thought this was profound!]

7. The "food of life" is the Eucharistic Body of the Church and life itself."

Seek My face is seeking the precepts of the infinite that God created;

See, seeking My Face is seeking My body in the Sacrificial Lamb of the redeeming love through the cross represented by the Eucharistic meal. Seeking My Face is life itself in that when one seeks My Face; they will be able to participate in the Redemption of humanity back to the intended time before Adam and Eve ate the apple. Seeking My Face will bring all life that is not life."

[While in received and penetrated all of my beings. I asked with all my heart.

See, Jesus is close to me, and I love Him, and He loves me, and I have a love that grows continually for Him. [Of course, He loved me first, giving me life and redeeming life through the cross]. Of course, I fall short in some instances because the tests are always beyond what we can imagine, though I get up once again and repent and am strengthened. Then I am better… His love for me in my humanness has made me more of a love in my entire being for and with humanity.]

II. Listen

1.I asked about America with my entire heart, pleaded with my entire being, and was received in the heavenly room as God's gift to humanity: "What should we do about America?" Jesus answered,

"Seeking My Face is the bringing of joy, love, and peace, little daughter."

2. I asked Jesus, "Father, what if I tell them that this seems to be simple ideas and concepts of words to use, Father?"

3. Jesus answers, " Little daughter, these are the most important to obtain to live by, and that is through seeking My Face in prayer, and the one will be a reflection of Me, and this will bring hope and [even miracle. I thought this while Jesus was speaking.] And this will bring hope and joy, peace, and love. In seeking My Face, they can find the solutions to truths and the intention of truth.   They will know the truths and solutions to redeem what has been taken away." [Whether it is family, friends, and each person in humanity to bring back and to the salvation in God, or whether it is the legacy of America's flourishing beauty of healing.]

4. Look and carry out scrumptiously into the solutions that I have given you, and in the solution, the solutions to these need to be scrupulously carried out. [These are the solutions for America Jesus is referring to.]

5. "What has been taken away from America has to be redeemed." See, My little daughter, those have turned away from My face and have not "looked" toward me and at My Face. Looking at My face is the redeeming solutions to America through it is a "continuous love fo the Sacred Heart of the Most Holy Sacrament at the Altar." Though it is not just in the adoration, everything we do should be the center. The center around all things should be in Christ. This a continuous offering of hope in and of the Spirit of God. We need to run the race and get stronger and stronger and stronger, not in might (though be healthy physically. Maybe some may have might, and the healing of might to bring healing is a spirit gift

given to use only in God's purpose.] All solutions will be found in seeking the Face of Me child.

6. See, My Child, God has an intention for humanity and all that exists and those who have looked away.

7. You cannot stop growing. I have allowed you to "look away." I asked, "Why, Lord, have I looked away." Jesus said, "so that you may understand the difference. You are the Eucharist body of Me. My child, your life must be centered around seeking My Face. [We have togetherness in the Sacred Heart of the Spirit of the Lord.]

8. "Those things in Me must be redeemed lost in each state and each community. "As I have told you in the book for solutions: go into in the communities and states and redeem what was lost in the businesses; because it has been taken away of it and was not God's intention that is why America has had problems, those have turned away from My Face little daughter. Therefore, they have lost and given America to those not intended. I have told them to seek My Face for the solutions and redemption of the community and the states. "

9. Jesus continues and says, "Checks and balances." What do you mean, Checks and Balances?" Jesus answered, "Check that thing in the government continuously." [This Jesus told me at the Park in La Canada Flintridge; I had it in the solutions previously when President Trump was put into office. Jesus Christ in the Holy Spirit told us that each part of government needs to be checked to ensure that monies and processes were negligent and taken from America fraudulently.]

10. "President Trump needs to be protected more than he has regularly. He needs to be prayed over regularly by Priests and Ministers and [one he feels that has great faith in God. Then he will have more

faith, belief, healing, and protection.] The children [not just all his children] also need to be prayed regularly."

11. I asked, "Why do they need to be prayed over regularly when the Holy Spirit is with them?" [I asked this because I wanted the people to understand the mysterious miracle because Jesus has told me before. I know through the molecules within the atmosphere that humans come into contact with.]

12. First, trust that praying over President Trump will give him protection and the following gifts, as it will you and the child while praying over them.

A renewing, a cleansing of the body's physical and spiritual positions of life itself.

i. Solutions to help and heal America

ii. Understanding, knowledge, and wisdom will be revealed

iii. Discernment, strength, and protection when one passes through dangers in life, whether brief or chronic.

iv. Transformation and reciprocation: giving oneself to be prayed for and then participating in life.

Second, the Divine Holy Spirit is with the vessel of the believers and even in the mist and with the children; through virtuous prayers, it is "calling out," "calling out " the Lord's true God.

Willing is giving oneself fully to God's purpose in His Holy Spirit. God manifests strength in weakness. Giving all your soul to God. When calling out in prayer for faith to be in protection, it is to seek God's Face because there is the psyche of the human soul and the psyche that needs to be changed in thought.

Just as one puts good and certain thoughts nurturing their development, the prayers of seeking God's Face and the truth of prayers over them will.

How can a chemical change of motion in the brain affect the thoughts, the body, and life? When the children are prayed for, they hear the calling as it brings faith, hope, and the essence of God's truth and truths so that they can decipher the truth and when in the world. Also, they will not be easily deceived and will desire God's intentions and plan and seek God's Face. When the swimmer swims, they learn to swim swiftly within the water, gliding in and floating smoothly, for they receive their purpose and destination with greater healthiness, though the tool is water. This may be likened to the way the Holy Spirit and the Spirit of God, the Virgin Mary, and the Saints come and soothe and heal and reveal solutions and truths to every part of one's life. Though they remember their actions when one is tested beyond humanness, they need even to give themselves more to be the reflection of God's Eucharistic body. "

Mary said, "President Trump, you have been called graciously, honorably, lovingly, trustingly, and devotionally to be the Eucharistic Body of Christ Jesus.

In your work, you describe the entire government of America and all other world governments. Seeking God's Face will bring the solutions to a broken world that needs to be healed. (If I may say, it needs to be mended (as Jesus Christ of the Sacred Heart and Cross told us) with the quintessential needle of God's truth. LOOK AT WORD IN SEEKING Christ's Face; God will give you that needle quintessential truth, President Trump, the Governmental Officials, and every one of us. When we seek God's Face, we will mend the torn world, and in doing so, we will heal the wound of Christ Jesus. That is redeeming humanity what was lost that is participating in the Eucharistic body of the true intention of the cross of Jesus wounds to mend the [sins] of the world that need healing and bring this loving, joy, and peace."

Visions I saw a covering of platinum diamonds shining on me while Jesus Christ told me about these Divine Messages for the people. I saw Him, Jesus' Face. It was all light, white shining with yellow. He gave me a key.

I went through that door I saw before and stepped into God's light of the Holy heavens While Jesus Christ was telling me that!.... Most of the time, I run to Him and go on Chariots of horses in the light of the Holy Spirit, which is the (energy and gas to form speed. Michael Archangel is the chief protection, and the angels are the rules that watch over the levels to heaven I am received." Remember, in prayer and miracles not seen even in healing, this is also where.

Today, I have had many spiritual experiences; I will not write about them in this book.

John 6 51 I am the living bread which has come down from heaven. Anyone who eats this bread will live forever, and the bread that I shall give is my flesh, for the world's life.'

CHAPTER SIX

Hitlerian World Controls Discussion of Karl Jaspers[51]

Notes on Jaspers and Divine Messages July 6, 2023 and before The following text was originally published in

Notes: 11.4.2023

October 8, 2023

Urgently, this is a discussion and response to the Hitlerian control of the Jewish Holocaust and, in comparison, today in America and the world.

Please see the chart of Paradigms of Pillars of Power and review it simultaneously while I speak of the urgencies. Remember, this is information that is vast and highly voluminous of complexities and ideas. Remember, these are pieces of information to enhance, direct, and empower, deliver sound solutions, and be a catalyst of truth to show you

---

[51] Horn, JASPERS (1883-1969) Prospects: the quarterly review of comparative education
KARL JASPERS (1883-1969) Hermann Hom1
(Paris, UNESCO: International Bureau of Education), vol. XXIII, no. 3/4, 1993, p. 721-739.
©UNESC O: International Bureau of Education, 2000
This document may be reproduced free of charge as long as acknowledgement is made of the source.
rn Herman, KA

how these urgencies affect your life and in the future. We must rapidly move ahead to protect our lives, country, and legacy.

In contemplation discussion, and comparison.

Stop World Control

Today, there are mirrors of the life of individuals and groups representing a Hitlerian life form.

We see today, on October 7th, 2023, and prior, the evilest atrocities in the domestic world since human existence.

Holocaust the definition Holocaust

The mass murder of Jews under the German Nazi regime during the period 1941–45. More than 6 million European Jews, as well as members of other persecuted groups, such as gypsies and homosexuals, were murdered at concentration camps such as Auschwitz. The term https://www.oxfordreference.com/display/10.1093/acref/9780198609810.001.0001/acref-9780198609810-e-3382

My Response:

Please, see other writings

www.lisaluciaarden.com

World Controls..

We have a choice now to change World Control and World injustices against our virgin nation what is now the danger of burning our life in The United States of America and humanity's world freedom and life; now we have to give our life to the "First Commandment love God with all our heart and soul and put no other god's before the" that is pure justice.

Prospects: the quarterly review of comparative education

His life and work were at risk during the Hitler dictatorship. He was compulsorily retired in 1937. Publication of his works was banned in 1938. The entry of the American troops into Heidelberg on 1 April 1945 saved him and his Jewish wife from deportation to a concentration camp. Hope and concern mingled in his critical appraisal of the reconstruction and political process in the new Federal Republic of Germany. When he moved to Basle in Switzerland in 1948, he found a new home in a traditional European center of liberty.

Pharmaceuticals, the United States benefit from war, and energy companies benefit from the people..

1. The Pandemic was created to de-populate and kill people .
2. 40 new billionaires' pharmaceuticals
3. Moderna and Pfizer made $1000 every second from the CCP vaccine
4. Listen Congress Controlled by Pharmaceutical Companies 2020 election congress received more than two-thirds of Congress received pharmaceutical monies from pharmaceutical companies
5. Pfizer leader said he was helping humanity he made a 100 billion The Pharmaceuticals need to be addressed
6. Economic System that Pharmaceuticals benefit hugely from medical emergencies
1. In a Military Emergencies war with Russia, three companies are making military tools.. to make money at the expense of people's life and .. the taxpayers' money. Putin wanted to negotiate in 2022

This is why AI, World health, the Elite, and other robust controls

I have intimated in my writings.

1. Scientific knowledge is organized knowledge, i.e., we know by what means it was arrived at and in what sense and within What limits it holds good; it is the exact opposite of unmethodical opinions and unquestioning belief;

2. Scientific knowledge, I am sure, stands the test of any reasoning; it must be distinguished from the convictions by which man lives and be prepared to risk his life.

3. Scientific knowledge has general validity, i.e., it is recognized with limitation by everyone who understands it; it stands in contrast to any other form of knowledge in which man may place unlimited faith." Page to Jaspers 2

'Only God can give us .. unlimited faith when we realize that HE IS THE ONE THAT CREATED SCIENCE. Because, then pure science of validity.. is unlimited when the hands, minds, and feet are in the path of the Pre-imminent of God's intention."

Jaspers investigates the limits of science by pointing out that: 'Objective scientific knowledge is not synonymous with existential knowledge.' 8 1923 ; 1961, P.45. It is concerned with the particular and not with the general. Scientific knowledge cannot set goals for life. Page 2 Jasper … It proclaims no valid values. Science is also unable to give any answer to the question as to its own meaning. Its motives cannot be scientifically proven.

For Jaspers: However, existence is not everything but remains related to the 'transcendental, which speaks in the "all embracing' is a structure in the process of reflection, firstly as 'being itself that is everything that we have our existence with.. Jaspers defines as 'world and the transcendental' and secondly as the 'being' that we are and in experience every form of existence. Jasper represents the 'all-embracing' as 'being', pure consciousness, spirit and possible existence.

On point is of particular importance for the purpose of Jaspers now establishes an inextricable link between existence and reason as the 'bond between all the manifestations of the all-embracing. 'Reason provides the only explanation of existence; reason only acquires content through existence."

Jasper went on to develop this rich network of relationships in his most comprehensive work entitled 'On Truth' 1947

See, he wrote during the time of Hitler and communism; his work was threatened, and his life was threatened. Today, we have the same ideology in America and across the nations, which is the control of Elite communists seeking to take control of the masses.

Today, we have the serious threat of the death of what it means to be human, from the abortion of a fetus and breath of human life to transgender to the control of the World Health decisions of controlling human mandates of vaccinations and medical treatment. Now, the measurement of AI, artificial intelligence, and how it is being used to identify and measure life and scientific findings of all aspects of life are also important.

I discussed this point of AI with my friend, a scientist of excellent knowledge and love for humanity. He believed that AI would answer many of our questions. He uses it now to study cancer and find solutions to cure cancer. However, I told him in different incidents that the soul has to be used for the fulfillment of what it needs to be human and even to find its authentic self in a relationship with God. He stopped and thought momentarily; the computer does not have a soul and hence cannot measure the truth about being human. Even today, the way they treat the American people is measured as if we are numbers and objects and do not have a soul or psyche. See, they tried to change what it truly means to be human .. and a man and a woman, and what the most beautiful valuable gift in life is.. is a human. And why would they promote abortion?

1.Injustice, American voters President Trump got accepted the second term.. They were afraid that President Trump and the American people, as well as parts of the world internationally, would bring freedoms to the masses, life, liberty, and justice. And the Elite Communist would have less control. Can you see why they do not want President Trump for the second time? They saw all his achievements with the team and the American people, his friendships, and the diplomatic respect he had for other countries, and in return, different countries have diplomatic respect. Cannot you see that many people were freed across the nations, and the masses were healthier on what it is to be human? President Trump and the team reflect the face of God's purpose for all humanity. Yet, we know that not one person is perfect.

2. Today, we need to realize that America needs much restoration. See, it shook the brittle bones of empty evil of the Elite communists.. they saw the future of a portion of what good and truth and pure justice. See they want to control the people. This is why there were so many evil atrocities against the people, and these Elite communists became so evil because they wanted world power. They planned each <u>catastrophic happening.. list them here; we know. .that for centuries, there has been a one-world government. However, it was only on American soil.. not since there are more world powers and many international works. The one-world government .. group is across nations of powerful and silent to the highest secret group of Elite communists seeking to control the world. This is why today now, they are seeking to convict President Trump and the team. of crimes they did not do. or overextending and blowing them up when they do not. Explain the story when I studied One World Government at LA VERNE UNIVERSTIY</u>. Of course, this is also understood as the geopolitical power China wants to control. WWII we supported the East and the West.. and we could have been an imperialistic nation.

3. Handling of the lockdowns and the mandates to take vaccinations.. without insufficient evidence to .. support their reasoning for the

lockdowns. I believe this was a .. cause to break down the American people and the people of the world .. to begin to have world control one world government. Many have proven the facts

4. The CCP virus was made in the lab.. an inside job. Fauci and CCP and others. These Elite Communist are part of the highest group of evil secret groups that is silent and do not let others know they seek to control the world

5. Afghanistan: I believe it was a strategic setup to pacify ISIS for some future to do more violence, selling the military tools and using the tools ...

I believe that... they wanted to use the tools and would use them for war.

    a. There, Isis, of the pagan god of evil .. and human torture and atrocity is an entry in Afghanistan is the foreshadowing of the world control of the deformity of freedom CCP VIRUS MADE TO KILL THE PEOPLE AND THE CCP VACCINATIONS…

6. War of Ukraine and Russia

7. They knew the contraindications of the CCP virus. However, I think they thought the masses would not be as resilient. And they have been. I have traveled to many places, and I have seen the strength and beauty of the faithfulness and humbleness of the people.

8. The powerful Elite Communist blatantly and secretly caused deformity and division amongst the. You heard well daughter.

9. **Transgender,** we need to realize it is a deformity. In this space of writing, we will not speak in detail. There are podcast that I have spoken on.. this topic.

    a. A scientific experiment to control to investigate the human body

    b. A deformed idea to form a new secondary being.

c. A deformed idea to cause violence and division

d. A deformed idea to serve the mentality that is lesser than the meaning of what I means to be human.

e. Division of the people.. protestors paid for..

f. But because of technology, the plans of action that control human existence .. can be maneuvered and controlled and changed rapidly. Moreover, the economy and health of a nation are predominantly controlled by emotional welfare and human emotions. God has allowed us to see all and all things exposed from crimes in each country and each government because He wants us to realize that we need to live, work, and vote in just and conservative leaders and law makers and state, federal, community, and business and educational leaders and every walk of life .. that .. that are first working for justice.

g. See Jesus is the answer God is the answer; yet, we are guardians of his love with Virgin Mary.. [52]

10. Cuba Military tools of China in and next to Puerto Rico. And the Russians went to Cuba… What did they do

11. Many other issues.. NOW DESTRUCTION OF WEATHERING USE TO DESTROY

12. Maui the disaster using science of destruction of the properties why.. The company is close to the border area.. where the disaster was.. burn used .. Technological destruction.. Why did this happen? They are giving back the properties.. Something is seriously in view.. for the reason they destroy the areas in Maui? It was not a natural disaster. I wrote on this in social .. reasons and

---

[52] Bing Videos, The Seven Sorrows of the Virgin Mary Devotion

questions.. Why did all the community officials leave and leave the children in their homes? Many deaths, many questions.

I believe most government, federal, state, and community officials do not realize this one-world Elite Communist at the highest level seeks to control. Remember, there are different levels of hierarchies Yet, now many do .. and realize we need to restore our country to self-sufficiency of life.

'Ojective scientific knowledge is not synonymous with existential knowledge 1923 ; 1961,p. 45. It is concerned with the particular and not with the general. Scientific knowledge cannot set goals for life P. 45 . It proclaims no valid values.' This is saying that scientific learning is not the value of "God." However, we realize that God accommodates humanity. He waits patiently for humanity to accept him. Other times he does not. .He gives us wisdom.. We must decide how we can best use it for humanity.

Children and education

1. 'Children must acquire skills and learn knowledge. Please see all the information; thank you, Lisa Lucia Arden. This is why we need to make sure they have a trade coming out of High School.
    Because of the robotic future of replacements.

2. 'Children must be educated according to their own inclinations and abilities.' This is why we need to have a general classical education for critical thinking, be exposed to hands-on experiments in reading, writing, music, and art, and study ecosystems, elements, literature, music, art, numbers related to accounting, etc.The essential role of the school in training children to become useful members of the community has two implications.

    a. Arousing the historical spirit of the community: Ethics in every class. Using successful private school paradigms.

b. The life of a child should be protected so they can have a pure environment to learn. An critical thinking should be paramount and self- sufficiency with a trade that they have .. I have spoken about this already.

Education Socratic education contains the deepest meaning since it involves 'no fixed doctrine, but an infinity of questions and absolute unknowing' (1947, p. 85). The teacher and his pupil are on the same level about ideas. 'Education is maieutic, i.e., it helps to bring the student's latent ideas into clear consciousness; the potential which exists within him is stimulated, but nothing is forced upon him from outside' (p. 85). Here education is understood as 'the element through which human beings come into their own through interpersonal contact by revealing the truth that is latent in them' (1957, p. 107).

1. See this will allow the children to think and see the truth .. instead of just following what is demanded. However, it is essential that truth towards biblical precepts and the definition between God's intention for humans and human nature of the first substance of being man and female. At the time Professor Jasper did not address the issues of transgender.. or male and female or LGBQT. However, I know mostly that he would disagree, proven by the fact of his classic understanding of his truths.

2. Education is in many different forms today that need to be intricately considered on how the children would be affected. Various movements affect the children's environment and definition of education since the world has had many changes of the human life of globalization, liberalism blatantly, world powers, exegesis of education and the meaning of education truths. Even cultural belief systems do not always have the same belief systems and even influence the modernity and liberal sciences on

what it means to be humans. Even the drugs of cruelty .. .. of promotion them to be a stylistic influence and

Jaspers believed that a limit resided in the fact that 'man must not in any way calculate his dealings with others' (1958, p. 245). The unique nature of Jaspers' reflection on education becomes remarkably clear when he speaks of love as the driving force and actual authority as the source of genuine education. He does not believe that these two factors are mutually exclusive. On the contrary, they are inseparable. Love protects education from the will to dominate and shape pupils for finite purposes and makes it a personal encounter.'

The educational content must be based on the great traditions of the human mind. Jaspers advocates the need **for moral content in all teaching; reading and writing will then cease to be mere technical attainments and become instead a spiritual act-a miracle.** When that spirit is alive, effort, hard work, practice, and repetition, often experienced as a burden, will acquire new meaning and become an absolute pleasure. Secondary schools must also pursue the same goal in all their different forms.

I also agree with these miraculous logical learning strategies, which are proven by past and even present history in private schools.

1. Great Traditions of the human mind Biblical Scriptures I believe should be taught.
2. Reading and writing a spiritual act a miracle Jaspers was in no doubt that the value of a school is directly bound up with the quality of its teachers who can only educate young people through lifelong self-education and training. 'The only true educator is the one who is permanently engaged in self-education through communication. Education can only be correct if its addressees acquire the ability to

educate themselves through stringent and tenacious learning.' (1958, p. 445). Page 7

What are the teachers learning today? Does it benefit the children for the 'great traditions of the human mind?' Student's 'tenacious learning' is paramount. We know many students are passed and allowed to go to each grade without passing high enough scores in reading, writing, and critical thinking. This shows that tenacious learning is essential to learning and developing basic skills to then develop gifts of the authentic being.

Think through the problems. Ask questions and prove. Does the result make the best for humanity of Judeo-Chrisian.. ethics and life principles.

2 Tim. 1: 7 God did not give us a spirit of timidity, but the Spirit of power and love and self-control.

God has given us a sound mind. We need to put Him first in our life.. And the justice, wisdom, and precepts of Biblical training is paramount .. First, have salvation in Jesus Christ.. and

What it means to be human

1. This is why they do not want us to think..
2. Being .. pure consciousness and the mind. .. is the being human.

Authority:

"Jaspers does not equate authority with violence and compulsion, but places it on a different level without completely detaching from these other aspects." Page 6

Authority is not violence compulsion and world control. "Authority is an indispensable element of all life in society. 'At all times, man is only able to live under some form of authority' (1957, p. 749). However, he does have the choice as to 'which content is to become the basis of his own life' (p.749)."

Man as existence: i.e. man in the irreplaceable historicity of his unique origin, in his unconditional resolve to become himself. Existence is the sign that being, pure consciousness and the mind cannot be understood on their own and do not have their reason, that man is not confined to immanence but remains essentially dependent on the metaphysical. However, existence is impossible without being, pure consciousness and the mind. These are essential conditions if existence is to come into its own and become a reality. 'It is embodied in being, made clear by the pure consciousness, and its content is revealed in the mind' (1947, p. 134). Page 11

November 4, 2023, New Notes

Jaspers gives a particularly impressive analysis of the relationship between science and philosophy in the third edition of 'The Idea of the University' in 1961 (see Jaspers, 1923). To bring out the essence of science, he highlights three basic principles: (a) scientific knowledge is organized knowledge, i.e. we know by what means it was arrived at and in what sense and within what limits it holds good; it is the exact opposite of unmethodical opinions and unquestioning belief; (b) scientific knowledge is absolutely certain, i.e. it stands the test of any reasoning; it must be distinguished from the convictions by which man may live and be prepared to risk his life; (b) scientific knowledge has general validity, i.e. it is recognized without limitation by everyone who understands it; it stands in contrast to any other form of knowledge in which man may place unlimited faith.

Jaspers investigates the limits of science by pointing out that: 'Objective scientific knowledge is not synonymous with existential knowledge' (1923: 1961, p. 45). It is concerned with the particular and not with the general. 'Scientific knowledge cannot set goals for life' (p. 45). It proclaims no valid values. 'Science is also unable to give any answer to the question as to its own meaning' (p. 45). Its motives cannot be scientifically proven.

The notion that man not only exists but wishes to be himself was developed by Jaspers in 1932 in his three-volume 'Philosophy' which is structured as follows: firstly, a worldly orientation as research into objective reality; secondly, the explanation of existence as an appeal for the individual to be himself; thirdly, metaphysics in relation to the transcendental

The 'all-embracing,"

This 'all-embracing' is structured in the process of reflection, firstly, as 'being' itself, which is everything in which and through which we have our existence and which Jaspers defines as the 'world and the transcendental' and, secondly, as thc 'bcing' which we are and in which we experience

Existence and Reason

"Reason provides the only explanation of existence." p. 3 every particular form of existence. Jaspers represents the 'all-embracing' as 'being,' pure consciousness, spirit, and possible existence.

One point of particular importance for the purpose of this study is that Jaspers now establishes an inextricable link between existence and reason as the 'bond between all the manifestations of the all-embracing'. 'Reason provides the only explanation.

Democracy, peace and the just world order are the problems around which Jaspers' philosophy revolves p. 3

Democracy Look up definition Freedom Liberty .. New .. subject for this book .. This has been my Podcast Speaking. Bring Peace and justice of solutions for humanity in the Divine intentions of God.

See this is my Four Truths .. from my second book

Peace

Justice

Reconciliation

Forward building in Compassion love

Also, it is in the outline.. of this present book

To acquire a perception of the unique nature of Jaspers' philosophy, the essential link which he establishes between science, existence, reason and the world must be recognized.

See, this is paramount. We have reason "to think, learn, contemplate, and create naturally in an environment that is no abusive, noncontrolling, and nonimpeding…

Hence, to exist is to be. And to be is to reason of thought and cultivate an understanding not impeded by restrains of bias or ideologies yet to have first ethics of truth.

Any isolated consideration of one of these factors seen as an absolute in itself will inevitably fail to perceive the totality of this thinking which is oriented towards the world that it nevertheless surpasses. These very links hold the key to the fruitful nature of Jaspers' philosophy. Pg. 3

Same as in my book the chart in 2011 look at and quote

CHAPTER SEVEN

Divine Message Leander Texas

Jesus said, You already know this because I am teaching you and this is already in your writing yet because many need to have a deeper faith and believe I need you to use these magnificent men and women that I have blessed in the parts of history to ..so that tradtion of truth lives My child.

You been singing more than writing the book catch up with the book..

In 1947, Jaspers drew a clear distinction between these forms of active conduct in relation to the world and education. 'At the level of inter-human relations (in particular between the older and the younger generations), education consists of everything that is imparted to young people by communicating contents, allowing them to share the substance of things and disciplining their conduct in such a way that this knowledge continues to grow within them and enables them to become free' (1947, p. 364). The process by which knowledge is imparted should lead young people 'imperceptibly to the origins, the genuine, the true foundations' (p. 364).

When one becomes free, they become their authentic being. See, discipline is essential for creation. Yet, discipline is also a form of not allowing oneself to become like the other or being controlled by the other or even the world, educational system, and societal systems.

"Allowing them to share the substance of things," yes, what does this refer to?

The substance of things is to understand and contemplate study and experiment and work in a strenuous endeavor to .. find the characteristics and makeup of things. .. They.. share the substance of things is a vast meaning

1. Allowing them to be empowered
2. Allowing them the freedom to know what the substance is
3. Allowing them to study and learn further without delay and continuous learning
4. Allowing them to present it to others in the community and be valued as a reason to exist.

This is essential and paramount in learning; otherwise, one will not be allowed to find the essence of who one is and what their cell makeup, spirit of life, and God-given gifts are for them.

See, I write this way to show that education is essential in the form always toward the purest truth. . ... to find the greatest meaning for God's purpose in the Divine Nature of things.

'Reality is honored as an unimpeachable authority by students who are totally submitted to him. Socratic education contains the deepest meaning since it involves 'no fixed doctrine, but an infinity of questions and absolute unknowing' (1947, p. 85). The teacher and his pupil are on the same level about ideas. 'Education is maieutic, i.e., it helps to bring the student's latent ideas into clear consciousness; the potential within him is stimulated, but nothing is forced upon him from outside' (p. 85). Here education is understood as 'the element through which human beings come into their own through interpersonal contact by revealing the truth that is latent in them' (1957, p. 107). Page 4

Jaspers discovered the unique nature of education as distinct from making, shaping, tending, and ruling. By 'making,' something usable is manufactured from a material based on a rational calculation; by 'shaping,' man creates a work whose form is infinite and impossible to calculate in advance. In our modern technical world, 'tending' or 'rearing' has acquired an uncanny resemblance with 'making'; nevertheless, they can only succeed by listening to the living being, which remains valuable as an organism. The process of 'ruling' means subjecting the other, be it nature or a human being, to an extraneous will and purpose.

Children .. process of learning has prior developments that are a foundation and vehicle for finding their purpose.

1. Children must acquire skills and learn knowledge' (1958, p. 30) pg. 5 Understanding this is why basic learning of education development is essential to develop a student's purpose and gifts. Yet, the skill should apply to the actuality of life in the potentiality of what is in the present and will be in the future. Hands-on projects that apply to the development of viable existence and entrepreneurial structure and the sustenance of the tools to be used in society now. Not just hypothetical. Of course, in the beginning, many studies are hypothetical to begin in the learning, and then apply to a true realistic living paradigm.

2. Children must be educated according to <u>their inclinations and ability (and develop their gifts. It is know that when a child is in an environment of conducive learning they learn. And develop individual gifts.)</u>

Additional ancillary .. science

Science is only additional. information yet (p. 32). Here, Jaspers objects to the idea that psychology as a science should be the 'foundation of pedagogical planning and decisions' (p. 32). However, he does concede that it has an 'ancillary role to play under the guiding hand of the educator' (p. 33).

1. The essential role of the school in training children to become valuable community members has two implications' (p. 33). Jaspers defines the first task as 'arousing the historical spirit of the community and life through the symbols of that community' (p. 33). his may be done by considering the previous history of such a community and through contact between young people and their educators. However, this aim cannot be a deliberate and reasoned intention. The second task, on the other hand, is to 'learn and practice everything necessary for work and a profession' (p. 33

This is a matter of deliberate planning. Both tasks are indispensable.

1. See preparation of deliberate planning .. the tools of study that apply today's technology and informative systems. We have not assessed our public system education to be .. enhanced. A tool for the present .. technological and informative .. vast information.. see in the schools, there are limitations.. and when the child goes out of the school, most of the applications they use in technology there. .is no congruence or enhancement of each. They do not apply or work in unison.. and then the work done in the .. .. school has or may have limitations and is is not used or adaptive to see how the tools can be used for the substance of learning different forms of subjects and genres. The children look on their phones. And technological apparatus about subjects that do not apply to their learning.. when they leave school only if they are disciplined to do their homework. Hence, discipline and deliberate planning to make sure the subjects apply and are taught, understood, and practiced permeate the learning of the student.

2. Questions: Do the children apply what they learned when they leave school?

3. Question: do they have the disciplinary actions to understand the concepts required for testing? That is essential.

Jaspers believes that education takes place at the intersection of tension between the past, present, and future. That unilateral preference must not be given to any of these time horizons. "He calls repeated attention to the fact that the substance of the present is rooted in the acquired tradition that forms part of human memory and that the path into the future runs through continuity with the past. **Education must not be abandoned to tradition, the passing moment or to some form of utopia as the only ultimate yardsticks.** It is only through concentration on the present moment accepted with a spirit of responsibility that the past and future can come truly into their own."

    a. Jaspers believes that education occurs at the intersection of tension between the past, present and future and that unilateral preference must not be given to any of these time horizons." This is why it is mandatory to have an excellent foundation with an invigorating curriculum that is first foundation of ethics and application for trades when leaving school .. and critical thinking. And also application to what is needed for society today; to solve problems in society today such as eco systems and infrastructure.

    b. Is the foundation of the tradition of truth from history, science, literature, and all subjects. To have tradition and truth in education, ethics must be in the foundation at every side, from the content to the delivery to the student understanding to the application. Also, to ask if the student understands it and can be tested on it in verbal and speaking questioning and writing, and some multiple choice.

4. Questions: How can the concepts taught be used directly related to the inclinations and abilities? Entrepreneurial training and

experiential subjects are needed to find the child's gifts, yet never limit one thing. This is why the standard training of all basic subjects is necessary. "The second task, on the other hand, is to 'learn and practice everything necessary for work and a profession' (p. 33)" pg. 3

5. Note: all learning should be taken down to the raw understanding basis since we have an infinite vast understanding of the concepts of life and all sciences. See, we missed points of information and can make a better way .. and purer, more quality way .. to use God's gifts properly.. for example, I have started to .. have each child .. required to make a notebook on eco-systems from the raw and all learnings. "The process by which knowledge is imparted should lead young people 'imperceptibly to the origins, the genuine, the true foundations' (p. 364)."

6. No woke systems and perpetual computerized integration of communication of selfies and shallow mindless speaking..

7. Ethics is essential

8. Recognizing that globalization has caused man .
    a. Geopolitical power
    b. Geopolitical economy
    c. Geopolitical technology
    d. Technology
    e. Globalization
    f. Nine criminal Billionaire Cartel Internationally and China is number approximately and brings all the crime to America and our boarders.. .. ..
    g. Elite Communist.

9. New restoration and for development of regulations for children
    a. Schools not woke..
    b. No acceptance transgender

c. No acceptance of teaching about sexual

d. No smoking drugs in schools

e. Limit phones of apps .

f. No pornography apps even in universities

g. Homework

    i. Reading

    ii. Writing

    iii. Speaking

    iv. Hands on projects

    v. Scheduled . planned field trips

    vi. Hand writing, charts comparisons

    vii. Application of Aristotle Categories

    viii. Applications to society as a whole

    ix. Solving current problems in society .. such as toxic foods, recycling, infrastructure of older buildings, agriculture, ect.

He calls repeated attention to the fact that the substance of the present is rooted in the acquired tradition that forms part of human memory and that the path into the future runs through continuity with the past. Education must not be abandoned to tradition, to the passing moment, or to some form of utopia as the only ultimate yardstick. It is only through concentration on the present moment, accepted with a spirit of responsibility, that the past and future can come truly into their own.pg 5

See, this is an essential tradition, yet, it needs to be a tradition that empowers and brings justice to the people to develop the opening of the "first substance of ideas." Some traditions of Communist and fascism and totalism and distribution of funds imbalance are traditions of a society that are part of injustice that impede human development and evolution ….

The process by which knowledge is imparted should lead young people 'imperceptibly to the origins, the genuine, the true foundations' (p. 364). Pg 2

This presupposes that young people will themselves come to terms with the surrounding reality, which has many different facets they may experience through play, work, and practical activities. The list of this experimental practice ranges from skills in work methods through physical training, clear speech, and disciplined discussion to an intellectual grasp of original contents in poetry, the Bible, and art, as well as an understanding of history and familiarity with the basic techniques of the natural sciences.

This is why there has to be an excellent orderly teaching of the pure history and facts of the absolute; because then the "genuine, the true foundations. . of knowledge of . . imperceptibly to the origins," will be

See the " spirit of responsibility, that the past and future come truly into their own." Today, because of postmodernity and blatant liberal belief of truths of tradition, they are changing.

Please stop

America, we are responsible for bringing proper ethics and what it means to be human.

Children are innocent .. and need to grow in an environment of their original gender at birth.

Athletes need to be protected from illogical crimes defining contestants as men in women's sports or transgender of men to women in women sports.

There are other emergencies that need to be considered.. these are just a few.

   1.Athletes of different gender compete on the opposite gender
   2.Transgender and teaching it in the schools system

3.Sexual education do not teach let children teach..

    TEACH AUTHENTIC PURPOSE ..

4.Woke .. systems look definition

5.Do not promote LGBQT

6.Safety .. public.. .. entry.. .. . protection of schools video and gun control.

7.Undercover police..

8.Incorrect history of America

9.See other points.

10.Not making sure that they are responsible for learning and passing tests.

11. Help those who need help with .. the exams..

See how the expression of life has changed with postmodernity after the technology of the computer.

The essential role of the school in training children to become useful members of the community has two implications' (p. 33).. . . The second task, on the other hand, is to 'learn and practice everything page 4

Necessary for work and a profession (p. 33). Jaspers defines the first task as 'arousing the historical spirit of the community and of life through the symbols of that community.'

Education:

November 5, 2023

Without faith, there can be no education but a mere technique of teaching' (1923: 1961, p. 86). In this book's earlier (1946) version, Jaspers recognizes that 'awe is the substance of all education. Without the pathos of an absolute, man cannot exist, else all would be meaningless' (p. 49). This absolute which creates meaning, may assume a variety of forms. Jaspers quotes caste, the State, religion or truth, independence, responsibility, and freedom. The absolute cannot simply be proclaimed but must be the subject of testimony in practical life. It can never be decreed but must be freely accepted. Moreover, it cannot be denied that in a pluralistic society, majority decisions cannot be made on a generally valid absolute; creating a consensus must remain a serious objective. Page 5

Let us review these most salient sentences that relate to the .. devastation of the severe deformity of peace and even stay alive and the fighting to retain the life of homes, finance, and goods of each person. This has past we now have our victory .. God is in control.

God's power in America will save our legacy.

Jaspers recognizes that 'awe is the substance of all education. Without the pathos of an absolute, man cannot exist, else all would be meaningless' (p. 49) Look up word absolute

When one does not use absolute what is made what is less than human when we do not have absolute we create less than life and even a deformity of what is of God's intention.

We even change the substance that is not defined as a human of God's intention yet and deformity of a lie of what life is. Such as transgender competing in a beauty pageant and winning first prize, and an athlete who is transgender who competes in an athletic game and wins.

Transgender

This is the deformity of the mind of men searching for curiosity that is of man, not of God. Many of the transgender operations were and are performed in hospital of high popularity and significance. This transgender is taking God's creation and corrupting it, and it, therefore, is really death to the real first substance of being a human. Transgender is death to the first substance of being of God's intention. The elite community supports transgender, and they use humans for their desire of deformity of life of their ideas and belief systems. Transgender is the murdering of the God intention of what it means to be male and female and a reflection of abortion; yet, abortion of The United States of America is the third highest country of abortions in the world after China first and second Russia is the greater evil and greater murder of the human seed of life. Scientists use babies in scientific studies, even proven by the fact of Pfizer.. high-level directors have accepted the use of babies for vaccinations and scientific tests.

Question: how can a child concentrate on their studies when they have un natural topics constantly in their environment.

Woke is an adjective . . . Vernacular English (AAVE) meaning "alert to racial prejudice and discrimination". Beginning in the 2010s, it came to encompass a broader awareness of social inequalities such as racial justice, sexism and LGBT rights.

https://en.wikipedia.org/wiki/Woke#:~:text=Woke%20is%20an%20adje ctive%20derived,justice%2C%20sexism%20and%20LGBT%20rights.

There are various meanings of woke. We will briefly discuss how the above definition is characteristic of a deficit in a natural and negative environment that affects a child's learning.

Children cannot be exposed to woke education of deformed lessor than life; A SECONDARY BEING .. YET GODS' HUMANITY..WE NEED TO BRING PEACE.. CHILDREN ARE TO YOUNG TO DECIDE ..; Most of all not be forced or change their true sexual identification. of entertainers of transgender and LBQT characteristics with sexual connotations.

This presupposes that young people will themselves come to terms with the surrounding reality, whose many different facets they may experience through play, work, and practical activities. The list of this experimental practice ranges from skills in methods of work through physical training, clear speech, and disciplined discussion to the intellectual grasp of original contents in poetry, the Bible, and art, and also to an understanding of history and familiarity with the basic techniques of the natural sciences.

Democracies (- sĭz). [F. démocratie, fr. Gr. δημοκρατία; δῆμος the people + κρατεῖν to be strong, to rule, κράτος strength.] 1. Government by the people; a form of government in which the supreme power is retained and directly exercised by the people. WEBSTER'S DICTIONARY (1913)

[אֵב] n.[m.] freshness, fresh green; concr., pl. green shoots.

24   אָבִיב n.m. coll.

1. fresh, young ears of barley;

2. month of ear-forming, or of growing green, Abib, month of Exodus & passover.[53]

BDB ABRIDGED

1576. גְּמוּל gmuwl, ghem-ool´; from 1580; treatment, i.e. an act (of good or ill); by implication, service or requital:—+ as hast served, benefit, desert, deserving, that which he hath given, recompense, reward.

1865. דְּרוֹר drown, deplore; from an unused root (meaning to move rapidly); freedom; hence, the spontaneity of outflow, and so clear:— liberty, pure.[54] by the fact that man is never totally conditioned by inheritance or by his environment. On the contrary, he has a vast hidden potential that can only be revealed by experimentation, hard work and firm resolve. In 1958, Jaspers expressed that a limit resided in the fact that 'man must not in any way calculate his dealings with others' (1958, p. 245). The

---

[53] BDB,Freshness, green shoot

[54] Hebrew STRONG'S DICTIONARY Strong's Hebrew and Chaldee Dictionary of the Old Testament (Hebrew Strong's) Public Domain Electronic text downloaded from the Bible Foundation e-Text Library:<http://www.bf.org/bfetexts.htm>Hypertexted and formatted by OakTree Software, Inc.
Hebrew text added by OakTree Software, Inc.Treatment, freedom

unique nature of Jaspers' reflection on education becomes remarkably clear when he speaks of love as the driving force and true authority as the source of genuine education. He does not believe that these two factors are mutually exclusive. On the contrary, they are inseparable. Love protects education from the will to dominate and shape pupils for finite purposes and makes it a personal encounter instead: Loving communication between individuals embraces all love of things, of the world and of God.

1. See that is because love is the creation of God's greatest beauty of life, humanity, and education identifies the character of the person and the development of the . .person the essence of what it is to be
2. See, there is hidden potential in people when exposed and confronted in an environment to... given hard work and firm resolve. This is why we need to help those who have these steps.
3. The woke systems and non absolutes and technological control and integrating sexual or no intention of God's regular creation of transgender and LGBTQ bring the first .. problem of, most importantly, what it is to be human, a man or a woman.
    a. When there is non-conflict caused by the environment or whom one represents as a human, it also has a current effect on what one can become in self-development, education, and potentiality.
    b. Identifying with the no absolute and nonclassical and non-truth and nonclassical understanding of ethical training and also identifying only as a male or female when causing impediment of the

"Love protects education from the will to dominate and shape pupils for finite purposes, and makes it a personal encounter instead: 'Loving communication between individuals embraces all love of things, of the world and of God." P. 5

Jaspers does not set out a program to design an education system but focuses on a few basic principles. He emphasizes the crucial role of primary school in laying the moral, intellectual, and political foundations for the entire population. The intellectual renewal imparted by teachers is the determining factor if the population and those in government are to recognize the justification of the necessary financial resources.

Education

1. Moral

2. Intellectual

3. Political (needs to be all toward justice that is love) – For America, our Constitutional Rights.. and . ethical Judeo Christian the "entire population; otherwise, there is disagreement on what is absolute. There need to be general absolutes of the truth of ethics, which are first and closest to what is to human male or female, and nothing in between.

4. Teachers. . need to .. express this and uphold these rules.. because there have been various changes in what it means to be human .. and even cultural designations that treat situations less than justice, proven by the fact of our schools and business communities and even leadership on the .. Presidential level .. Executive and Judicial levels.. and even the complexities of the globalization of different nationalities and cultural belief systems, as well as the fetus's survival.

Hence, many do not make the proper decisions closest to the best for humanity as individuals and as a whole.

See, I know that I continue to .. tell you my coin ideas that why we need to recourse and reassess the systems because these movements are so vast that they cannot be pushed back or impeded to allow the human to be who the human is God's intention

- Distribution of funds imbalance
- Corporate censorship
- Find that list of World Groups
- World powers
- Geopolitical power.
- Geopolitical economy
- Geopolitical military
- Geopolitical Culture
- Globalization

Note that this can always be varied because it is mandatory for those who want to save them.

We added the additional point of the Distribution of funds in this context to reveal that the Distribution of Funds causes many to need more resources or an environment. Dr. Jasper mentions the "experimental" of education and ethical moral living to see their potential.

You can see what they, particularly China and the dragon, of deception, evil, and her blatant counterparts.

A. They want to make the country weak and sick with drugs, fentanyl, and drugs
B. They want to take away the economic positions by manufacturing
C. They use our governmental business loans.
D. They even enter into treasonous criminal contracts with large companies to enter into loans.
E. Third, they integrate with more criminals of human trafficking and fraud

God's power, America, our miracle

We are being protected and now having .. victory.

Three Pillars of Happenings.

Decisive importance is attached to the educational content, which must be based on the great traditions of the human mind. Jaspers advocates the need for moral content in all teaching; reading and writing will then cease to be mere technical attainments and become a spiritual act- a miracle. When that spirit is alive, effort, hard work, practice, and repetition, often experienced as a burden, will acquire new meaning and become an absolute pleasure. In all their different forms, secondary schools must also pursue the same goal." Page 7

I have also pleaded for moral development in ethical checkpoints and ethical foundations, which is required in each course and each system.

The Truth in Jesus Christ, the Wisdom of His love

Luke 22:19 Then he took bread, and when he had given thanks, he broke it and gave it to them, saying, 'This is my body given for you; do this in remembrance of me.' 20 He did the same with the cup after supper, saying, 'This is the new covenant in my blood poured out for you.

CHAPTER EIGHT

Discussion on China Business

Brief Notes

January 3, 2022

From the Desk of Lisa Lucia Arden, MDIV

Discussion January 1, 2, 3, 2022 Communist China Business

Something is not right .. with the Communists.. worse than ever. I am concerned. There will be a lineup of countries that are evident in their beliefs. All leaders need to be careful on all sides.

October 29, 2024

These notes help you see the importance of our future to protect America with excellent leadership.

I pray the Leader of China seeks the God of Abraham. Also, he leads his people with justice. The Chinese are my brothers and sisters. I .. lived in San Marino, California, where many live.

1. First, with God in serving Him first, then serving the people.
2. Second, how do they serve first with God's Justice
3. Third, be careful of entering their country's workings inside.
4. Fourth, be careful with all the enter workings with other countries

Divine Message

General Communism will not last .. in a time of seeking attempt of the globalized holocaust of human freedoms.. It will be the Communist of destruction in the darkness of continuous.. injustice attached to their ideologies. Their deformed ideology will be a battle that they will never rest and become more the darkness of life and even less human and even less of God's people.

I am concerned about them and their people. And their land.

See, remember, even in lands that are not identified as Communist, there are Communist societies of control. I pray and promote justice, safety, and deliverance.. for people of Communistic ideologies and their victims.

See that these Communist and, as a matter of fact, any persons of ideological beliefs that do not believe in God, the God of Abraham, have then an open door to other "gods," per se, other beliefs that are secondary to the truth..; hence, this is a danger because there is an open door of the "powers and principalities of the (darkness)." It is not the correct way of living. Even though there seems to be production, it is destructive. Eventually, it comes to death, seen in all ways and sciences of life from the present Holocaust attempt of humanity in deteriorating the population to the belief systems and acceptance of the high rates of abortion in Domestic Countries such as China, the USA, and Russia to the foods that we make entering as "biogenetically made," destroy the body, to the control and manipulation of our Constitutional human's daily freedoms.

Countries that have Communist ideas could change, and may they bring peace, justice, and well-being to their countries. I hope for the future. It is possible.

See if they evolve to a more just plan to capitalistic ideas that the people can become, and the countries can be self-sufficient.

See, there can be an evolution of a better way and a follow-through justice built to develop human dignity, human development, human freedom, human traditions, and the empowerment of humanity.

We as a people have internationally awakened and addressed several of the severe Communistic ideologies and strategic secretive plans to control humanity in many different ways.

Consequently, upon the investigation, it has been proven that these Communist ideas and powers and nations are a treacherous threat to the world globally; therefore, the consequences of the danger to all humanity of all nations that the Communist powers have done gives the international representatives the right to continue to treat Communist China Leaders and her counterparts the action of: being refused the merits and honors of trading business and diplomacy and even removed and excommunicated from certain parts of business life.

It is human nature to work for man's ideas because we are given the gift and responsibility to care for each other and our land at creation. However, we do it in the love and toward the love of God in the best way. Even if we are imperfect and incomplete, we continue to redeem each minute by the grace of God and our neighbors so that we can continue living a just and compassionate life according to God's intentions for each life and way of life. (Will continue the discussion). Please get in touch with Lisa Lucia Arden, MDIV, luciaarden1@gmail.com

CHAPTER NINE

Military Comparisons

A BRIEF NOTE OF EMERGENCY

Do you think the DEMOCRATIC ELITE COMMUNIST UNDER KAMALA COMMUNIST COULD UNDERSTAND OR EVEN HELP WITH THIS ..

SHE HAS CONCENTRATED ON MAKING THE USA A THIRD-WORLD COUNTRY, DESTROYING OUR STRENGTH AND ABUSING EVEN IMMIGRANTS, BRINGING THEM HERE WHEN THEY NEED EXISTENCE, AND SHE HAS NO PLAN EXCEPT TO BRING DEATH TO THE AMERICAN CITIZEN'S LIVES. EXISTENCE .. NOT TAKING CARE OF THE AMERICANS..FIRST

IT IS OUR RESPONSIBILITY TO SPEAK IN TRUTH AND BELIEVERS AND AMERICAN CITIZENS

THE DEMOCRATIC POWER OF DEATH TO AMERICA NEEDS TO BE REMOVED, AND A NEW GOVERNMENT UNDER

THE REPUBLICAN PRESIDENT TRUMP AND TEAM TO SAVE USA GOD FIRST AMERICANS FIRST

LISA LUCIA ARDEN POLITICIAN

A worst-case Taiwan scenario for Chinese leader Xi Jinping would be a significant military operation in which the People's Liberation Army fails spectacularly or displays shocking incompetence akin to Russia's in

Ukraine. Could this happen? The bad news is that even if China's armed forces fail spectacularly, this does not necessarily mean a shorter, less bloody, or less costly conflict. Xi is unlikely to call off his military if the People's Liberation Army stumbles badly. Where Taiwan is concerned, Xi can expect to press his armed forces to persist in the fight, producing a protracted conflict in the center of the Indo-Pacific and profoundly disrupting commerce and stability across the region.

Civil-Military Disfunction in Dictatorships

Dictators face notable obstacles when it comes to ensuring the combat effectiveness of their armed forces. These generally manifest in two problems: anxieties over allegiances and the dearth of reliable information. Because they are prone to paranoia, dictators tend to select and promote officers based on their perceived personal allegiance rather than their records or qualities as commanders. This instinct drove Xi to launch a significant anti-corruption campaign in the earliest years of his tenure, resulting in hundreds of generals being ousted. While bribery and fraud undoubtedly constituted severe problems within the Chinese military, Xi's campaign had all the hallmarks of a purge, allowing the commander-in-chief to sweep aside perceived opponents throughout the officer corps.

Prioritizing coup-proofing at the expense of readiness creates other problems, too. Dictators prefer centralizing decisions on postings and promotions, and troop movements in their own hands. They often establish multiple centers of military and paramilitary power to prevent any one military leader or bureaucratic entity from accumulating too much power and to encourage competition over cooperation among subordinates. This is one reason why Putin permitted the emergence of the Wagner Group. While not embracing private security companies to the same degree as Putin's Russia, Chinese Communist Party leaders have long maintained a set of muscular internal security apparatuses funded in recent years at a level exceeding China's official national defense budget.

Military Modernization: Targeting Taiwan

Even before Russian President Vladimir Putin's 2022 invasion of Ukraine, senior U.S. officials and analysts were warning that Xi had accelerated his timeline for unification with Taiwan and prioritized the military means to attain it. 2027 is widely referenced, and one prominent expert has dubbed the 2020s "the decade of living dangerously." Of course, Xi, like his purported pal Putin, could order his armed forces to launch a major military operation any time he chooses, and his generals would almost certainly obey. However, most experts on China's military consider that a decision by commander-in-chief Xi to invade Taiwan is unlikely in the near term, at least barring some dramatic change in the Chinese Communist Party's calculus of regime security. Indeed, the 2027 date mentioned in Chinese documents appears to be a milestone to attain benchmarks in the military's ongoing multi-decade modernization drive rather than a deadline for an attack on Taiwan.

In January 2022, for example, Putin seemed utterly convinced that his armed forces were well-trained, well-equipped, well-led, and would acquit themselves well in a military operation against Ukraine. Why? Because no one had led him to believe otherwise. Indeed, the Russian dictator had been beguiled by multiple subordinates employing elaborate ruses and charades. His generals had constructed a Potemkin military. Some 350 years earlier, Grigory Potemkin reportedly conjured up impressive facades in Crimea to hide the rural reality of dire poverty and dilapidated conditions from his sovereign, Catherine the Great. Putin, too, had visited showcase barracks and mess halls, witnessed precisely orchestrated field exercises, and watched impressively choreographed parades — all intended to hide the corrosive effects of corruption, fraud, and incompetence on a monumental scale.

The Alchemy of Combat Effectiveness

Dysfunction and doubts aside, what is the secret to success in war? The specific recipe for combat-effective armed forces is somewhat mysterious, and you can't simply bet on the side with the most fancy weapons. In recent years, the commissioning of vast quantities of new aircraft and seacrafts in China's armed forces has been impressive. It commands the most excellent attention at home and abroad and is straightforward to identify and quantify. But system specifications and inventories do not by themselves ensure success in battle. Other "soft" factors, such as personnel quality, training effectiveness, morale, and command-and-control culture, are also critical yet challenging to measure. Moreover, meaningful combat effectiveness is the result of multiple elements all combined. To be effective, a military needs sound doctrine, organization, weaponry, personnel training, logistics, and culture; each component must work strategically together.

Such an outcome would humiliate China's commander-in-chief, provoke a domestic political-military crisis, and propel Beijing to escalate. As the world has witnessed in Ukraine, a dictator shocked by a very public display of gross incompetence by his military may react in a range of worrisome ways. This includes—but is not limited to—threatening the use of nuclear weapons.

In the final analysis, even an unsuccessful Chinese military operation against Taiwan would send seismic geostrategic shockwaves worldwide across the Indo-Pacific region. A botched Chinese attack would bring small consolation to the island and likely elevate cross-strait tensions for decades. Moreover, China's relations with incredible powers and small powers, notably the United States, would be irreparably damaged. As I have argued elsewhere, a failed invasion would still trigger a new Cold War.

https://warontherocks.com/2023/05/xi-jinpings-worst-nightmare-a-potemkin-peoples-liberation-army/

Look at the differences in military numbers.

Xi Jinping's Worst Nightmare: A Potemkin People's Liberation Army

Andrew Scobell

May 1, 2023

Xi Jinping's Worst Nightmare: A Potemkin People's Liberation Army

Andrew Scobell

May 1, 2023

Xi Jinping's Worst Nightmare: A Potemkin People's Liberation Army

Andrew Scobell

May 1, 2023

According to the International Institute for Strategic Studies

Country	Active military	Reserve military	Paramilitary	Total	Per 1,000 capita (total)	Per 1,000 capita (active)
People's Republic of China	2,185,000	1,170,000	660,000	4,015,000	2.9	1.6
Japan	247,150	56,000	14,350	317,500	2.5	2
United States	1,328,000	744,950	0	2,072,950	6.3	4
Russia	1,154,000	2,000,000	554,000	3,708,000	26.1	8.1

If Japan and USA work together, they can win

https://www.iiss.org/press/2024/02/the-military-balance-2024-press-release/#:~:text=About%20The%20International%20Institute%20for,Middle%20East%20Regional%20Security%20Summit).

https://www.statista.com/statistics/264443/the-worlds-largest-armies-based-on-active-force-level/#:~:text=As%20of%20January%202024%2C%20China,the%20top%20five%20largest%20armies.

- Economy & Politics›
- Politics & Government

Premium

Largest armies in the world by active military personnel 2024

Published by

Einar H. Dyvik,

Jul 4, 2024

As of January 2024, China had the world's most significant armed forces by active-duty military personnel, with about 2 million active soldiers. India, the United States, North Korea, and Russia rounded out the top five largest armies.

Difference between active and reserve personnel

Active personnel, also known as those on active duty in the United States and those in active service in the United Kingdom, are individuals whose full-time occupation is part of a military force. Active duty is in contrast to a military's reserve force, individuals with both a military role and a civilian career. The number of active duty forces in the U.S. is much larger than its reserve membership.

What is the strongest army?

The strength of a country's armed forces is determined by how many personnel they maintain and the number and quality of their military equipment. For example, looking only at personnel does not factor in the overwhelmingly higher number of nuclear warheads owned by Russia and the United States compared to other countries. One way to answer this question is to look at the total amount of money each country spends on its military, including personnel and technology. In terms of countries with the highest military spending, the United States leads the world with an annual budget almost three times larger than second-placed China.

Largest armies in the world ranked by active military personnel as of January 2024

CHAPTER TEN

PILLARS OF PARADIGMS OF POWER[55]

GOD

Below pillars

Technology and information systems

Regulation and law

God, the existence of life in the center

Existence of all human's daily life

World Controls and Government

PILLAR TECHNOLOGY INFORMATION SYSTEM	PILLAR REGULATIONS LAW	PILLAR ON EARTH AND HEAVEN	PILLAR EXISTENCE DAILY LIFE	PILLAR WORLD POWERS

NEED ETHICS

JUSTICE IS ETHICS.

ETHICS ARE GOD'S PRECEPTS

MASSIVE OF MOVEMENTS CONTROLS   MASSIVE CONTROLS

---

[55] Arden, Lisa, Lucia, MDIV, Pillars of Power 2024 get original date.. and copy right

GEOPOLITICAL POWER
GEOPOLITICAL ECONOMY
G7 AND BRICS 50 COUNTRIES
GEOPOLITICAL TECHNOLOGY
TECHNOLOGY
GLOBALIZATION
NINE BILLIONAIRE
CRIMINALS

ELITE CRIMINALS

ELITE CRIMINAL POLITICIANS
POLITICIANS INFLUENCERS
FOODS AGRICULTURAL
GATES – AGRICULTURE 260,000
acres approx
BEZOS – AGRICUTLUE GET
OTHER

SECRET GROUPS MASONS

ENTERTAINERS

NEWSCASTERS

SOCIAL MEDIA CORPORATE
CONTROLS

PEOPLES CONTROLS

ELON, BEZOS, ZUCKERBERG,
SOROS, GATES, FINK, PRINCE,

Largest Landowners in the United States in 2024[56]

Largest Landowner Name	Approximate Acreage Owned
The U.S. Government	650 million acres
Native American Tribes	56 million acres
The Emmerson Family	2,411,000 acres
John Malone	2,200,000 acres

---

[56] Largest Land Owners, https://www.landgate.com/news/largest-landowners-in-the-united-states-2024

Ted Turner	2,000,000+ acres
Stan Kroenke	1,700,000+ acres
The Reed Family	1,600,000+ acres
The Irving Family	1,300,000+ acre

FOODS 13 FAMILIES
AMERICAN COMPANY POWER

BLACK ROCK	GATES – AGRICULTURE
VANGUARD	BEZOS – AGRICULTURE
STATE STREET	

S& P 81 percent

Housing 61 percent approx

<u>BOARDERS GENERAL OUR GEOPOLITICAL POWER. PLEASE SEE THE DEFINITION OF GEOPOLITICAL IN MY BOOK ARISE TO GOD'S TRUTH, RESTORE AND KEEP AMERICA FREE.[57]</u>

DEATH OF OUR AMERICA WITH OPEN BORDERS Even the Elite communists and the Democratic communists use the land itself to bring ideologies of liberal and communistic controls of world one, the world power of hierarchies of death.

OTHER LIST OF WORLD POWER GROUPS

World Economic Forum

World Health Forum

---

[57] Arden, Lisa, Lucia MDIV, Arise to God's Truth, Restore and Keep America's Freedom, Lisa Lucia Arden, December 2020 ,geopolitics

Elite Communist Controllers

Note: These are Brief notes. They introduce the mighty pillars of the velocity of life today.

NOTE THAT THIS HAS TO BE ON THE SIDE PAGE. OF THE .. .. NOTES.

February 29, 2024

Discussion of the Pillars of Power

Please see my Podcasts and writings. I discuss these salient systems controlling our world.[58]

Note: I will only speak briefly on these topics. I can write entire volumes on these subjects. However, the purpose is to show you what has developed and evolved in humanity's existence and life happenings and why there needs to be assessments and actions of justice for the people.

Pillars of Technology and Information Systems

Today, we have more advanced technology and information systems than ever. We have used them to live in all aspects of life. Some used technology for their intended need to do fair and just business and development; some did not realize their work in technology and information systems has many effects in all different ways, beauty to beauty, life making life, death making life, innovation to an even better life, deterioration to quantity to the power of pure highest quality to life. We thought we knew. And some did know. And others are afraid to see the truth. And others were forced to continue. And now many see the truth. And many see it correctly. We do not know all the motives, and even those who developed the technology and information did not know all the contraindications. Yet, remember there is a document called the "Secret Covenant." 7 God did not give us a spirit of timidity, but the Spirit of

---

[58] Arden, Lisa, Lucia, MDIV, www.arisetogodstruth.com

power and love and self-control." This document is called the "secret Covenant" and speaks of the control of the people. Elite Communist World Controls.

President George Washington.

We cannot forget the beauty of the beginning of President George

Remember, we are speaking about America correctly: the people, her land, and her legacy. America was given to those who needed a home and safety from their leaders and country.

Ask God first, and seek a relationship first with God.

I need to regularly Pray, read the Bible, Journal, worship, and see where I need to become closer to God and do righteousness. What, why, who, and when is causing my situation the way it is? What do I want? Ask God what His will is.

Prayer is paramount. Please see my writing .. on worship in my books.

I believe it is our relationship with God in Jesus Christ is our salvation and the answers to restore and access how to drive with urgencies to protect our See in the First and Second Commandment that we can heal our being:

1. Look with an intricate eye
2. Search for the truth and find the fruit of truth.
3. And take care of the people and do great justice. there can be miracles
4. Then, we can bring death to life. In God's power.
5. For me, of course, we arise to live in the power of God's sovereign power. It is better than we even realize. See a beauty more extraordinary than ever created because God creates His beauty in us. And it is the most extraordinary beauty. And God creates in you the most remarkable life. And God creates in you the most

incredible justice. And God creates a miracle that lives in you, bringing the most extraordinary life.

Pillars of Regulations and laws of life and Mediations of Diplomacy of Justice of truth and Freedom of the people.

Because of the vast power of technology and information systems, different choices and even perfect developments of greater justice and benefit for humanity's welfare must be directed by the mighty hands of truth. If this is not done, then death, deformity, and even worse actions can develop and form.

Abortions Reiterating.

Abortions are at the highest in the world after China and Russia. See, they use babies in scientific research. They promote abortions the powerful pharmaceutical companies and politicians use .. Pfizer's leader was questioned about using the fetuses for the hum.

Wars

The wars of no negotiations (name them .. Russia and Ukraine, Israel and Hamas, and others.

Boarders

The war on the borders of the United States of America is the war for her people and safety. More, get the number. Fentalyn. And the human trafficking of the people. Why do we protect all other areas worldwide, including our homes and the government? We need to protect the border.. we do not want what comes in. There are geopolitical powers and nine criminal billionaires. www.lisaluciaarden.com

Foods

The laws and regulations of CCP virus and CCP vaccinations and lockdowns. The food system is the way they are processed. These are to mention a few. See, this is how .. the quantity, monetizing foods, and not considering people's welfare.

Pharmaceuticals

I will just briefly speak about this topic, yet it is mandatory after safety, food, housing, and world health go into a tantrum with Pharmaceuticals. I can speak volumes about this. They make pharmaceuticals that are not best for the people. Many of the pharmaceuticals cause more significant diseases, and they need to be re-addressed. We know that much of their work is for the cure of diseases. Yet, much is not suitable for the people. During the CCP vaccinations, We know that 100 billion dollars were made from Pfizer, and 40 people became billionaires during this period. We also know that there have been facts many who believe that vaccinations were made to destroy, weaken, and kill people. Get

Pillars of existence of life

Economic Controls

World Health

Stopping Communication with people locks down.

Globalization

Today, there is globalization and multi-cultural belief systems .. Many populations of different beliefs, and most people do not understand the systems of

Geopolitical powers are geopolitical controls and political ideologies that want to control America.

Today, many people in the United States have different belief systems and understand what it means to be human.

Liberal and Conservative

Moreover, many liberal ideas are practiced in all parts of life, which have changed how people communicate and live and have affected our justice system, education system, economic system, and even our religious belief system.

Transgender

Such as the example of Transgender and woke ideas .. these are forces of secondary life. .less than life that

See all the .. peoples.. controls of the .. people.

Children Trafficking

900,000 approximately

Why Question these happenings?

Ask ourselves why they are doing this. Why are they deteriorating human life? There are several leaders and controllers. Some say they want to depopulate, and others, I believe, are doing what they think is justice and fair business for the people.

If we do not address these questions urgently, the nature of molecular science itself will destroy their work. See, molecules of the same kind also attack each other, and molecules by nature mix and become what is allowed, forming a hierarchy in definition and formation.

March 12, 2024

Yet, God wants to redeem the "molecules" of His creation. He believes in miracles and realizes that His creation is understood to see the truth He created for. This is why men of His people suffer, and it is because of the purpose of God's love.

Let me be clear: if the Divine Nature of life in God's hands allows it, an immense evil can overtake them.

Most millionaires, billionaires, and influential people did not want these tragic atrocities, the greatest evils in humanity's existence, such as the wars and many of the world's controls. God only knows their hearts and purposes, yet many actions have been revealed. We need to reconcile, restore, and reform the truth of justice again to the clear Divine law of humanity first and the authentic purpose to empower and live in peace and justice.

I discuss these titles above because they work all in unity, whether in harmony or agreement or opposing sides; these are great movements that are happening and need to be taken into DYNAMIC AND [59]STRATEGIC AND REFORMATION AND RESTORATION TO THE CLOSEST DIVINE JUSTICE FOR HUMANITY.

WATER MICROPLASTICS SEE ANIMALS AND HUMANS

Before 2007, I spoke and knocked on business doors to raise awareness of the water crisis and microplastics.

I published our Need to Give to the World, Heal America Love in God, in 2016. And I.

Arise to God's Truth, Restore and Keep America's Freedom, 2020[60]

[59] Our Need to Give to the World: America Love in God, Heal America- Kindle edition by Arden, Lisa Lucia. Politics & Social Sciences Kindle eBooks @ Amazon.com., Arden, Lisa Lucia, MDIV

[60] https://www.amazon.com/ARISE-GODS-TRUTH-LUCIA-ARDEN-ebook/dp/B08T8LJ8TR/ref=sr_1_3?crid=6SLHFQ1ND2FV&dib=eyJ2IjoiMSJ9.xtnuqkBr2J VwfsZJzfYFXvR9uvMZNWtuV_HxjEuwOvfGjHj071QN20LucGBJIEps.BdlOV17fMuCB5UaG KHXzRVhCRaXwjn1uxaR_D-OW1R4&dib_tag=se&keywords=lisa+lucia+arden&qid=1731487580&sprefix=%2Caps%2 C213&sr=8-3, Arden Lisa Lucia, MDIV

God First, America our Miracle, Vote Freedom Vote Trump (Recent Book October 31, 2024[61]

AGRICULTURE IMPORTANT SPEAK ABOUT

Again, realize that this is just a brief discussion. My mission is to bring these pillars of life to restore and regain the natural purpose and system used efficiently and naturally in justice for nature itself, what it represents as an original concept, and how to use it to its best form for today's world. Companies all over America and the world are considering these aspects.

1. Amounts of land lost why, whom, and what will they do with it 536,545 farms gone .. at the same time .. 165 million acres of farmland gone
2. Different sustaining Two Bar Sheep .. get the website to explain
3. Foods the way they are prepared for fast foods and the general consumer. For example, ground beef produces "Ammonia" in ground beef. Beef slime. McDonald's French Fries are also toxic. Chick Flix also has toxins. Chickens, beef, and all dairy products humans ingest these foods. They also injure the substance and cause a reaction in the human systems that could be detrimental. These foods are processed pharmaceuticals and chemicals that could affect and have been scientifically tested to harm humans.

See, after safety and housing, there is food. We know now and hear of the emergencies and

I realize that an authentic person is responsible for upholding justice and looking with an intricate eye and wisdom.

FEAR TURNS TO SURVIVAL OF THE FETUS, AND SOMETIMES THE HUMAN CHOOSES LESS THAN WHAT IS OF

---

[61] GOD first, America Our Miracle: Vote Freedom, Vote President Trump: Arden MDIV, Lisa Lucia: 9798345121887: Amazon.com: Books, Arden, Lisa Lucia, MDIV

GOD, AND SOMETIMES GOD WANTS US TO DO THAT DOES NOT SEEM LOGICALLY BECAUSE HE NEEDS TO BRING HIS TRUTH IN THE NORMAL THAT IS STAGNATE AND THE SUCCESS THAT NEEDS TO HAVE A CATALYST OF HIS GIFTS HIDDEN AND EVEN THAT WHAT NEEDS TO BE RELIVED TO LIVE AND MAKE UP TIME AND BRING TO WHAT HAS BEEN WOUNDED, NOT UNDERSTOOD, AND EVEN DEFORMED NEEDS TO BE REDEEMED

You can already see they are scared. They are building the bunkers for the war. They are made for several reasons. The electric grid issues, war, technological disasters, environmental

However, I believe that not everyone is involved, which is powerful. I think many want to create and develop, and they do not realize their life become deformities. Even the life present that God allowed them to build was used to develop deformities and deaths and even constant danger in our country and across the world.

Written February 29, 2024

I interject these notes to show you the reality of the ownership of the economy that controls many movements and aspects of the people and nations. Because much of the ownership of funds is allocated to only certain companies, we need to look at this reality to protect the masses, the Americans and children across the world, and even poor women and men.

How can we benefit from this? How can we create and bring life? For me, in God in the Trinity in Jesus Christ, the First Commandment is: Love God with all your heart and soul and love your neighbor as yourself.

First, look with an intricate eye for understanding.

Second, reveal the truth and find the truth.

Third, see how they can care for the people and the world in great justice. I call it miracles.

Fourth, how can we bring death to life and give mercy to others so they can rise to life? They can live in "living justice."

First, look with an intricate eye for understanding.

What is looking at the intricate eye of understanding to you .. Understanding is the highest wisdom to bring life to humans in development and peace in quality of life that brings .. freedom to be a person in society that respects others and the laws and supports conservative values and children and families with wholesome develop; however, at the same time allowing to become the individual to create and bring justice of creation and life. Question of an example: did the making of the CCP virus bring life or death? Did the unproven scientific fact that vaccinations should be used to save a life because it is proven that they would protect and save a life? We saw the truth.. by the facts.

Second, reveal the truth and find the truth.

Third, see how they can care for the people and the world in great justice. I call it miracles.

Fourth, how can we bring death to life and give mercy to others so they can rise to life? They can live in "living justice."

New system:

Explain education.

United States Companies will not have contracts for 10 to 30 years if they do not bring back manufacturing under proper regulation that serves humans first in the quality and safety of natural products.

Also, they need to develop SMALL BUSINESS

What are the different global systems?

There are four principal global systems: environmental, political, economic, and social, which are intrinsically connected. These are the ones in charge of shaping the world, from a local scale to a global scale, and yes, humans play a significant role in intervening somehow in all the systems already mentioned.

Here are the latest .. statistics[62]

Of country

Find the outline of the geopolitical power information I will work on.

Looking at the information, discuss the characteristics briefly.

Most Powerful Countries | U.S. News (usnews.com)

United States

China

Russia

Germany

"The world's most powerful countries also are the ones that consistently dominate news headlines, preoccupy policymakers, and shape global economic patterns. Their foreign policies and military budgets are tracked religiously. When they pledge, at least some in the international community trust – or fear – they will keep it. These countries project their influence on the world stage.

The Power sub-ranking is based on an equally weighted average of scores from six country attributes that relate to a country's power: a

---

[62] Most Powerful Countries | U.S. News (usnews.com)

leader, economically influential, with strong exports, politically influential, strong international alliances, and a strong military. For more information on how we rank, read the Best Countries methodology.

Past. Statistics .. what do you think?

Top 10 Companies by Market Cap in 2023[63]

https://www.google.com/search?q=WORLD+COMPANY+POWERS&rlz=1C1CHZN_enIT1045IT1045&oq=WORLD+COMPANY+POWERS&gs_lcrp=EgZjaHJvbWUqBggAEEUYOzIGCAAQRRg70gEJNTUxM2owajE1qAIAsAIA&sourceid=chrome&ie=UTF-8

COMPANY	SECTOR	MARKET CAP (USD)
Apple	Technology	2.776 trillion
Microsoft	Technology	2.588 trillion
Saudi Aramco	Oil & Gas	2.138 trillion
Alphabet (Google)	Technology	1.601 trillion

India's post-pandemic demand revival powered its economy to become the fifth-largest globally, surpassing the UK. However, the stock market was down marginally from a year ago, with the biggest dampener being a weaker rupee, which fell by 10 percent over the same period. Despite this,

---

[63]See title proper documentation
https://www.google.com/search?q=WORLD+COMPANY+POWERS&rlz=1C1CHZN_enIT1045IT1045&oq=WORLD+COMPANY+POWERS&gs_lcrp=EgZjaHJvbWUqBggAEEUYOzIGCAAQRRg70gEJNTUxM2owajE1qAIAsAIA&sourceid=chrome&ie=UTF-8

India's 100 richest combined wealth grew by $25 billion to touch $800 billion.[64]

https://www.forbesindia.com/article/india-rich-list-2022/the-rupee-may-be-weaker-but-the-rich-are-richer/81427/1

Here are the top 10 largest U.S. companies for 2022, ranked by Fortune.[65]

https://www.cbsnews.com/news/fortune-500-list-biggest-companies-walmart-amazon-apple/

1. Walmart

According to Fortune, the world's largest retailer posted $611 billion in revenue last year. Walmart has held the top spot for 11 years straight.

2. Amazon

The online retailer generated $514 billion in revenue last year. Amazon has been second on the list for four years.

3. Exxon Mobil

The oil company also had a banner year in 2022, raking in $413 billion in revenue and $55 billion in profit. Exxon Mobil moved into the third spot after bumping off Apple.

---

[64] https://www.forbesindia.com/article/india-rich-list-2022/the-rupee-may-be-weaker-but-the-rich-are-richer/81427/1

[65] https://www.cbsnews.com/news/fortune-500-list-biggest-companies-walmart-amazon-apple/

4. Apple

The tech giant had $394 billion in revenue for 2022. Apple may have fallen to fourth, but the iPhone seller is still the most profitable company on the list, claiming that title for the eighth time in nine years, according to Fortune.

5. UnitedHealth Group

The health insurance company generated $324 billion in revenue last year, making it the highest-ranking health care company on Fortune's list.

6. CVS Health

The pharmacy chain reported 2022 revenue of $322 billion, making it the highest-ranked company on Fortune's list run by a woman. CEO Karen Lynch took the helm in 2021.

7. Berkshire Hathaway

Warren Buffett's holding company had $302 billion in revenue last year, with the conglomerate holding on to its No. 7 spot on Fortune's list.

8. Alphabet

Google's parent company brought in nearly $283 billion in revenue, allowing Alphabet to maintain its No. 8 ranking on the list.

9. McKesson

The medical supplies company generated $264 billion in revenue last year, according to Fortune. McKesson also ranked 9th in last year's list.

10. Chevron

The San Ramon, Calif.-based energy company saw its revenue soar 52% last to $246 billion.

Which is the biggest company in the world?[66]

https://www.google.com/search?q=WORLD+COMPANY+POWERS&rlz=1C1CHZN_enIT1045IT1045&oq=WORLD+COMPANY+POWERS&gs_lcrp=EgZjaHJvbWUqBggAEEUYOzIGCAAQRRg70gEJNTUxM2owajE1qAIAsAIA&sourceid=chrome&ie=UTF-8

- #1 Walmart Inc. (WMT)
- #2 Amazon.com Inc. (AMZN)
- #2 China Petroleum & Chemical Corp. (SNP)
- #4 PetroChina Co. Ltd. (PCCYF)
- #5 Apple Inc. (AAPL)
- #6 Exxon Mobil Corp. (XOM)
- #7 Shell PLC (SHEL)
- #8 CVS Health Corp. (CVS)

What company has made the most money?

Ranking of the 50 most profitable companies worldwide 2022

In 2022, the Saudi Arabian oil company Saudi Aramco posted the highest net revenue of any company in the world, with profits of over 300 billion U.S. dollars .Aug 22, 2023

What company makes the most money per day?[67]

Top 10 Most Profitable Companies on Earth

Saudi Aramco: $304.04 M daily - Earns $1 M in 4.7 minutes.

Apple: $163.1 M daily - Earns $1 M in 8.8 minutes.

---

[66]https://www.google.com/search?q=WORLD+COMPANY+POWERS&rlz=1C1CHZN_enIT1045IT1045&oq=WORLD+COMPANY+POWERS&gs_lcrp=EgZjaHJvbWUqBggAEEUYOzIGCAAQRRg70gEJNTUxM2owajE1qAIAsAIA&sourceid=chrome&ie=UTF-8

[67] Most Powerful, https://theconversation.com/who-is-more-powerful-states-or-corporations-99616

Industrial & Commercial Bank of China: $123.29 M daily - Earns $1M in 11.7 minutes.

Samsung Electronics: $109.3 M daily - Earns $1 M in 13.2 minutes.

Which country has the richest corporation in the world?

The 10 wealthiest corporations include the likes of Saudi Aramco, Apple, Amazon and Microsoft, with seven of the top 10 based in the United States. However, Saudi Arabia takes the top spot with Saudi Aramco.

https://theconversation.com/who-is-more-powerful-states-or-corporations-99616

Just think about the private and public power of global giants like Google or Apple. When Donald Trump recently met Apple chief executive Tim Cook to discuss how a trade war with China would affect Apple's interests, it demonstrated that the leading multinationals are political actors, not bystanders.

Brief question and discussion: What are the amounts needed to uphold their companies transactions and sustaining development projects and payouts? Why have many companies lost and shut down or congloborated

Look at companies process of actions

Yes, experts and all alike know the contraindication and the catalyst to companies actions and positions and now that we have .. actions of geopolitical powers evident and factual from just to state a brief happening

1. Chinese geopolitical powers
2. Russia geopolitical powers
3. Saudia Arabia geopolitical powers
4. North and South Korea geopolitical powers
5. India
6. Germany
7. And others ..
8. Africa

CHECK THIS LIST AND JUST BRIEFLY SPEAK ABOUT IT.. SEE THE .. ..

COMPANIES HAVE CHANGED BECAUSE . THE .. CCP VIRUS AND WORLD POWERS

https://foreignpolicy.com/2016/03/15/these-25-companies-are-more-powerful-than-many-countries-multinational-corporate-wealth-power/

The Top 25 Corporate Nations

BY DAVID FRANCIS

Note these are different.

We live in an era where the interplay between state and corporate power shapes the reality of international relations more than ever. In combination with the current nationalist and protectionist backlash in large parts of the world, this may yet lead to a revival of global rivalries: states using corporations to achieve geopolitical goals in an increasingly hostile environment and powerful corporations perhaps using more aggressive strategies to extract profits in response. If this is where we're heading, it could have a lasting impact on the world order.

https://theconversation.com/who-is-more-powerful-states-or-corporations-99616

Jaspers distinguishes this 'all-embracing' phenomenon of the world and transcendental essence specifically human phenomena which he divides into being, pure consciousness, intellect and possible existence.

Being is given absolute form in pragmatism, biologism, psychologism, and sociologism, the pure consciousness in rationalism, the spirit in education, the existence in existentialism (which becomes nihilism), the world in materialism, naturalism, idealism, and pantheism, and the metaphysical in acosmism (p. 141). Page 10

Man as a being: the man who is conceived and born, grows up, achieves maturity, and dies as a living being, an individual. The individual is characterized personally by the specific form of his animated body, which is able to function through the complex interplay of chemical and physical processes. Man is determined by his inclinations and the environment, and each individual differs from all others. He shares this characteristic with animals, but this vital reality still does not define his true human nature. He is, in fact, something other than an animal. He differs from animals in that he combines, at the same time, nature and history, while inheritance and tradition play a large part in determining his characteristics. This qualitative difference between man and animals is underscored by other forms of the 'all-embracing' that characterize the living nature of man.

"The individual is characterized personally by the specific form of his animated body, which is able to function through the complex interplay of chemical and physical processes. Man is determined by his inclinations and the environment, and each individual differs from all others." while inheritance and tradition play a large part in determining his characteristics.

Yet, as we know, that does not determine men's lives and purposes, especially because God's life in humans is infinite. God's breath, the Messianic breath, is continually growing and never stopping.

Chemical and physical processes: We know humans need to have a process and environment to be that person in wholesomeness and develop as their "individual" from others. Hence, it is paramount the environment is in a magnitude and balance to uphold the "chemical,"

Man as pure consciousness: this term denotes man with the unique possibility of moving beyond his consciousness as an individual living creature and focusing that consciousness on the nature of being as such, which is made the subject of critical perception and enjoys general validity. This consciousness is the 'locus of valid thinking' (1947, p. 67), of which only man is capably9 e. Understanding refers to objective existence and grasps this objective world through its categories. This general consciousness is necessarily specific to each living being in which it must exist.

Man as intellect: i.e., a man who can 'generate ideas' that create order among the confusing profusion of disparate knowledge that can be extended at will, highlighting the relationship between individual factors and whose aim is to establish unity among the diversity of phenomena. Intellectual understanding is more than mere logical thinking. The mind is the force of understanding that seeks to perfect the totality of its interiority and shape the world. This mind is objectively perceptible through science, poetry, art, the legal order, and moral life. The mind needs the intellect rooted in the living being, but the intellect is not everything.

Intellectual understanding is more than mere logical thinking. The mind is the force of understanding that seeks to perfect the totality of its interiority and shape the world. This mind is objectively perceptible through science, poetry, art, the legal order, and moral life. The mind needs the intellect rooted in the living being, but the intellect is not everything.

Man as existence: i.e., a man in the irreplaceable historicity of his unique origin, in his unconditional resolve to become himself. Existence is the sign that being, pure consciousness, and the mind cannot be understood independently and do not have their reason, that man is not confined to immanence but remains essentially dependent on the metaphysical. However, existence is impossible without being, pure consciousness, and the mind. These are essential conditions if pure consciousness's content is revealed in the mind (1947, p. 134). Pure consciousness and the mind cannot be understood on their own and do not have their reason, that man is not confined to immanence but remains essentially dependent on the transcendental Page11

Geopolitical Land Mass of Power

Note that I am attempting to prove a point, and I also want you to think about these facts.

How can we restore our freedoms and the potentiality of human development of the masses to be the authentic person, continue to strive to have liberty and life to be that person as individual gifts and endeavors and missions, and also bring it to society, the community, and the world in a way that is not constrained and controlled by world orders?

I believe that when the people have leaders who serve justice and what it means to be human, as defined in our discussion .... Get a sentence on what it means to be human.

Even the land monopoly of geopolitical power control is evident. Look at Russia, the land mass, and then Ukraine. Russia, under Putin and his counterparts, took Ukraine.. under a holocaust of evil. During the presidency of President Trump and President Reagan, we were able to be protected by the

See, they have enough. They want "world control," as evident in their actions. Today, I am writing this book, Hamas of the Hands of Death, to take Israel and use the USA as the force attempting to weaken the world of freedoms since Iran knows the USA seeks to protect the freedoms of get quote of the history of Hamas.

https://www.linkedin.com/feed/update/urn:li:activity:7142340902252916 736/

Hamas never wanted to put down its war tools. They continue to

This is also reflected in the companies that make the most gross national and international products, take most of the funds for them, and simultaneously seek to control the people, to name a few.

<u>Please look at the chart, and you can fill in all the World and Geopolitical Urgencies—these are just a few.</u>

1. They took away the vote from the people when President Trump won because President Trump serves the people. NOTE WE HAVE TO HAVE VOTER ID. NO IMMIGRANT VOTING
2. Pharmaceutical Company Controls
3. CCP Virus made to kill the people
4. CCP Vaccines
5. Lockdown
6. CCP Business owned in the USA and the world
7. Individual Elite Communist controls Billionaires
8. Private Companies Black Rock, State Street Vanguard, Funnel U.S. Investment To Chinese Shipyard That Built Third CCP Aircraft Carrier CPA NEWSROOM AUGUST 18, 2022 https://prosperousamerica.org/vanguard-blackrock-funnel-u-s-investment-to-chinese-shipyard-that-built-third-ccp-aircraft-carrier/

SUMMARY

"As of June 2022, BlackRock, Vanguard, and other Wall Street financial firms are exploiting American investors and helping the Chinese Communist Party (CCP) build and modernize the Chinese military.

Currently, these firms offer Exchange Traded Funds (ETFs) and other investment products to U.S. investors that track indices containing Chinese companies building and modernizing the CCP's military. For example, CSSC Holdings Ltd. was listed as a constituent of the following index: MSCI Emerging Markets, MSCI ACWI, FTSE Emerging, and FTSE All-World. These indices are tracked by trillions of assets under management globally through associated ETFs.

✕ PROBLEM: American investors, via ETFs and Mutual Funds, are actively funding Chinese entities that are modernizing China's People's Liberation Army (PLA) and Navy and that have been sanctioned (or are linked to a company that has been) by the U.S. government for human rights abuses or national security risk.

√ SOLUTION: Require transparency and disclosure from index providers and fund managers, and prohibit sanctioned and known bad actor Chinese companies from inclusion in indexes and investment products like ETFs and Mutual Funds."[68]

Ask the question. Remember, we are only going to give a few catalysts to open our minds to understanding some. Some know all their reasons. Yet, remember, even those who appear to be allies.

1. " Do you think China and the USA will be allies or friends to find against another country in the future." There is some discussion about this. Actually, what do you think? China is our ally friend.. when we know they are starting a cyber-attack of war on our country.. and many other
2. Was China used to help kill off the people's population? Remember, Gates speaks about this periodically, Schwab Karl.. and many others. Soros funds Democrats. Fauci

---

[68] Private Companies Black Rock, State Street Vanguard, BlackRock Funnel U.S. Investment To Chinese Shipyard That Built Third CCP Aircraft Carrier CPA NEWSROOM AUGUST 18, 2022
https://prosperousamerica.org/vanguard-blackrock-funnel-u-s-investment-to-chinese-shipyard-that-built-third-ccp-aircraft-carrier/

a. Fentanyl allowed to have open borders .. drugs came through
b. Immigrants invasion: we do not know how many criminals and war preparers, treason planning America after they become citizens. I agree… to stop payment of foreign aid and. We must open up "Title 42," President Trump's agreement.
c. CCP virus was made with other individuals involved just now in China
d. People such as Fauci and others.
e. CCP vaccinations to kill people 40 people became billionaires in the pharmaceutical companies.
f. Lockdowns to take away income and control of their life
g. Want to make digital money
h. Food controls
i. List of companies whose information was raided in the USA and China
j. . a
k. Maui.. Biowarfare on the people to .. take the land from the people to build the World control powers life of ideas
l. Ukraine-Russia War
m. Israel and Hamas war
n. Weathering Controls Disaster
o. EMF killing of human cells
p. Chemical Sprau
q. World Health Controls Pharmaceutical Toxins
r. World Economic Controls

3. World Control
https://internationalbusinessguide.org/corporations/
4. List of forums and associates.
    a. World Economic Forum Børge Brende is the President and member of the Managing Board of the World Economic Forum
    b. https://inp.harvard.edu/people/b%C3%B8rge-brende. He is on the board of the International Negotiation Program at

Harvard, and look how they have allowed the protestors to bring the violent expression of Israel and the protection of freedom. Where is he? Should he have spoken? Footnote. Also, we see they want one world government and world control.

   c. The UN funds Palestinian children's schools to teach terrorism and hatred of Jews and kill them. https://sdgs.un.org/panelists/he-mr-borge-brende-29218 get footnote.

   d. https://live.worldbank.org/en/experts/b/borge-brende-0Who

   e. World Health Control https://www.who.int/newsroom/questions-and-answers/item/pandemic-prevention--preparedness-and-response-accord

   f. Do not control our health. We should have the choice. Many people died because of the weakness of the body and death. Get footnotes

   g. Who is more powerful – states or corporations?[69]

   h. Published: July 10, 2018, 11:14 am EDT

   i. https://theconversation.com/who-is-more-powerful-states-or-corporations-99616

Who holds power in international politics? Most people would probably say the largest states in the global system. The current landscape of international relations seems to affirm this intuition: new Russian geopolitics, "America First," and Chinese state-led global expansion, among others, seem to put state power back in charge after decades of globalization.

Yet multinationals like Apple and Starbucks still wield phenomenal power. They oversee huge supply chains, sell products worldwide, and help mold international politics to their interests. In some respects, multinationals have governments at their beck and call –

---

[69] Who is more powerful – states or corporations? Published: July 10, 2018 11:14am EDT https://theconversation.com/who-is-more-powerful-states-or-corporations-99616

We compare states and corporations based on their deep pockets. The following table ranks the 100 largest corporations and countries based on their revenues in 2016. Revenues, in the case of states, are mainly collected taxes.

States occupy the top rankings, with the US first followed by China and Japan (the eurozone ranks first with more than US$5,600 billion if we treat it as a single political entity). However, plenty of corporations are on par with some of the largest economies in the world: Walmart exceeds Spain and Australia, for example. Of the top 100 revenue generators, our ranking shows 71 are corporations.[70]

People need to ask, and leaders of states and governmental officials are th

Look at this: we will make it, brothers and sisters.

We, the people, will live in justice and liberty for all.

However, we need to correct and restore these urgencies, which are chiseling and deforming the seat of justice in America.

We need first to seek justice in each one of us.

We cannot accommodate what we measure to take advantage of others behind other's backs.

People cannot use the innocent for their desires.

The eyes of God are watching people, and we better not use the people for our desires without them knowing what is happening. This is the elite controls and communists that are even lay people that abuse others. God is watching all of us.

---

[70]Who is more powerful – states or corporations?Published: July 10, 2018 11:14am EDT
https://theconversation.com/who-is-more-powerful-states-or-corporations-99616

Some sins and crimes are done behind others' backs, whether it is weapons of mass destruction preparation, drugs prepared to bring over the border, or masons using evil tactics.

Becareful; there are secrets and ways they hurt people .. no child should be around the smoke of drugs and smoke and even adults. They can get cancer and brain damage and even the "demons" that the people carry. It is known now that demons are taken in the smoke of the criminal smoking to hurt or enter into the space of another.

Ephesians 6:10 Finally, grow strong in the Lord, with the strength of his power. 11 Put on the whole armor of God to resist the devil's tactics. 12 For it is not against human enemies that we have to struggle, but against the principalities and the ruling forces who are masters of the darkness in this world, the spirits of evil in the heavens. 13 That is why you must take up all God's armor, or you will not be able to put up any resistance on an evil day, or stand your ground even though you exert yourselves to the full.

Ephesians 6:14 So stand your ground, with truth a belt round your waist, and uprightness a breastplate, 15 wearing for shoes on your feet the eagerness to spread the gospel of peace 16 and always carrying the shield of faith so that you can use it to quench the burning arrows of the Evil One. 17. Then you must take salvation as your helmet and the sword of the Spirit, that is, the word of God.

Ephesians 6:18 In all your prayer and petition, keep praying in the Spirit on every possible occasion. Never get tired of staying awake to pray for all God's holy people, 19 and pray for me to be allowed to open my mouth and fearlessly make known the mystery of the gospel 20 of which I am an ambassador in chains; pray that in proclaiming it I may speak as fearlessly as I ought to. 21 So that you know, as well, what is happening to me and what I am doing, my dear friend Tychicus, my trustworthy helper in the Lord, will tell you everything. 22 I am sending him to you precisely for this purpose, to give you news about us and encourage you thoroughly.

Ephesians 6:23 May God the Father and the Lord Jesus Christ grant all the brothers peace, love, and faith. 24 May grace be with all who love our Lord Jesus Christ in life imperishable.

Note: Let us ask about the revenue of the different countries. See, now we need to consider the CCP Virus. Also, during the wars, these exact numbers may have changed.

The 15 Best Military Commanders In Human History, Ranked | Watch (msn.com)

CHAPTER ELEVEN

Catholic Justice

Brief Notes in Living in Truth

Commanded by Christ in the Great Commission, we are called to bring first Christ, and in Christ, there is Justice *

The Lord's command was in me when I spoke out from my heart in the Latin prayers in Saint Thomas Aquinas, Rome, Italy, in June 2012

I have followed my heart, the "listening heart," and spoke out in Prayer in the middle of the Latin prayers, and the Holy Spirit in my heart gave me His Words in the truth to say,

Pope Benedict XVI and the Bishops of the Catholic Church go across the world to Preach the Gospel of Christ to tell the

Good News ***

Our life is faith in Christ at His heart, living in His effulgent, powerful presence.

Our devoted love for our Catholic Church in unity is in His omnipotent Hands.

Our Eucharistic mass of miracles and power, yet the sweet, forgiving peace of Christ's presence within us, sustains us to live in truth in His purpose and quintessential Love.

Our Holy Spirit of Mystery, Jesus Christ, sends us to live in us and through us in truth, love, wisdom, good works, power, tenderness, protection, and healing.

Our Holy Scriptures are the voice and Almighty hand of Christ's of God's Alpha and Omega omniscience to our life.

Our prayer is to help us be pure examples of your Love, Christ so that the humanity of people can know You and live in Your presence.

Our America stands in pureness and truth, our United States, United; we stand in urgency for our Faith, our Families, our Freedom, and our world.

Yes, my brother and sister stand in pureness in Truth in the Lord Jesus Christ.

1. Pope Benedict elaborated on St. Augustine's famous saying in his encyclical Deus Caritas est. St. Augustine insisted on justice because "justice is both the aim and the intrinsic criterion of all politics." (No. 28).

2. St Thomas says that every science seeks after the proper causes of its subject. We should direct each science to the " proper causes of its subject." When we do not "seek after the proper causes of its subject," we do not have justice. Then, the subject becomes nothingness because it is not "the proper cause" for its existence. As believers in what it is to be human

3. "Success is subordinate[before] to the criterion of justice. The will to do what is right and to understand what is right."[71] We have the free will to do what is right. Even if it seems yet the minuteness of action and no one sees, our Lord sees He watches from the heavens. This minuteness of action is powerful because it lives and has truth.

4. Today, people put success of materialism, social status, cultural or religious beliefs, and personal desires before justice. Each of us needs to vote in and support a politician, defined as: "Fundamental

---

[71] Listening Heart, https://www.cambridge.org/core/books/abs/pope-benedict-xvis-legal-thought/listening-heart/6C618CBEDA73C18DDB92708A47AE76DA

tasks of the politician is to serve right and fight against the dominion of wrong."[72] We need to ask ourselves, as Most Holiness Pope Benedict XVI reminds us, is our present leader: are our politicians serving the right and fighting against the dominion of wrong?

*We have all we need to bring in the Great Commission:

See, the Lord Jesus Christ gave His life to us, to all of humanity, so that we can have life and life abundantly through Christ, Life, Crucifixion, death, Resurrection, and the sending of the Holy Spirit. He alone is the only one to bring True Justice! Jesus Christ has given us living precepts of being human and how to bring justice to His teachings. Furthermore, He sustains us through His Eucharistic Mass and the Holy Spirit and the Holy Scriptures, the Saints, the Catholic Teachings, and the Leaders of the Church, and the unity of peoples of the Church and believers and all the sacraments. Let's list in the hearts of the people. Recollect their love for their Lord and the power of His words of truths to bring the reason of faith and reason of religion in Christ.

The Lord has given us these miraculous, omnipotent gifts from heaven and earth. Let us be purified: "God purifies the Hearts" Proverbs 17:3 Purifying the heart brings justice because it brings love, and love brings compassion. Compassion brings seeking out solutions to care for others in the wellbeing of humanity. For we do not wrestle against flesh and blood, but against principalities, against powers, against the rulers of the darkness of this age, against spiritual hosts of wickedness in the heavenly places.(Eph. 6:11,12)

5. Just as the Medieval period of San Thomas Aquinas promotes, "justice is both the aim and the intrinsic criterion of all politics." Intrinsic justice in politics: Justice has to be in politics to be actual politics. Even if it is small, we can speak out, break the silence, and communicate the truth and justice in our voices and actions.

---

[72] Listening Heart

6. " To Augustine, more than any other man, the church throughout this troubled period owes the preservation of its doctrine of man's dependence on God for deliverance and salvation.[73]

7. "One of the decisive developments in the Western philosophical tradition was the eventually widespread merging of the Greek intellectual tradition and the Judeo-Christian Religious and scriptural traditions.

Augustine is one of the leading figures through and by whom this merging was accomplished."[74] Today, we need to preserve the Catholic Church's precepts and scriptural traditions. Individually, our heart and soul are likened to Jaspers' "metaphysical guilt." We must be responsible for our actions, speak out in wisdom, and communicate. We need to break our silence about injustices, even if we know some may not believe.

Today, we must preserve the Holy Scriptures and Christian Catholic doctrine from the modern complexities of confusion, syncretism, and assimilation. We must live in Christ, in man's dependence on God for deliverance and salvation.

We need strategic commanding heights to pour justice upon this atrocity in History. Humans cannot live to their fullest because they are oppressed, manipulated, and even deceived.

1. Pope Benedicto XVI asks how "can we discern between good and evil?" How can we promote justice? "Regulated by law in the support of the majority can serve as a sufficient criterion." The dignity of man and humanity is at stake, and the majority principles are not enough; everyone in a position of responsibility must seek out the criteria to be followed when framing laws. The convictions of Christians to keep divine laws in the ruling of the Scythians were what motivated resistance movements to act opposing the Nazi regime and disparate totalitarian regimes, thereby being

---

[73] Gould Baring, Rev. S, Lives of Saints https://www.gutenberg.org/files/46947/46947-h/46947-h.htm, p. 107

[74] Ibid, Lives of Saints, p. ?

champions of justice and humanity as a whole.[75] Today, we need to do the same and be champions of justice. We need to speak out in truth in Christ's teachings and act in our daily living in the precepts of the Catholic Christian teachings, asking ourselves if our living is expressing what our Lord Jesus Christ would desire. We need to do this actively! Just as St. Thomas had to promote justice in the Medieval period.

2. No other time has humans been at the level of reason information system that is the most powerful recorded in history. However, as a community and world, we have yet to use these information sciences in the most efficient paradigms for the basic needs of humanity socially, mentally, physically, economically, and educationally. Today, the world is in an economic tragedy and uproar. These are times when we need to be lifted in the power of the Holy Spirit to witness our Lord, the world's salvation, and be an expression of strength and love.

3. The law of truth. We need to have the law of truth. We know the truth in our relationship with the Lord: "O Beauty of ancient yet so new." St. Augustine illuminates this in his Confessions. God's "Beauty of ancient," His everlasting covenant with His people from generation to generation, and living today in the people's hearts. Bishop Morerod reminds us to ask ourselves: Why is our Church still existing? Bishop Morerod answers that people must have a personal relationship with their Lord God. People of the Church have a living relationship with their God. Because they continually seek His relationship. Therefore, we know these precepts and seek to follow them. We are responsible for bringing this truth of God's 'O Beauty" to the world's laws in justice. Yes, to get, to fight, to run that race. Thus, to serve justice when framing laws has never been simple, and today, given the vast extent of our knowledge and capacity, it has become still more complicated.

4. When we know what is right for a just Good Governance, we know what Truth is:

---

[75] Pope Benedicto, XVI Listening Heart

a. INSPIRATION AND TRUTH OF SACRED SCRIPTURE- The Profession of Christian Faith (I believe in God the Father) - Live seeking His precepts and covenantal commandments and accepting Him as Lord and Savior Purifying us through the Eucharistic Mass.

b. GOD, "HE WHO IS," IS TRUTH AND LOVE- When we believe in God, He is truth and Love. He gave us love by life on the Cross and new life through the resurrection.

The existence of angels — a truth of faith

1. LIVING IN THE TRUTH
2. TO BEAR WITNESS TO THE TRUTH
3. OFFENSES AGAINST TRUTH
4. RESPECT FOR THE TRUTH
5. TRUTH, BEAUTY, AND SACRED ART

1. We need to communicate as Dr. Karl Jasper teaches and speak out individually to the others.Today, as discussed above, it is our responsibility to be human to promote the "cause" of what it is to be human. We know what it is to be human because we know what truth is. We know as Catholics what it is to be human based on Christ's precepts. Promoting human rights and Christian precepts.

2. We know the truth. God is living in the Church and the hearts of the people. It is our responsibility to break that silence so that we can speak out and communicate. There is a "Holocaust" of economic abuse in government and banks and even businesses taking from the essential labors. Furthermore, the protection of human life and dignity. This present leader has many injustice issues. I pray that he steps down. I pray for him. "Human rights" have been abused in many facets, such as religion, abortion, euthanasia, and many other atrocities, such as governmental, economic, and governance failure. [76] "All human beings are born

---

[76] —Article 1 of the United Nations Universal Declaration of Human Rights (UDHR)[9 Human rights are commonly understood as "inalienable fundamental rights to which a

free and equal in dignity and rights. They are endowed with reason and conscience and should act towards one another in a spirit of brotherhood. "From this foundation, the modern human rights arguments emerged over the latter half of the twentieth century. Gelling as social activism and political rhetoric in many nations put it high on the world agenda.[8]

3. There is a lack of "good governance" to carry out laws to promote justice in a society and protect the people. Politicians have a heavy challenge to make justice live today. However, we need to be honest about what is taking place; the statistics we see of many tragedies of the people: unemployment, poverty, social issues, faith and religious abused and denied, syncretism, traditional values abused, traditional values assimilated in modernity, family non-support, and many other atrocities. (Pray for our Military men. They have the highest rate of suicide 20.00% approximately, higher than the national average of 19.0%) Old paradigms of Politics are obsolete; we need to take what is suitable from the old and vote for a Politician with a record that can at least keep us from going deeper into the tragedy of every entity of life.

4. Today, we have the tools as people to promote justice. Most of all, we have our relationship with Jesus Christ in the mystery of the Eucharistic Mass. The Lord has given us the Holy Scriptures and the Catholic teachings: the Pope, Bishops, Priests, Nuns, Deacons, the lay people. We have the Saints. Believers are strong, faithful, educated, diplomatic, and upright citizens. We have a voice! We have our strength in Christ. Christ manifests strength in weakness.

---

person is inherently entitled simply because she or he is a human being."[1]The idea of human rights[3] states, "if the public discourse of peacetime global society can be said to have a common moral language, it is that of human rights." Despite this, the strong claims made by the doctrine of human rights continue to provoke considerable skepticism and debates about the content, nature and justifications of human rights to this day. Indeed, the question of what is meant by a "right" is itself controversial and the subject of continued philosophical debate.[4]Many of the basic ideas that animated the movement developed in the aftermath of the Second World War and the atrocities of The Holocaust, culminating in the adoption of the Universal Declaration of Human Rights in Paris by the United Nations General Assembly in 1948.

This means that if we humble ourselves to His precepts, we will have the strength to bring justice because Christ's precepts in the Holy Scriptures bring life and life abundantly. Christ's precepts bring good, orderly purpose for the love and care for all humanity. Not only do we have Judeo-Christian precepts in the Holy Scriptures, but we also have a relationship with our God, and Catholics have our Lord Jesus Christ and Him as Lord and Savior. Human Rights- and dealing with issues

1. What does it mean to be human?
2. It can be challenging to define what right is.
3. Each culture has different beliefs.
4. With Globalization, there is a syncretism, assimilation, and a mixing of cultural ideas.
5. Therefore, it would take a lot of work to define humans. It would take a lot of work to define what is right.
6. Traditional values begin to water down and starting to adopt other beliefs, secreting
7. Positivism: Hans Kelsen: "An aggregate of objectives linked together in terms of cause and effect". Then, indeed, no ethical indication of any kind can be derived from it." Then, no ethical indication of any kind can be derived from it.
8. "Justice preserves the happiness, or the parts of the happiness, of the political community."[77]

'In God, power, essence, will, intellect, wisdom, and justice are all identical; nothing can be in God's power that could not be in his just will or his wise intellect."[78]

We ask ourselves then, in our (power), if we promote justice if it is in God's will, then injustices can be broken from the bonds of hidden secrecy of sin. Essence in the (nature) of who we are, our purpose in all that we do, and our desire to live in Christ? Will in our (will) is it in the right

---

[77] Catholic Catechism Book V13
[78] Ibid, Catholic Catechism, Article 3 271.

relationship with Christ's will? Intellect, do we use are (intellect) or reason for justice? When we express our compassion and love, compassion, essence, will, intellect, and wisdom in Christ through the power of the Holy Spirit, then it can become life to others, giving hope and protecting their rights for justice. This is why we need to have a "just intellect," a reason in Christ's redeeming purpose for the present, bringing all to the cross of Christ for living in life in truth.

Catholic Justice Prima Facie

In The Question of German Guilt, Dr. Karl Jaspers reminds us that the Nazi government has fallen for now more than half a century.

However, today within our modern governments of today there are malformations of a "Nazi government" per se of a "holocaust" toward the zygote coming from the zenith of all wonderment in God's creation in the humanness of a human being formed, forcing sterilization, abortion and euthanasia and other deformities to humanity. Even the President seeks to use innocent hands to carry out his 'nothingness' of death upon the human essence and What it means to be human.

But also in the economics of loot stolen literally from the innocent and ignorant mouths and minds, from the life of each human's existence and authentic identity that may have been. The economic abuse, failure to even balance the financial problems, using the middle class for good for evil , and using the poorest of ignorance for a position in the Presidency.

Then the international solidarity of justice not only cannot be avoided that the bloodbaths of innocent indigenous peoples of (destitution) deprived of the necessities of life, (poverty-stricken) beggars, prostitution and hopeless of generational oppression (impoverished) exhausted of all vitality and life soil for the heart and sustaining nutrients of life. If we look at the globalization of the world markets, it is at a height of dynamic motion than anytime in history. For the majority of people in the world, globalization has great possibilities. It has one of the greatest impacts on justice for people today.

Catholic Justice[79]

Social Justice:

This responsibility for the carnage(massacre) of the Second World War.

"Echoes of tragedy will linger... children then have perished." [80] Today we have the responsibility to prevent the carnage of the precious carcasses to be in a "holocaust" of the mind of Politicians of "nothingness."

Solidarity of Nations Justice:

Today, we have the responsibility to promote justice on an international level. Unlike the history of our world, our countries have developed globalization and are multicultural within communities. Therefore, it is all the more paramount we live and work in "God's power, essence, intellect, will, wisdom [working and breathing in each entity in justice]"[81] to promote   justice of solidarity[82] In the complexities of these new multicultural communities. Because justice is relevant in all cultures, when it is justice in the true nature of the human being, it will bring justice and happiness and flourishing in peace. When we apply each part of our life to God, we will permeate justice. However, again, we need to support leaders and Politicians who have a "listening heart." what the people need is to fight for justice within our international relations within the boundaries right reason, natural law, social law, human law, ethical law, political law all embraced in the divine law of reason in faith and reason in religion and for us Catholics the Holy Scriptures.

This century is the century to come back to the Cross. We need to open our eyes wide to see truth, clear our ears open to hear the voice of wisdom

---

[79] Catholic Catechisma, Article 3 1928

[80] The Question of Guilt, Introduction

[81] Catholic Catechisma, Article 3

[82] Bauzon, Stephen Professor, Political Ethics Lectures, Pontifical Saint Thomas Aquinas, Rome, Italy, Fall 2011

of our Lord, feel that miracle of the power of the Holy Spirit guiding us for others to come to the cross and heart of Christ, taste that Eucharistic miracle right to the deepest part of our soul for ongoing transformation and unity in Jesus Christ and His Church and bend down on our knees that we are part of that foundation of Jesus Christ's Church.

Responsibility

"Metaphysical guilt the responsibility that survivors often feel toward those who suffered and died."

Responsibility, oh my Lord, I write these words little yet so grand, seeking the master's hand of care and hope of justice that I may take responsibility to bring justice to the world's peoples. See we know you made these precious people you made each one out of love. We are your children and because we are from you we seek out to do your will and that is to be responsible for the ones that you created. Responsible so you can rely on us to pour out your living justice in the hearts and lives of the people. Responsible for telling, showing, bringing, guiding, and feeding them in the Love of God's salvation in Jesus Christ. This is the only way to true justice. You said you have humanity at your heart. You said you love humanity. You said for us to love humanity as You love us.

" Jesus is the way the truth and the life and know one will come to the Father except through Him."

Let our daily lives be reminiscent of the daily beauty we fight for freedom of justice.

God never changes because He knows the ultimate truth. God in Christ is the ultimate justice. As we know the Lord accommodates His people in their humanity. Issues today that are atrocious as a "holocaust" to humanity can be resurrected and made renewed in the power and miracle in Jesus Christ through the Holy Spirit working in the Hearts of the believers. Responsibility for justice let it be at our finger tips of our hearts to give and work for the true justice in Jesus Christ.

Catholic Justice Prima Facie

In The Question of German Guilt, Dr. Karl Jaspers reminds us of the Nazi government has been fallen for now more than a half a century.

Catholic Justice[83]

Social Justice

1928   Society ensures social justice when it provides the conditions that allow associations or individuals to obtain what is their due, according to their nature and their vocation. Social justice is linked to the common good and the exercise of authority.

I. RESPECT FOR THE HUMAN PERSON

1929   Social justice can be obtained only in respecting the transcendent dignity of man. The person represents the ultimate end of society, which is ordered to him:What is at stake is the dignity of the human person, whose defense and promotion have been entrusted to us by the Creator, and to whom the men and women at every moment of history are strictly and responsibly in debt.35[84]

Economic Justice:

ARTICLE 7: THE SEVENTH COMMANDMENT

Do not steel.

2401   The seventh commandment forbids unjustly taking or keeping the goods of one's neighbor and wronging him in any way with respect to his goods. It commands justice and charity in the care of earthly goods and the fruits of men's labor. For the sake of the common good, it requires respect for the universal destination of goods and respect for the right to

---

[83] Catholic Catechisma, Article 3 1928

[84] Ibid, Catholic Catechisma Article 3 Social Justice

private property. Christian life strives to order this world's goods to God and to fraternal charity.[85]

Justice and Solidarity Among Nations :

2437 On the international level, inequality of resources and economic capability is such that it creates a real "gap" between nations.224 On the one side there are those nations possessing and developing the means of growth and, on the other, those accumulating debts.

Today we have the responsibility to promote justice on an international level. Unlike the past history of our world our countries have developed globalization and are multicultural within communities. Therefore, it is all the more paramount we live and work in "God's power, essence, intellect, will, wisdom[working and breathing in each entity in justice]"[86] to promote is justice of solidarity in the complexities of these new multicultural communities. Because, justice truly is relevant in all cultures when it is justice in the true nature it fulfills the human being. When we apply each part of our life in God we will permeate justice. However, again we need to support leaders and Politicians that have a "listening heart" what the peoples needs are to fight for justice within our international relations within the boundaries.

Justice:

In God, Holiness, divine intimacy [salvation], Harmony, wisdom, peace, wellbeing of humanity, flourishing of human being, reality, action in wisdom of the Holy Spirit's strength.

Responsibility as Catholics

We need to take risks.

As Catholic Christians:

---

[85] Ibid, Catholic Catechisma, Article 7 Seventh Commandment IV. Economic Activity and Social Justice

[86] Catholic Catechisma, Article V. Justice and Solidarity Among Nations

Responsibility, I write these words little yet so grand seeking the master's hand of care of hope of justice that I may take responsibility, to bring justice to the peoples of the world. See we know you made these precious people you made each one out of love. We are your children and because we are from you we seek out to do your will and that is to be responsible for the ones that you created. Responsible so you can rely on us to pour out your living justice in the hearts and lives of the people. Responsible to tell them, show them, bring them, guide them, feed them in the Love of God's salvation in Jesus Christ this is the only way to the true justice.

" Jesus is the way the truth and the life and know one will come to the Father except through Him."

Let our present lives be reminiscent of each day to be beauty we fought for freedom of justice.

Let our immediate present lives be active in responsibility

God never changes because He knows the ultimate truth. God in Christ is the ultimate Justice. As we know the Lord accommodates to His people in their humanity. Issues today that are atrocious as a "holocaust" to humanity can be resurrected and made renewed in the power and miracle in Jesus Christ through the Holy Spirit working in the Hearts of the believers. Responsibility for justice be flowing from each the breath and beat of our heart to give and work for the true justice in Jesus Christ.

We, as believers seeking to live by the precepts of Jesus Christ outlined for us in the Holy Scriptures and the Catholic teachings, have the responsibility to seek to maintain justice and bring about justice for the values of "What it means to be human?" Different cultures have different ideas of

The best way we can bring Justice is to get Jesus into the lives of the people.

We have a command to Preach the Word across the world.

I was praying in the Spirit-filled Pontifical San Thomas Aquinas, and the Spirit of the Lord commanded me to speak out: Pope Benedicto and the

Bishops should go across the world and preach the Gospel, tell the Good News of Jesus. We, as Catholics, need to go to the ends of the Earth to preach the word of God. Pope Benedicto and the Church.

Note: make sure you make a difference in the section for Catholic Christian points.

Symbol the Lord's plan for his Church, namely that all the hierarchical order of Christ's Church, all "sacred power" exercised in the Church, is nothing other than service, service with a single purpose: to ensure that the whole People of God shares in this threefold mission of Christ and permanently remains under the power of the Lord; a power that has its source not in the powers of this world, but instead in the mystery of the Cross and the Resurrection.

The absolute, yet sweet and gentle, power of the Lord responds to the depths of the human person, to his loftiest aspirations of intellect, will, and heart. It does not speak the language of force but expresses itself in charity and truth."Allow me to wet my lips in spring water, to feel its freshness, reviving freshness."

Philosophy is the principle of concentration through which man becomes himself by partaking in reality.[87]

We need to define man to

Language Birth Spirituality Integrating Communication Truth Living Justice Responsibility

God → Christ → Humanity → Family → Faith → Social Happiness → Tradition → Well Being → Reality

Freedom " The neutrality of the state authority on questions of world views guarantees the same ethical freedom to every citizen." [88]

---

[87] Jaspers, Way of Wisdom, p. 7

[88] Ratzinger and Habermas
=,https://books.google.com/books?hl=en&lr=&id=ERzoAPsS9usC&oi=fnd&pg=PA3&dq=

Commandments :

Justice's First commandment is to love the Lord with all your heart and put no other God before thee

Then, the Second Commandment says, "Love your neighbor as yourself." See, you want your neighbor to have what you have, and that is the love Relationship you have with Jesus Christ, the Son of God, in the power of the Holy Spirit.

Today in Evangelizing, bring all to the Cross of Christ .. to the Eucharist table. ..

Faithful Love and Loyalty join together, Saving Justice and Peace embrace.

11Loyalty will spring up from the earth, and Justice will lean down from heaven. Yahweh will himself give prosperity, and our soil will yield its harvest. Justice will walk before him, treading out a path.Psalm 85:10-13(14)

In Jesus Christ we have the message of the truth and the gospel of our salvation, and having put our trust in Christ we have been stamped with the seal of the Holy Spirit of the Promise.

Traditions. Individually are heart and soul likened to Jaspers' "metaphysical guilt" we need to be responsible for our actions and speak out in wisdom and communicate. Break our silence of any injustices even if we know that some may not believe.

Today we have to preserve the Holy Scriptures and Christian Catholic doctrine from the modern complexities of confusion and syncretism and assimilation. Today we need to be living in Christ in the dependence of man on God for deliverance and salvation.

---

ratzinger+and+habermas,+p.+33+dialectic+secularization&ots=uBFPyS54Jq&sig=IBnDv1
6gES-kXbR-pomMKO4cwks#v=onepage&q&f=false

Yes, we need strategic commanding heights to pour out justice upon this present atrocities in History. Humans cannot live to their fullest because they are oppressed, manipulated and even deceived.

Pope Benedicto XVI ask us how "can we discern between good and evil?" How can we promote justice? "Regulated by lw in the support of the majority can serve as a sufficient criterion." Dignity of man and humanity is at stake, the majority principles not enough; everyone in a position of responsibility must personally seek out the criteria to be followed when framing laws.

The convictions of Christians to keep divine laws in the ruling of the Scythian, was what motivated resistance movements to act opposing the Nazi regime and disparate totalitarian regimes, thereby being champions of justice and to humanity as a whole.[89] Today we need to do the same and be champions of justice. We need to speak out in truth in Christ's teachings, act in our daily living in the precepts of the Catholic Christian teachings asking ourselves is our living expressing what our Lord Jesus Christ would desire. We need to do this actively! Just as St. Thomas had to promote justice in the Medieval period .

No other time in History that humans are at the level of reason of information system at the most powerful recorded in History. However, as a community and world we have not used these sciences of information in the most efficient paradigms for the basic needs of humanity, socially, mentally, physically, economical and educationally. Today the world is in a economic tragedy and uproar. These are times we need to be lifted up in the power of the Holy Spirit to be witness of our Lord the salvation of the world and be an expression of strength and love.

The law of truth . We need to have the law of truth. We know truth in our relationship with the Lord "O Beauty of ancient yet so new". St. Augustine illuminates in his Confessions. God's "Beauty of ancient", His everlasting covenant with His people from generation to generation and living today in the hearts of the people. Bishop Morerod, reminds us we can ask

---

89 Pope Benedicto, XVI Listening Heart

ourselves: Why is our Church shill existing? Bishop Morerod answers, people must have a personal relationship with their Lord God. People of the Church have a living relationship with their God. Because they continually seek for His relationship. Therefore we know these precepts and seek to follow them. Now it is our responsibility to bring this truth of God's 'O Beauty" to the world's laws in justice. Yes, to bring, to fight, to run that race. Thus to serve justice when framing laws it has never been simple, and today in view of the vast extent of our knowledge and our capacity, it has become still harder.

When we know what is right for a just Good Governance we know what Truth is:

II. INSPIRATION AND TRUTH OF SACRED SCRIPTURE- The Profession of Christian Faith (I believe in God the Father) - Live seeking His precepts and covenantal commandments and accepting Him as Lord and Savior Purifying us through the Eucharistic Mass.

III. GOD, "HE WHO IS", IS TRUTH AND LOVE- When we believe in God, He is truth and Love . He gave us love through giving us life on the Cross and giving us new life through the resurrection.

The existence of angels — a truth of faith

1. LIVING IN THE TRUTH
2. TO BEAR WITNESS TO THE TRUTH
3. OFFENSES AGAINST TRUTH
4. RESPECT FOR THE TRUTH
5. TRUTH, BEAUTY, AND SACRED ART

We need to communicate as Dr. Karl Jasper teaches and speak out individually to the others. Today as discussed above there is a It is our responsibility to be human to promote the "cause" of what it is to be human. We know what it is to be human because we know what truth is. . We know as Catholics what it is to be human on Christ precepts. Promoting human rights and Christian precepts.

We know the truth. God is living in the Church and the hearts of the people. It is our responsibility to break that silence to speak out and communicate . There is a "Holocaust" of economic abuse in government and banks and even business taking from the basic labors. Furthermore, the protection of human life and dignity. This present leader has many injustice issues. I pray that he steps down.   I pray for him. "Human rights" have been abused in many facets such as religious, abortion, euthanasia, and many other atrocities such as governmental economical and governance failure. [90]

"All human beings are born free and equal in dignity and rights. They are endowed with reason and conscience and should act towards one another in a spirit of brotherhood."From this foundation, the modern human rights arguments emerged over the latter half of the twentieth century. Gelling as social activism and political rhetoric in many nations put it high on the world agenda.[8]

There is a present lack of "good governance" to carry out laws to promote justice in a society to protect the people.

Politicians have a heavy challenge to make justice live today.

However, we need to be honest about what is taking place, the statistics we see of many tragedies of the people: unemployment, poverty, social issues, faith and religious abused and denied, syncretism, traditional values abused, traditional values assimilated in modernity, family non-

---

[90] —Article 1 of the United Nations Universal Declaration of Human Rights (UDHR)[9 Human rights are commonly understood as "inalienable fundamental rights to which a person is inherently entitled simply because she or he is a human being."[1]The idea of human rights[3] states, "if the public discourse of peacetime global society can be said to have a common moral language, it is that of human rights." Despite this, the strong claims made by the doctrine of human rights continue to provoke considerable skepticism and debates about the content, nature and justifications of human rights to this day. Indeed, the question of what is meant by a "right" is itself controversial and the subject of continued philosophical debate.[4]Many of the basic ideas that animated the movement developed in the aftermath of the Second World War and the atrocities of The Holocaust, culminating in the adoption of the Universal Declaration of Human Rights in Paris by the United Nations General Assembly in 1948.

support and many other atrocities. (Pray for our Military men they have the highest rate of suicide 20.00% approximately, higher than the national average is 19.0% approximate) Old paradigms of Politics are obsolete, we need to take what is good from the old and vote in a Politician with a record that can at least sustain us from going deeper into tragedy of every entity of life.

Today we have the tools as people to promote justice. Most of all we have our relationship in Jesus Christ in the mystery to the Eucharistic Mass. The Lord has given us the Holy Scriptures and the Catholic teachings. The Pope, Bishops, Priest, Nuns, Deacons, the lay people. We have the Saints . Believers are strong and faithful and educated and diplomatic and upright citizens. We have a voice! We have our strength in Christ.. Christ manifest strength in weakness. Meaning if we humble ourselves to His precepts we will give us the strength to bring justice. Because, Christ's precepts in the Holy Scriptures bring life and life abundantly. Christ precepts bring good orderly purpose for the love and care for all humanity.

Not only do we have the Judeo-Christian precepts in the Holy Scriptures; but we have the Relationship with our God, and for Catholics we have our Lord Jesus Christ and Him as Lord and Savior.

Human Rights- and dealing with issues

1. What it means to be human?
2. Difficult to define what right is.
3. Each culture has different believes.
4. Now with Globalization there is a syncretism, assimilation, a mixing of cultural ideas.
5. Therefore, it would be hard to define human. It would be hard to define what is right.
6. Traditional values begin to water down and beginning to adopt other beliefs, secreting
7. Positivism: Hans Kelsen: " an aggregate of objective linked together in terms of cause and effect" then indeed no ethical indication of any kind can be derived from it." Then no ethical indication of any kind can be derived from it.

8. "Justice preserves the happiness, or the component parts of the happiness, of the political community."[91]

'In God, power, essence, will, intellect, wisdom, and justice are all identical nothing there can be in God's power which could not be in his just will or his wise intellect."[92]

We ask ourselves then in our (power) do we promote justice if it is in God's will, than injustices can be broken from the bonds of hidden secrecy of sin. Essence in the (essence) of who we are our purpose in all that we do seeking to live in Christ? Will in our (will) is it in right relationship with Christ will? Intellect do we use are (intellect) or reason for justice? When we express our compassion and love, compassion, essence, will, and intellect,wisdom in Christ through the power of the Holy Spirit, then it can become life to others, giving hope protecting their rights for justice. This is why we need to have a "just intellect," a reason in Christ's redeeming purpose for the present, bringing all to the cross of Christ for living in life in truth.

Catholic Justice Prima Facie

In The Question of German Guilt, Dr. Karl Jaspers reminds us of the Nazi government has been fallen for now more than a half a century.

However, today within our modern governments of today there are malformations of a "Nazi government" per se of a "holocaust" toward the zygote coming from the zenith of all wonderment in God's creation in the humanness of a human being formed, forcing sterilization, abortion and euthanasia and other deformities to humanity. Even the President seeks to use innocent hands to carry out his 'nothingness' of death upon the human essence and What it means to be human.

But, also in the economical of loot stolen literally from the innocent and ignorant mouths and minds, from life of each human's existence and

---

[91] Catholic Catechism Book V13

[92] Ibid, Catholic Catechism, Article 3 271.

authentic identity that may of been. The economic abuse, failure to even balance the economic problems, using the middle class for good for evil and using the poorest of ignorance for a position in the Presidency.

Then the international solidarity of justice not only cannot be avoided that the bloodbaths of innocent indigenous peoples (destitution) deprived of the necessities of life, (poverty-stricken) beggars, prostitution and hopeless of generational oppression, (impoverished) exhausted of all vitality and life soil for the heart and sustaining nutrients of life. If we look at the globalization of the world markets, it is at a height of dynamic motion than anytime in history. For the majority of people in the world, globalization has excellent possibilities. It has one of the most significant impacts on justice for people today.

Catholic Justice[93]

Social Justice:

This responsibility for the carnage(massacre) of the Second World War.

"Echoes of tragedy will linger... children then have perished." [94] Today, we have the responsibility to prevent the carnage of the precious carcasses from being in a "holocaust" of the mind of Politicians of "nothingness."

Solidarity of Nations Justice:

Today, we have the responsibility to promote justice on an international level. Unlike our world's past history, our countries have developed globalization and are multicultural within communities. Therefore, it is all the more paramount that we live and work in "God's power, essence, intellect, will, wisdom[working and breathing in each entity in justice]."[95]

---

[93] Catholic Catechisma, Article 3 1928

[94] The Question of Guilt, Introduction

[95] Catholic Catechisma, Article 3

to promote   justice of solidarity[96] In the complexities of these new multicultural communities. Because justice truly is relevant in all cultures, when it is justice in the true nature of the human being, it will bring justice and happiness and flourishing in peace. Applying each part of our life to God will permeate justice. However, again we need to support leaders and Politicians who have a "listening heart" and what the people's needs are to fight for justice within our international relations within the boundaries of right reason, natural law, social law, human law, ethical law, political law all embraced in divine law of reason in faith and reason in religion and for us Catholics the Holy Scriptures.

This century is the century to come back to the Cross. We need to open our eyes wide to see the truth, clear our ears open to hear the voice of wisdom of our Lord, and feel that miracle of the power of the Holy Spirit guiding us for others to come to the cross and heart of Christ, taste that Eucharistic miracle right to the deepest part of our soul for ongoing transformation and unity in Jesus Christ and His Church and bend down on our knees that we are part of that foundation of Jesus Christ's Church.

Responsibility

" Metaphysical guilt is the responsibility that survivors often feel toward those who suffered and died."

Responsibility oh my Lord I write these words little yet so grand seeking the master's hand of care of hope of justice that I may take responsibility, to bring justice to the peoples of the world. See we know you made these precious people you made each one out of love. We are your children and because we are from you we seek out to do your will and that is to be responsible for the ones that you created. Responsible so you can rely on us to pour out your living justice in the hearts and lives of the people. Responsible to tell them, show them, bring them, guide them, feed them in the Love of God's salvation in Jesus Christ this is the only way to the

---

[96] Bauzon, Stephen Professor, Political Ethics Lectures, Pontifical Saint Thomas Aquinas, Rome, Italy, Fall 2011

true justice. You said you have humanity at your heart. You said you love humanity. You said for us to love humanity as You love us.

" Jesus is the way the truth and the life and know one will come to the Father except through Him."

Let our daily lives be reminiscent of the daily beauty we fight for freedom of justice.

God never changes because He knows the ultimate truth. God in Christ is the ultimate justice. As we know the Lord accommodates to His people in their humanity. Issues today that are atrocious as a "holocaust" to humanity can be resurrected and made renewed in the power and miracle in Jesus Christ through the Holy Spirit working in the Hearts of the believers. Responsibility for justice

let it be at our finger tips of our hearts to give and work for the true justice in Jesus Christ.

Catholic Justice Prima Facie

In The Question of German Guilt, Dr. Karl Jaspers reminds us of the Nazi government has been fallen for now more than a half a century.

Catholic Justice[97]

Social Justice:

1928   Society ensures social justice when it provides the conditions that allow associations or individuals to obtain what is their due, according to their nature and their vocation. Social justice is linked to the common good and the exercise of authority.

I. RESPECT FOR THE HUMAN PERSON

1929   Social justice can be obtained only in respecting the transcendent dignity of man. The person represents the ultimate end of society, which is ordered to him:What is at stake is the dignity of the human person,

---

[97] Catholic Catechisma, Article 3 1928

whose defense and promotion have been entrusted to us by the Creator, and to whom the men and women at every moment of history are strictly and responsibly in debt.35[98]

Economic Justice:

ARTICLE 7: THE SEVENTH COMMANDMENT

Do not steel.

2401   The seventh commandment forbids unjustly taking or keeping the goods of one's neighbor and wronging him in any way with respect to his goods. It commands justice and charity in the care of earthly goods and the fruits of men's labor. For the sake of the common good, it requires respect for the universal destination of goods and respect for the right to private property. Christian life strives to order this world's goods to God and to fraternal charity.[99]

Justice and Solidarity Among Nations :

2437   On the international level, inequality of resources and economic capability is such that it creates a real "gap" between nations.224 On the one side there are those nations possessing and developing the means of growth and, on the other, those accumulating debts.

Today we have the responsibility to promote justice on an international level. Unlike the past history of our world our countries have developed globalization and are multicultural within communities. Therefore, it is all the more paramount we live and work in "God's power, essence, intellect, will, wisdom[working and breathing in each entity in justice]"[100] to promote is justice of solidarity in the complexities of these new multicultural communities. Because, justice truly is relevant in all cultures when it is justice in the true nature it fulfills the human being. When we

---

[98] Catholic Catechisma Article 3 Social Justice
[99] Ibid, Catholic Catechisma, Article 7 Seventh Commandment IV. Economic Activity and Social Justice

[100] Ibid, Catholic Catechisma, Article V. Justice and Solidarity Among Nations

apply each part of our life in God we will permeate justice. However, again we need to support leaders and Politicians that have a "listening heart" what the peoples needs are to fight for justice within our international relations within the boundaries.

Justice:

In God, Holiness, divine intimacy [salvation], Harmony, wisdom, peace, the well-being of humanity, flourishing of human beings, reality, action in the wisdom of the Holy Spirit's strength.

Responsibility as Catholics

We need to take risks.

As Catholic Christians:

Responsibility, I write these words little yet so grand seeking the master's hand of care of hope of justice that I may take responsibility, to bring justice to the world's peoples. See, we know you made these precious people. You made each one out of love. We are your children and because we are from you we seek out to do your will, which is to be responsible for the ones you created. Responsible so you can rely on us to pour out your living justice in the hearts and lives of the people. Responsible to tell them, show them, bring them, guide them, feed them in the Love of God's salvation in Jesus Christ is the only way to the proper justice.

"Jesus is the way, the truth, and the life, and no one will come to the Father except through Him."

Let our present lives be reminiscent of each day to be beautiful. We fought for the freedom of justice.

Let our immediate present lives be active in responsibility

God never changes because He knows the ultimate truth. God in Christ is the ultimate Justice. As we know, the Lord accommodates His people in their humanity. Issues today that are atrocious as a "holocaust" to humanity can be resurrected and made renewed in the power and miracle in Jesus Christ through the Holy Spirit working in the Hearts of the believers. Responsibility for justice flows from each breath and beat of our hearts to give and work for true justice in Jesus Christ.

We as believers seeking to live by the precepts of Jesus Christ outlined for us in the Holy Scriptures and the Catholic teachings have the responsibility to strive to maintain justice and bring about justice for the values of "What it means to be human?" Different cultures have different ideas of

The best way we can bring Justice is to get Jesus into the lives of the people.

We have a command to Preach the Word across the world.

I was praying in the Spirit-filled Pontifical San Thomas Aquinas, and the Spirit of the Lord commanded me to speak out: Pope Benedicto and the Bishops should go across the world and preach the Gospel, tell the Good News of Jesus. We, as Catholics, need to go to the ends of the Earth to preach the word of God. Pope Benedicto and the Church.

Note: make sure you make a difference in the section for Catholic Christian points.

Symbol the Lord's plan for his Church, namely that all the hierarchical order of Christ's Church, all "sacred power" exercised in the Church, is nothing other than service, service with a single purpose: to ensure that the whole People of God shares in this threefold mission of Christ and always remain under the power of the Lord; a power that has its source not in the powers of this world, but instead in the mystery of the Cross and the Resurrection.

The absolute, and yet sweet and gentle, power of the Lord responds to the whole depths of the human person, to his loftiest aspirations of intellect, will, and heart. It does not speak the language of force but expresses itself in charity and truth."Allow me to wet my lips in spring water, to feel its freshness, reviving freshness".

Philosophy is the principle of concentration through which man becomes himself by partaking in reality.[101]

We need to define man to

Language Birth Spirituality Integrating Communication Truth Living Justice Responsibility

God → Christ → Humanity → Family → Faith → Social Happiness → Tradition → Well Being → Reality

Freedom " The neutrality of the state authority on questions of world views guarantees the same ethical freedom to every citizen." [102]

Commandments:

Justice's First commandment love the Lord with all your heart and put no other God before thee

Then, the Second Commandment says, "Love your neighbor as yourself." See, you want your neighbor to have what you have, and that is the love Relationship you have with Jesus Christ, the Son of God, in the power of the Holy Spirit.

Today in Evangelizing bring all to the Cross of Christ .. to the Eucharist table. ..

Faithful Love and Loyalty join together, Saving Justice and Peace embrace.

11Loyalty will spring up from the earth, and Justice will lean down from heaven. Yahweh will himself give prosperity, and our soil will yield its harvest. Justice will walk before him, treading out a path.Psalm 85:10-13(14)

---

[101] Jaspers, Way of Wisdom, p. 7
[102] Ratzinger and Habermas, p. 33

In Jesus Christ we have the message of the truth and the gospel of our salvation, and having put our trust in Christ we have been stamped with the seal of the Holy Spirit of the Promise.

CHAPTER TWELVE

Nicomachean Ethics

It is clear, therefore, that in the opinion of all events of men of action, virtue is a greater good than honor and is the end of the Political Life. pg 15 I.v. 2-6

April 4, 2024

See, in God, we have Him and His life in us to receive and do the precepts and truth in justice to bring what was intended at creation. We know basic ethics have the answers to peace and happiness. Peace brings life, growth, reconciliation, and abundance in the truth of the Divine Nature.

Please see books Lisa Lucia Arden www.lisaluciarden.com also a new book

God First America Our Miracle by Lisa Lucia Arden

The Word of God. The Revelation.

See how we know what and how and govern and correct and restore and redeem.. our country and communities a

See, history is the continuation of all of us and the present being of us. The future and the distant future .. History has the Spirit of the Living God of the Highest.. that lives on creating the most beauty and love that surpasses all things.. and the History of God with the people is the actions of the most incredible mercy, most marvelous grace, great healing, greatest truth, most significant covenant, most tremendous power, most astonishing beauty, most extraordinary life, greatest happiness, greatest joy, most incredible wisdom, greatest strength, greatest love, and the greatest and highest in all things.

This is why I have shown you many translations of ancient words of God and His people or words in translations directly associated with the original languages and how they are still alive today.

See, our countries and our nations are living in the Highest LOVE AND HIGHEST POWER AND HIGHEST LIFE AND HIGHEST JUSTICE IN THE GOD OF ABRAHAM .. BECAUSE THEY STILL exist, AND WE CAN REDEEM WHAT WAS LOST NOW

YET, WE NEED A NEW LEADER IN AMERICA .. WE NEED A LEADER THAT puts AMERICANS FIRST, GOD FIRST … THAT IS VOTING IN The Word is the Holy Scriptures. Also, those holy writings and the Word integrate and uphold the life of the experiences of God and His people and humanity.

Psalms 119:105   Your word is a lamp for my feet, a light on my path. 1

PRESIDENT TRUMP 2024 AND IN THE FUTURE VOTING IN LEADERS THAT ARE HIGHEST IN WISDOM AND JUSTICE, make sure you get the chart of the holocaust .. economy from the first book

See the word justice, which is defined as DIVINE LAW.

κρίσις krisis, kree´-sis; decision (subjectively or objectively, for or against); by extension, a tribunal; by implication, justice (especially, divine law): — accusation, condemnation, damnation, judgment.

3413. Μιχαήλ Michael, mikh-ah-ale´; of Hebrew origin (H4317); Michael, an archangel: — Michael.

 See, Michael Archangel is known to be a protector .. DIVINE PROTECTOR

God has protected us.

Angels. And thus the grace of humility belongs to the highest angel before the throne, being as he is a creature yea, even to the Lord of Glory Himself.

In his human nature, He must be the pattern of all humility, of all creaturely dependence;[103]

Judges 2:1 The Angel of Yahweh went up from Gilgal to Bethel and said, 'I have brought you out of Egypt and led you into this country, which I promised on oath to your ancestors. I said, "I shall never break my covenant with you.

America God has brought us out of "Egypt," out of the clutches of the British .1776.

Now, America, let us get out of the clutches of the Democratic communist elite and World Controls of "2024."… Let us return to the Covenant of the Love Loving God and putting other gods before and loving our neighbor as ourselves. First and Second Commandments and the Covenant we made in Prayer of Continental Congress of 1774[104] We Americans can and are responsible for bringing justice, truth, freedom, and happiness. This is even in our Declaration and our Constitution.

See all the gifts we have from God, America .. ask Him Seek, you Shall Find, Know and the Door Shall be Open, Ask and you Shall Receive, in your humble dependence in righteousness, knowing and respecting Almighty God, and put no other God before Himn

Notice God's names are connected to humanity and His relationship and purpose. See, nothing is impossible for God. Nothing is too small or large for Him to bring redemption and restoration.

22. אֲבִיאֵל ʾAbiyʾel, ab-ee-ale´; from 1 and 410; father (i.e. possessor) of God; Abiel, the name of two Israelites:—Abiel.

WE HAVE GOD AS OUR FATHER

---

[103] TRENCH: SYNONYMS OF NT Synonyms of the New Testament (Trench-Synonyms)by Richard Chenevix Trench, D.D. Public Domain Digitized by Ted Hildebrandt, Gordon College, Wenham, MA
Electronic text hypertexted and prepared by OakTree Software, Inc.Version 1.5, Angels,

[104] Prayer of Continental Congress of 1774

222. אוּרִיאֵל ʾUwriyʾel, oo-ree-ale´; from 217 and 410; flame of God; Uriel, the name of two Israelites:—Uriel.(ANGEL OF LIGHT)

GOD IS OUR FLAME

420. אֶלְדָּעָה ʾEldaʿah, el-daw-aw´; from 410 and 3045; God of knowledge; Eldaah, a son of Midian:—Eldaah.

GOD IS OUR KNOWLEDGE

384. אִיתִיאֵל ʾIythiyʾel, eeth-ee-ale´; perhaps from 837 and 410; God has arrived; Ithiel, the name of an Israelite, also of a symbolical person:—Ithiel.

GOD HAS ARRIVED

449. אֱלִידָד ʾEliydad, el-ee-dawd´; from the same as 419; God of (his) love; Elidad, an Israelite:—Elidad.

GOD IS LOVE

475. אֶלְיָשִׁיב ʾElyashiyb, el-yaw-sheeb´; from 410 and 7725; God will restore; Eljashib, the name of six Israelites:—Eliashib.

GOD IS OUR RESTORATION

2870. בָּאֵל tabʾel, taw-beh-ale´; from 2895 and 410; pleasing (to) God; Tabeel, the name of a Syrian and of a Persian:—Tabeal, Tabeel

GOD IS PLEASED

3094. יְהַלֶּלְאֵל Yhallelʾel, yeh-hal-lel-ale´; from 1984 and 410; praising God; Jehallelel, the name of two Israelites:—Jehalellel, Jehalelel.

GOD IS PRAISED

410. אֵל ʾel, ale; shortened from 352; strength; as an adjective, mighty; especially the Almighty (but also used of any deity):—God (god), x goodly, x great, idol, might(-y one), power, strong. Compare names in "-el."

GOD IS OUR STRENGTH

GOD IS MIGHTY

GOD IS ALMIGHTY

GOD IS GREAT

GOD IS GOODLY

GOD IS POWER

GOD IS STRONG

GOD IS THE MIGHTY ONE

430. אֱלֹהִים ʾelohiym, el-o-heem´; plural of 433; gods in the ordinary sense; but specifically used (in the plural thus, especially with the article) of the supreme God; occasionally applied by way of deference to magistrates; and sometimes as a superlative:—angels, x exceeding, God (gods)(-dess, -ly), x (very) great, judges, x mighty

GOD IS SUPREME

GOD IS VERY GREAT

GOD EXCEEDING ALL gods

GOD IS JUDGE

GOD IS EXTRA MIGHTY

3164. יַחְדִּיאֵל Yachdiyʾel, yakh-dee-ale´; from 3162 and 410; unity of God; Jachdiel, an Israelite:—Jahdiel.

GOD IS UNITY

448. אֱלִיאָתָה ʾEliyʾathah, el-ee-aw-thaw´; or (contraction); אֱלִיָּתָה ʾEliyathah, el-ee-yaw-thaw´; from 410 and 225; God of (his) consent; Eliathah, an Israelite:—Eliathah.

GOD GIVES CONSENT

3043. יְדִיעֲאֵל Ydiyʿa ʾel, yed-ee-ah-ale´; from 3045 and 410; knowing God; Jediael, the name of three Israelites:—Jediael.

GOD IS KNOWING

2995. יַבְנְאֵל Yabnʾel, yab-neh-ale´; from 1129 and 410: built of God; Jabneel, the name of two places in Palestine:—Jabneel.

GOD ALLOWS BUILDING IN HIM

3068. יְהֹוָה Yhwh; from 1961; (the) self-Existent or Eternal; name of God:—the Lord. Compare 3050 and 3069.

GOD IS SELF- EXISTENT

GOD IS ETERNAL

GOD IS LORD

3094. יְהַלֶּלְאֵל Yhallelʾel, yeh-hal-lel-ale´; from 1984 and 410; praising God; Jehallelel, the name of two Israelites:—Jehalellel, Jehalelel.

GOD IS PRAISED

3157. יִזְרְעֶאל Yizrʿeʾl, yiz-reh-ale´; from 2232 and 410; God will sow; Jizreel, the name of two places in Palestine and of two Israelites:—Jezreel.

GOD WILL SOW

3168. יְחֶזְקֵאל Ychezqeʾl, yekh-ez-kale´; from 2388 and 410; God will strengthen; Jechezkel, the name of two Israelites:—Ezekiel, Jehezekel.

GOD WILL STRENGTHEN

3171. יְחִיאֵל Ychiyʾel, yekh-ee-ale´; or (2 Chron. 29:14) יְחַוְאֵל Ychavrel, yekh-av-ale´; from 2421 and 410; God will live; Jechiel (or Jechavel), the name of eight Israelites:—Jehiel.

GOD WILL LIVE

3177. יַחְלְאֵל Yachl'el, yakh-leh-ale´; from 3176 and 410; expectant of God; Jachleel, an Israelite:—Jahleel.

GOD EXPECTS

6214. עֲשָׂהאֵל ʿAsah'el, as-aw-ale´; from 6213 and 410; God has made; Asahel, the name of four Israelites:—Asahel.

GOD HAS MADE

6490. פִּקּוּד piqquwd, pik-kood´; or פִּקֻּד piqqud, pik-kood´; from 6485; properly, appointed, i.e. a mandate (of God; plural only, collectively, for the Law):—commandment, precept, statute.

GOD APPOINTS

GOD MANDATES

GOD COMMANDS

GOD HAS PRECEPTS

STOD HAS STATUES

GOD FOR THE LAW

6439. פְּנוּאֵל Pnuw'el, pen-oo-ale´; or (more appropriately,) פְּנִיאֵל Pniylel, pen-oo-ale´; from 6437 and 410; the face of God; Penuel or Peniel, a place East of Jordan; also (as Penuel) the name of two Israelites:—Peniel, Penuel.

GOD PROPERLY

GOD HAS A FACE

6602. פְּתוּאֵל Pthuw'el, peth-oo-ale´; from 6601 and 410; enlarged of God; Pethuel, an Israelite:—Pethuel.

GOD ENLARGES

6909. קַבְצְאֵל Qabts'el, kab-tseh-ale'; from 6908 and 410; God has gathered; Kabtseel, a place in Palestine:—Kabzeel. Compare 3343.

GOD HAS GATHERED

See, this is what God does for humanity when they are in righteousness, and even when they are not, he accommodates. He is sovereign yet could strike at any time.

See these actions of God .. that are the .. substance of ethics in the foundations of the virtues and precepts.

6409. פַּלְטִיאֵל Paltiy'el, pal-tee-ale'; from the same as 6404 and 410; deliverance of God; Paltiel, the name of two Israelites:—Paltiel, Phaltiel.

GOD OF DELIVERANCE

6317. פּוּטִיאֵל Puwtiy'el, poo-tee-ale'; from an unused root (probably meaning to disparage) and 410; contempt of God; Putiel, an Israelite:—Putiel.

GOD OF CONTEMPT

6918. קָדוֹשׁ qadowsh, kaw-doshe'; or קָדֹשׁ qadosh, kaw-doshe'; from 6942; sacred (ceremonially or morally); (as noun) God (by eminence), an angel, a saint, a sanctuary:—holy (One), saint.

GOD SACRED CERMONIALLY

GOD SACRED MORALLY

GOD OF ANGELS

GOD OF SAINTS

GOD BY EMINENCE

GOD IN SANCTUARY

GOD HOLY

GOD HOLY ONE

GOD IN SAINTS

69m18. קָדוֹשׁ qadowsh, kaw-doshe´; or קָדֹשׁ qadosh, kaw-doshe´; from 6942; sacred (ceremonially or morally); (as a noun) God (by eminence), an angel, a saint, a sanctuary:—holy (One), saint.

GOD OF SACRED CEREMONIALLY

GOD OF MORALLY

GOD OF ANGELS

GOD OF SAINTS

GOD A SANCTURAY

GOD HOLY ON E

GOD ONE

GOD SAINT

6936. קָדְקֹד qodqod, kod-kode´; from 6915; the crown of the head (as the part most bowed):—crown (of the head), pate, scalp, top of the head.

GOD THE CROWN OF THE HEAD

GOD BOWED DOWN CROWN HEAD

GOD OF PATE (A PERSONS HEAD)

GOD OF SCALP (A PERSONS SCALP)

GOD TOP OF THE HEAD

7055. קְמוּאֵל Qmuw'el, kem-oo-ale´; from 6965 and 410; raised of God; Kemuel, the name of a relative of Abraham, and of two Israelites:—Kemuel.

GOD HAS RAISED

GOD NAME OF ABRAHAM

6965. קוּם quwm, koom; a primitive root; to rise (in various applications, literal, figurative, intensive and causative):—abide, accomplish, x be clearer, confirm, continue, decree, x be dim, endure, x enemy, enjoin, get up, make good, help, hold, (help to) lift up (again), make, x but newly, ordain, perform, pitch, raise (up), rear (up), remain, (a-)rise (up) (again, against), rouse up, set (up), (e-)stablish, (make to) stand (up), stir up, strengthen, succeed, (as-, make) sure(-ly), (be) up(-hold, - rising).

7467. רְעוּאֵל Rʻuw ʾ el, reh-oo-ale´; from the same as 7466 and 410; friend of God; Reuel, the name of Moses' father-in-law, also of an Edomite and an Israelite:—Raguel, Reuel.

GOD A FRIEND

GOD OF MOSES

GOD OF MOSES'S FATHER-IN-LAW

7501. רְפָאֵל Rphaʾel, ref-aw-ale´; from 7495 and 410; God has cured; Rephael, an Israelite:—Rephael.

7597. שְׁאַלְתִּיאֵל Shʾaltiyʾel, sheh-al-tee-ale´; or שַׁלְתִּיאֵל Shaltiyʾel, shal-tee-ale´; from 7592 and 410; I have asked God; Shealtiel, an Israelite:—Shalthiel, Shealtiel.

7592. שָׁאַל shaʾal, shaw-al´; or שָׁאֵל shael, shaw-ale´; a primitive root; to inquire; by implication, to request; by extension, to demand:—ask (counsel, on), beg, borrow, lay to charge, consult, demand, desire, x earnestly, enquire, + greet, obtain leave, lend, pray, request, require, + salute, x straitly, x surely, wish.

8017. שְׁלֻמִיאֵל Shlumiyʾel, shel-oo-mee-ale´; from 7965 and 410; peace of God; Shelumiel, an Israelite:—Shelumiel.

8050. שְׁמוּאֵל Shmuwʾel, sehm-oo-ale´; from the passive participle of 8085 and 410; heard of God; Shemuel, the name of three Israelites:—Samuel, Shemuel.

8085. שָׁמַע shamaʻ, shaw-mah´; a primitive root; to hear intelligently (often with implication of attention, obedience, etc.; causatively, to tell, etc.):—x attentively, call (gather) together, x carefully, x certainly, consent, consider, be content, declare, x diligently, discern, give ear, (cause to, let, make to) hear(-ken, tell), x indeed, listen, make (a) noise, (be) obedient, obey, perceive, (make a) proclaim(-ation), publish, regard, report, shew (forth), (make a) sound, x surely, tell, understand, whosoever (heareth), witness.

HEBREW STRONG'S DICTIONARY Strong's Hebrew and Chaldee Dictionary of the Old Testament (Hebrew Strong's) Public Domain Electronic text downloaded from the Bible Foundation e-Text Library:http://www.bf.org/bfetexts.htm Hypertexted and formatted by OakTree Software, Inc.Hebrew text added by OakTree Software, Inc.Version 3.3Melek Kreesis

6.192 στέφανοςα, ου m: a wreath consisting either of foliage or of precious metals formed to resemble foliage and worn as a symbol of honor, victory, or as a badge of high office — 'wreath, crown.' ἵνα φθαρτὸν στέφανον λάβωσιν 'in order to be crowned with a wreath that will not last' 1Cor 9:25. It may be important in some contexts to indicate clearly the significance of the wreath worn on the head, for example, 'a wreath to show victory.' To describe 'a wreath' merely as 'a circle of leaves' would hardly be sufficient to indicate its cultural significance. In order to do justice to the cultural relevance of such a wreath, it may be important to add some type of marginal note (compare διάδημα 'diadem crown,' 6.196). LOUW & NIDA

Greek-English Lexicon of the New Testament Based on Semantic Domains (Louw & Nida)Johannes P. Louw and Eugene A. Nida, Editors

Copyright © 1988, 1989 by the United Bible Societies, New York, NY 10023

Second Edition. Used by permission.

Landkarten zur Bible, prepared by Karl Elliger, revised by Siegfried Mittmann. Designed by Deutsche Bibelgesellschaft Stuttgart and Kartographisches Institut Helmut Fuchs Leonberg. Copyright ©1963, 1978, 1990 by Deutsche Bibelgesellschaft, Stuttgart. Used by permission.

Electronic text hypertexted and prepared by OakTree Software, Inc.

Version 4.4

Immaculate Consumption Church, Monrovia

While praying the gorgeous Immaculate Consumption Church in Monrovia I was in a deep ecstasy .... Message from St. Peter that, "the Catholic Church have the keys to the Kingdom of God. The Catholic Church has to be a great example to all the believers of Christ and humanity and the world as God's people. Even if there is division we as the Catholic Church have to work toward unity and God's love and truth in Christ."

Message from St. Peter that, the Catholic Church (in unity with all the Christian Churches that profess Jesus Christ is the Son of God and Saviour and Lord) have the keys to the Kingdom of God. That the Catholic Church has to be a great example to all the believers and humanity and the world as God's people.

Seal of the State of the Vatican City "Since the XIV Century, the two crossed keys have been the official insignia of the Holy See. The gold one, on the right, alludes to the power in the Kingdom of the heavens, the silver one, on the left, indicates the spiritual authority of the papacy on the earth. The mechanisms are turned up towards the heaven and the grips turned down, in other words into the the hands of the Vicar of Christ. The cords with the bows that unites the grips alludes to the bond between the two powers." i   [Code of Arms of the State of Vatican City Cf.Fundamental law of the State of Vatican City dated c26.11.2000 (Acta Apostolicae Sedis, Supplement, 01.02.2001, Attachment B).]

Carmel of Church Sedona

Sedona… we have the Keys to love the Keys of love

(The Spirit said) "I have given you (My Chruch) the keys to open the lock of the treasure is waiting for you to use for My glory."ii

"Blessed is anyone who mediates on wisdom and reason with intelligence, who studies her ways in his heart and ponders her secrets." (Ecc. 14: 20)

This is why the Lord our God is asking you all to build a personal relationship with Him to will be "blessed." We will then have more kindling lights to help American and the world in this urgent need for the existence in life.

We can not be as Lot. God "did not spare people with whom Lot lived; He abhorred them, rather, for their pride." (Ecc. 16:8,9)

"Listen to me, my child, and learn knowledge, and give your whole mind to My words. I shall expound discipline methodically and proclaim knowledge with precions." (Ecc. 16: 24)

Distribution of Funds to and for the Restoration and America

First, notes for the Article for book about America.

August 27, 2023

Note: I discussed the Distribution of funds .. before .. in my writings 2009

To solve the deathly distribution of funds ..

See the billionaires and the great companies are those who know how to make funds.. successful.

1. **Not directly regulated by the government:** Not government regulated these funds allocated. The funds should be regulated by the owners of Billionaires and Great Companies are required to give the WORK TOGETHER WITH THE GOVERNMENT HOWEVER MINIMUM HOURS FOR GOVERNMENT AND CANNOT GET PAID .. UNTIL CONTRACT

2. **Designated that have proven success and development of the empowering of humanity Americans and employees.** There can be regulations that funds are allocated to those in need and human urgencies.. not biased yet for the protection of Americans and employees.

God wants to save all people

'I have reared children and brought them up, but they have rebelled against me. Isaiah 1: 2

This is the core of what has happened to our America..

BDB Abridged (Hebrew Content)

Qal 1. rebel, revolt, of nations, c. בְּ against; abs.; פָּשְׁעוּ בִי (Isr. under fig. of ״'s sons).

BDB Abridged (Hebrew Content)

Qal 1. rebel, revolt, of nations, c. בְּ against; abs.; פָּשְׁעוּ בִי (Isr. under fig. of ״'s sons).

2. transgress against God, abs., for (עַל) a bit of bread; בַּדָּבָר הַזֶּה in this thing; עַל תּוֹרָתִי; elsewhere c. בְּ against God. Niph.

6588   פֶּשַׁע n.m. transgression —

1. transgression against individuals.
2. of nation, against nation: of land. Elsewh.
3. against God: a. in gen, ‖ חטאת; personified as evil spirit. Satan and spirit of evil of lies.

   A. as recognized by sinner; he knows it, makes known concerning it to ״, does not cover it (כסה); turns from it; casts it away from him.
   B. God deals with it: by visiting it (פקד), dealing with one according to it, making it known to sinner; punishing in various ways: מִן׳ because of it; c. עַל acc. to it; for it, c. בְּ; עַל פ׳ yoke of transgression; personified; he does not grant forgiveness to it.
   C. God forgives (נשא) it; pardons (סלח); passes over (עבר עַל); removes (הרחיק); covers over (כפר); God blots out (מחה); delivers from, הצּיל מן.

4. guilt of transgression (cf. עון), בְּלִי פּ׳ without (guilt of) transgression.

5. punishment for transgression, cf. עון 3.

6. offering for transgression, האתן בכורי פשעי shall I give my first-born as an offering for my transgression (cf. חטאת 4

Hebrews strong

6586. פָּשַׁע pasha‹, paw-shah´; a primitive root (identical with 6585 through the idea of expansion); to break away (from just authority), i.e. trespass, apostatize, quarrel:—offend, rebel, revolt, transgress(-ion, -or).

6587. פֶּשַׂע pesa‹, peh´-sah; from 6585; a stride:—step.

6588. פֶּשַׁע pesha‹, peh´-shah; from 6586; a revolt (national, moral or religious):—rebellion, sin, transgression, trespass.

Kohlen

GK H7321 | S H6586 פָּשַׁע pāša‹ 41x

v. [root of: 7322]. Q to rebel, revolt (against human or divine authority).

☞ NIV | ESV | CSB | NRSV | JPS | NKJV | KJV

6583. פַּשְׁחוּר Pashchur [832d]; from 6582; five Isr.:—Pashhur(14).

Nas Hebrew dictionary 6582. פָּשַׁח pashach [832d]; a prim. root; to tear in pieces:—torn to pieces(1).

6586. פָּשַׁע pasha‹, paw-shah´; a primitive root (identical with 6585 through the idea of expansion); to break away (from just authority), i.e. trespass, apostatize, quarrel:—offend, rebel, revolt, transgress(-ion, -or).

Strongs dictionary

פָּשַׁע (pāša‹), q. rebel, violate, transgress; ni. be offended (H7321); פֶּשַׁע (peša‹), nom. rebellion, transgression (H7322).

OT

1. As part of the terminology for sin, פֶּשַׁע, transgression, has a narrower meaning than חָטָא and עָוֹן. Originated from the political sphere to mean "rebellion" (e.g., 2 Kgs 1:1) and used 136x in OT, it normally implies willful violations by an inferior against a superior (e.g., Prov 28:24). In biblical theology, the term refers to an open and brazen defiance of God by humans. In Ezek 2:3, its use in parallel with מָרַד, rebel, reinforces its primary connotation: "Son of man, I am sending you to . . . a rebellious nation that has rebelled against me; they and their fathers have been in revolt (פֶּשַׁע) against me." The use of this term in Gen 50:17 by the brothers to acknowledge their "sins" against Joseph does not indicate an exception of its normal usage; rather, it highlights the difference of their social positions. However, the meaning of חָטָא and עָוֹן are less restrictive and can often refer to the wrong of a superior against an inferior (e.g., חָטָא in 1 Sam 19:4; 26:21). Though עָבַר (H6296) is often translated in some versions as "transgress," as a term for sin it is not used as frequently as פֶּשַׁע. It depicts overstepping the boundaries set by the commandments (e.g., Num 14:41; 1 Sam 15:24).

2. For a discussion of sin, חָטָא (sin, commit a sin; make a sin offering, purify, H2627).

Alex Luc

Niddotte

Prov. 28:24

Whoever robs his father or his mother

and says, "That is no transgression,"

is ra companion to a man who destroys.

Ezek. 2:3 And he said to me, "Son of man, I send you to the people of Israel, to gnations of rebels, who have rebelled against me. hThey and their fathers have transgressed against me to this very day.

Gen. 50:17 'Say to Joseph, "Please forgive the transgression of your brothers and their sin, because they did evil to you.'" And now, please forgive the transgression of the servants of fthe God of your father." Joseph wept when they spoke to him.

1Sam. 26:21 Then Saul said, r"I have sinned. Return, my son David, for I will no more do you harm, because my life was precious in your eyes this day. Behold, I have acted foolishly, and have made a great mistake."

חָטָא (ḥāṭāʾ), q. miss, sin, commit a sin; pi. bear loss, make a sin offering, purify; hiph. miss the mark, cause to sin; hitp. miss oneself, purify oneself (H2627); חֵטְא (ḥēṭʾ), nom. sin, guilt, punishment of sin (H2628); חַטָּא (ḥaṭṭāʾ), adj./nom. sinful, sinner (H2629); חֲטָאָה (ḥᵃṭāʾâ), nom. sin, sin offering (H2631); חַטָאָה (ḥaṭṭāʾâ), sinful thing (H2632); חַטָּאת (ḥaṭṭāʾt), nom. sin, sinful state, punishment of sin, sin offering (H2633).

Needs to be purify.. reconciliation in Jesus Christ.

7321 [6586] פָּשַׁע, pāšaᶜ, v. [root of: 7322]. [Q] to rebel, revolt (against human or divine authority)

7322 [6588] פֶּשַׁע, pešaᶜ, n.m. [7321]. rebellion, revolt, sin, transgression (against human or divine authority)

Revolt "of nations," the world control .. all is under the eyes of God

Revolt undercover slave.. lideel and Scott

Luke 4:19 eto proclaim the year of the Lord's favor."

Matt. 26:28 for xthis is my zblood of the3 covenant, which is poured out for amany bfor the forgiveness of sins.=

Matt. 26:28 for xthis is my zblood of the3 covenant, which is poured out for amany bfor the forgiveness of sins.

Matt. 12:25 zKnowing their thoughts, ahe said to them, "Every kingdom divided against itself is laid waste, and no city or house divided against itself will stand.

Rom. 6:10 For the death he died he died to sin, eonce for all, but the life he lives he lives to God.

Disaster, sinful nation, people weighed down with guilt, race of wrong-doers, perverted children! They have abandoned Yahweh, despised the Holy One of Israel, they have turned away from him.

Is. 2:2 It will happen in the final days that the mountain of Yahweh's house will rise higher than the mountains and tower above the heights. Then all the nations will stream to it, 3 many peoples will come to it and say, 'Come, let us go up to the mountain of Yahweh, to the house of the God of Jacob that he may teach us his ways so that we may walk in his paths.' For the Law will issue from Zion and the word of Yahweh from Jerusalem.

Is. 1:5 Where shall I strike you next, if you persist in treason? The whole head is sick, the whole heart is diseased,

Treason .. Government and peoples.. againsit USA

Is. 1:11 'What are your endless sacrifices to me?' says Yahweh. 'I am sick of burnt offerings of rams and the fat of calves. I take no pleasure in the blood of bulls and lambs and goats. 12 When you come and present yourselves before me, who has asked you to trample through my courts? 13 Bring no more futile cereal offerings, the smoke from them fills me with disgust. New Moons, Sabbaths, assemblies— I cannot endure solemnity combined with guilt.

Sin of our country and our people and our churches.

Is. 1:18 'Come, let us talk this over,' says Yahweh. 'Though your sins are like scarlet, they shall be white as snow; though they are red as crimson, they shall be like wool. 19 If you are willing to obey, you shall eat the good things of the earth. 20 But if you refuse and rebel, the sword shall eat you instead— for Yahweh's mouth has spoken.'

God is asking for our to love Him first.

Is. 1:22   Your silver has turned into dross, your wine is watered. 23 Your princes are rebels, accomplices of brigands. All of them are greedy for presents and eager for bribes; they show no justice to the orphan, and the widow's cause never reaches them.

Is. 1:27   Zion will be redeemed by fair judgment, and those who return, by saving justice. 28 Rebels and sinners alike will be destroyed, and those who abandon Yahweh will perish.

Is. 2:4   Then he will judge between the nations and arbitrate between many peoples. They will hammer their swords into ploughshares and their spears into sickles. Nation will not lift sword against nation, no longer will they learn how to make war.

There will be a time when no longer will they learn how to make war… Let those against the innocent be the first .. to stop the war

Is. 2:6   You have rejected your people, the House of Jacob, for it has long been full of sorcerers like the Philistines, and is overrun with foreigners. 7 The country is full of silver and gold and treasures unlimited, the country is full of horses, its chariots are unlimited; 8 the country is full of idols. They bow down before the work of their hands, before what their own fingers have made.

Filled our country with 'immigrants," "overrun with foriegners, and "sorceers." "They have rejected, the House of Jacob the House of USA."

Is. 2:20   That day, people will fling to moles and bats the silver idols and golden idols which have been made for them to worship, 21 and go into the crevices of the rocks and the clefts in the cliffs, in terror of Yahweh, at the brilliance of his majesty, when he arises to make the earth quake.

Is. 2:18   When the idols all disappear, 19 they will go into the caverns of the rocks and into the fissures of the earth in terror of Yahweh, at the brilliance of his majesty, when he arises to make the earth quake.

Building bunkers

Is. 3:18 That day the Lord will take away the ornamental chains, medallions, crescents, 19 pendants, bracelets, trinkets, 20 diadems, ankle-chains, necklaces, scent bottles, amulets, 21 finger-rings, nose-rings, 22 party dresses, cloaks, scarves, purses, 23 mirrors, linen clothes, turbans and mantillas.

Musicians and wealth of controlers

Is. 4:2 That day, Yahweh's seedling will turn to beauty and glory, what the earth brings forth will turn to the pride and ornament of Israel's survivors. 3 Those who are left in Zion and remain in Jerusalem will be called holy, all those in Jerusalem noted down to live. 4 When the Lord has washed away the filth of Zion's daughters and with the wind of judgement and the wind of burning cleansed Jerusalem of the blood shed in her, 5 Yahweh will create, over every house on Mount Zion and over those who assemble there, a cloud by day, and by night smoke with the brightness of a flaring fire. For overall will be the Glory as canopy 6 and a tent to give shade by the day from the heat, refuge, and shelter from the storm and the rain.

See God is waitng for all to turn away from out sins to be washed by His love.

Is. 5:8 Woe to those who add house to house and join field to field until there is nowhere left and they are the sole inhabitants of the country. 9 Yahweh Sabaoth has sworn this in my hearing, 'Many houses will be brought to ruin, great and fine ones left untenanted; 10 for ten acres of vineyard will yield only one barrel, and ten bushel of seed will yield only one bushel.'

No homes for the people taken .. take homes …

Is. 5:15 Human nature has been humbled, humankind brought low, and the eyes of the proud have been humbled.

We do not know when our life is that last breathe let us come to truth and peace.

Why did they do this? Using war to bring chaos amongst nations. He has brought us low to where we are now seeking him…

Is. 5:18 Woe to those who drag guilt along by the reins of duplicity, drag along sin as though with a cart rope; 19 to those who say, 'Why doesn't he do his work quickly so that we can see it; why doesn't the Holy One of Israel's design hurry up and come true so that we can experience it?'

Is. 5:20 Woe to those who call what is bad, good, and what is good, bad, who substitute darkness for light and light for darkness, who substitute bitter for sweet and sweet for bitter.

What they did to the Military… . what they did to America

June 12, 2024

Review Isaiah .. and write points on it.

Is. 5:22 Woe to those whose might lies in wine bibbing, their heroism in mixing strong drinks, 23 who acquit the guilty for a bribe and deny justice to the upright. 24 Yes, as the flame devours the stubble, as the straw flares up and disappears, their root will be like decay and their shoot be carried off like dust, for having rejected the law of Yahweh Sabaoth, having despised the word of the Holy One of Israel.

Is. 5:25 This is why Yahweh's anger has blazed out against his people; and he has raised his hand against them to strike them; why the mountains have shuddered and why corpses are lying like dung in the streets. After all this, his anger is not spent. No, his hand is still raised!

We the people want to now bring justice and upright.. "For having rejected the law of Yahweh Sabaoth, having despised the Word of the Holy one Israel." See even those whom profess the .. truth .. of God and seek .. God's love and wisdom.. and life and accept the Salvation in Christ Jesus… are even judged because .. we are human and being sanctified day by day.. .. Remember many and most cannot fulfill each commandment .. they need the Spirit of God…of His love..

Is. 7:13 He then said: Listen now, House of David: are you not satisfied with trying human patience that you should try my God's patience too? 14 The Lord will give you a sign in any case: It is this: the young woman is with child and will give birth to a son whom she will call Immanuel. 15 On curds and honey will he feed until he knows how to refuse the bad and choose the good. 16 Before the child knows how to refuse the bad and choose the good, the lands whose two kings are frightening you will be deserted. 17 Yahweh will bring times for you, your people and your ancestral House, such as have not been seen since Ephraim broke away from Judah (the king of Assyria)

Jesus Christ… prophecy .. and .. knows bad and good.. .

Is. 9:5 For a son has been born for us, a son has been given to us, and dominion has been laid on his shoulders; and this is the name he has been given, 'Wonder-Counsellor, Mighty-God, Eternal-Father, Prince-of-Peace' 6 to extend his dominion in boundless peace, over the throne of David and over his kingdom to make it secure and sustain it in fair judgment and integrity. From this time onwards and forever, the jealous love of Yahweh Sabaoth will do this.

Is. 9:12 But the people would not come back to him who struck them, they would not seek out Yahweh Sabaoth; 13 hence Yahweh has topped and tailed Israel, cutting off palm and reed in a single day. 14 (The 'top' is the elder and the man of rank; the 'tail' is the prophet teaching lies.) 15 This people's leaders have led them astray, and those who are led by them are swallowed up. 16 Hence the Lord will no longer take delight in their young people, or pity on their orphans and widows, since all of them are godless and evil, and everything they say is madness. After all this, his anger is not spent. No, his hand is still raised!

Is. 9:17 Yes, wickedness has been burning like a fire, devouring bramble and thorn-bush, setting the forest thickets ablaze— up they go in billowing smoke! 18 The country has been set on fire by the fury of Yahweh Sabaoth, and the people are like food for the flames. No one spares a thought for his brother. 19 They have sliced to the right and are still hungry, they have eaten to the left and are not satisfied; each devours the flesh of his own arm. 20 Manasseh devours Ephraim, Ephraim Manasseh, together they turn against Judah. After all this, his anger is not spent. No, his hand is still raised!

Is. 9:12 But the people would not come back to him who struck them, they would not seek out Yahweh Sabaoth; 13 hence Yahweh has topped and tailed Israel, cutting off palm and reed in a single day. 14 (The 'top' is the elder and the man of rank; the 'tail' is the prophet teaching lies.) 15 This people's leaders have led them astray, and those who are led by them are swallowed up. 16 Hence the Lord will no longer take delight in their young people, or pity on their orphans and widows, since all of them are godless and evil, and everything they say is madness. After all this, his anger is not spent. No, his hand is still raised!

People against .. freedoms..

Is. 9:17 Yes, wickedness has been burning like a fire, devouring bramble and thorn-bush, setting the forest thickets ablaze— up they go in billowing smoke! 18 The country has been set on fire by the fury of Yahweh Sabaoth, and the people are like food for the flames. No one spares a thought for his brother. 19 They have sliced to the right and are still hungry, they have eaten to the left and are not satisfied; each devours the flesh of his own arm. 20 Manasseh devours Ephraim, Ephraim Manasseh, together they turn against Judah. After all this, his anger is not spent. No, his hand is still raised!

Buring of the .. deforested .

Is this also what has happen with Hezobolla and Palestian Hamas..

Is. 10:1 Woe to those who enact unjust decrees, who compose oppressive legislation 2 to deny justice to the weak and to cheat the humblest of my people of fair judgement, to make widows their prey and to rob the orphan. 3 What will you do on the day of punishment, when disaster comes from far away? To whom will you run for help and where will you leave your riches, 4 to avoid squatting among the captives or falling among the slain? After all this, his anger is not spent. No, his hand is still raised!

We are responsible … for the people…the children..

Is. 11:6 The wolf will live with the lamb, the panther lie down with the kid, calf, lion and fat-stock beast together, with a little boy to lead them. 7 The cow and the bear will graze, their young will lie down together. The lion will eat hay like the ox. 8 The infant will play over the den of the adder; the baby will put his hand into the viper's lair. 9 No hurt, no harm will be done on all my holy mountain, for the country will be full of knowledge of Yahweh as the waters cover the sea.

Protect.. the children.. God help us.. .. Help us.. even though evil.. is next to us the children..

Is. 11:6 The wolf will live with the lamb, and the panther lies down with the kid, calf, lion, and fat-stock beast together, with a little boy to lead them. 7 The cow and the bear will graze, and their young will lie down together. The lion will eat hay like the ox. 8 The infant will play over the adder's den; the baby will put his hand into the viper's lair. 9 No hurt, no harm will be done on all my holy mountain, for the country will be full of knowledge of Yahweh as the waters cover the sea.

Is. 19:16 That day Egypt will be like women, trembling and terrified at the threatening hand of Yahweh Sabaoth, when he raises it against her. 17 The land of Judah will become Egypt's shame; whenever she is reminded of it, she will be terrified, because of the plan which Yahweh Sabaoth has laid against her. 18 That day in Egypt there will be five towns speaking the language of Canaan and pledging themselves to Yahweh Sabaoth; one of them will be called City of the Sun. 19 That day there will be an altar dedicated to Yahweh in the centre of Egypt and, close to the frontier, a pillar dedicated to Yahweh, 20 and this will be a sign and a witness to Yahweh Sabaoth in Egypt. When they cry to Yahweh for help because of oppressors, he will send them a Saviour and leader to deliver them. 21 Yahweh will reveal himself to Egypt, and the Egyptians will acknowledge Yahweh that day and will offer sacrifices and cereal offerings, and will make vows to Yahweh and perform them. 22 And if Yahweh strikes Egypt, having struck he will heal, and they will turn to Yahweh who will hear their prayers and heal them. 23 That day there will be a highway from

Egypt to Assyria. Assyria will have access to Egypt and Egypt have access to Assyria. Egypt will serve with Assyria.

Vission of this I have look on my website I put the prayer there

21 When that day comes, Yahweh will punish the armies of the sky above and on earth the kings of the earth; 22 they will be herded together, herded together like prisoners in a dungeon and shut up in gaol, and, after long years, punished. 23 The moon will be confused and the sun ashamed, for Yahweh Sabaoth is king on Mount Zion and in Jerusalem, and the Glory will radiate on their elders.

See Jesus will cause death on the war mongers of greatest atrocities .

Is. 25:6 On this mountain, for all peoples, Yahweh Sabaoth is preparing a banquet of rich food, a banquet of fine wines, of succulent food, of well-strained wines. 7 On this mountain, he has destroyed the veil which uscd to veil all peoples, the pall enveloping all nations; 8 he has destroyed death for ever. Lord Yahweh has wiped away the tears from every cheek; he has taken his people's shame away everywhere on earth, for Yahweh has spoken.

See God.. does" take the veil off the people of blindness and or bondage .. and destroys death for ever..

It was a Divine Command to make … the best food dishes that you are able to make.. ..

Is. 25:9 And on that day, it will be said, 'Look, this is our God, in him, we put our hope that he should save us, this is Yahweh, we put our hope in him. Let us exult and rejoice since he has saved us.' 10 For Yahweh's hand will rest on this mountain, and Moab will be trodden under his feet as straw is trodden into the dung-heap. 11 He may stretch his hands wide on the hill like a swimmer stretching out his hands to swim. But he will humble his pride despite what his hands may attempt. 12 And the impregnable fortress of your walls, he has overthrown, laid low, flung to the ground, in the dust.

God has saved us.

Is. 26:1 That day, this song will be sung in Judah: 'We have a fortress city, the walls and ramparts provide safety. 2 Open the gates! Let the upright nation come in, the nation that keeps faith! 3 This is the plan decreed: you will guarantee peace, the peace entrusted to you. 4 Trust in Yahweh forever, for Yahweh is a rock forever. 5 He has brought low the dwellers on the heights, the lofty citadel; he lays it low, brings it to the ground, flings it down in the dust. 6 It will be trodden under foot, by the feet of the needy, the steps of the weak.'

Fortress city walls protect our boarders we wil have a song of Faith.. that God will bring us peace and there shall be "gates .. . that are open "upright nations come in. A nation that keeps faith." We need to protect our country and .. borders with walls of strong fortress, and .. then there are gates for the upright nation (immigrants to come in that keep faith. Respect and hope in God.".

2 'Yahweh Sabaoth, the God of Israel, says this, "I have broken the yoke of the king of Babylon. 3 In exactly two years I shall bring back all the vessels of the Temple of Yahweh which Nebuchadnezzar king of Babylon took away from here and carried off to Babylon. 4 And I shall also bring back Jeconiah son of Jehoiakim, king of Judah and all the exiles of Judah who have gone to Babylon, Yahweh declares, for I shall break the yoke of the king of Babylon."'

Let us .. redeem the USA .. and make all the Churches and the tables .. in God's of Israel, Usa has eaten at the table of evil and defilement of the legacy God has built.. because they have turned from God. And most were working and trusting the leaders and then realized they had been deceived.. and some had eaten from both tables because of the softhearted .. liberalism… ..and even turning from God. It Is not judging. It is asking all to give their heart to God... And make each meal and each purpose God's purpose. ..

I saw .. a persons heart. It was ashes, and all of us saw other things of ashes around it. It had an ash color.. See, Jesus Christ .. showed me the picture .. when the person was abusing me.. and told me I want to redeem this heart.. . daughter... you know this person has been through .. many things..

yet has not given their heart to God.. and is in death of life of the sacred heart of Jesus Christ.

Jer. 28:5 The prophet Jeremiah then replied to the prophet Hananiah in front of the priests and all the people present in the Temple of Yahweh. 6 'So be it!' the prophet Jeremiah said, 'May Yahweh do so! May he fulfil the words that you have prophesied and bring all the vessels of the Temple of Yahweh and all the exiles back to this place from Babylon. 7 Listen carefully, however, to this word that I am now going to say for you and all the people to hear: 8 From remote times, the prophets who preceded you and me prophesied war, disaster and plague for many countries and for great kingdoms; 9 the prophet who prophesies peace can be recognized as one truly sent by Yahweh only when his word comes true.'

Jer. 28:10 The prophet Hananiah then snatched the yoke off the neck of the prophet Jeremiah and broke it. 11 In front of all the people Hananiah then said, 'Yahweh says this, "This is how, in exactly two years' time, I shall break the yoke of Nebuchadnezzar king of Babylon and take it off the necks of all the nations."' At this, the prophet Jeremiah went away.

Is. 26:16 Yahweh, in distress they had recourse to you, they expended themselves in prayer, since your punishment was on them. 17 As a pregnant woman near her time of delivery writhes and cries out in her pangs, so have we been, Yahweh, in your eyes: 18 we have been pregnant, we have writhed, but we have given birth only to wind: we have not given salvation to the earth, no inhabitants for the world have been brought to birth. 19 Your dead will come back to life, your corpses will rise again. Wake up and sing, you dwellers in the dust, for your dew will be a radiant dew, but the earth will give birth to the shades.

New life of the people's heart.. look up the words "writhed."

Is. 26:20 Go, my people, go to your private room, shut yourselves in. Hide yourselves a little while until the retribution has passed. 21 For see, Yahweh emerges from his dwelling to punish the inhabitants of earth for their guilt, and the earth will reveal the blood shed on it and no longer hide its slain.

Is. 27:1 That day Yahweh will punish, with his unyielding sword, massive and strong, Leviathan the fleeing serpent, Leviathan the coiling serpent; he will kill that dragon that lives in the sea.

Is. 27:2 That day, sing of the splendid vineyard! 3 I, Yahweh, am its guardian, from time to time I water it; so that no harm befall it, I guard it night and day.

I pray with God in the Trinity and the Angels and Saints of God "night and day. " God's purpose the nights many of those that need to be saved in the Salvation of Jesus Christ .. are pierced in the burning ashes of hell parts of their personhood.. satan does not go to sleep until.. he seeks to torture .. others. God sees and is watching and will redeem. He wants to redeem all humanity.

God has won the war already on sin in His Resurrection. Yet, we are prayer warriors, and many spiritual gifts God gives to His believers to proclaim His Salvation .. God allows trials because those who are warriors and believers help this type .. of people who need redemption; the Holy Spirit is in and with and through the physical body also and the spiritual. Body.. the physical body .. because part of the Spiritual body of the Holy Spirit.. especially for God's purpose .. See, we are the" body of Christ," those who seek His Holiness.. and redemption.. and there are different gifts of this is and sometimes very mysteriously understood and cannot all be revealed… because .. this is infinite and everlasting no stopping of life. It heals death.. the Holy Spirit of God in the Trinity in the Cross of Jesus Christ sees we guard the doors of heaven and even wait at the gates of hell to help those to get out of the hell, "hell," different levels and different attitudes.. of life.. even those actions people do are "hell, " they make on earth.. in their life is hell and the heart .. because hell and is in hell. I saw this in a person's heart last night and before. That is living. Yet they shall have the life of breath of God.. and God wants to save them.

Is. 27:2 That day, sing of the splendid vineyard! 3 I, Yahweh, am its guardian, from time to time I water it; so that no harm befall it, I guard it night and day.

Is. 27:4 —I do not have a wall. Who can reduce me to brambles and thorn-bushes? —I shall make war and trample on it and simultaneously burn it.

Is. 27:5 Or should they beg for my protection, let them make their peace with me, peace let them make with me.

June 15, 2024

Jesus told me. You have heard my voice and Mary.

Peace must be done now, USA, toward your relationship with Jesus Christ…

This is why… we need to go to the cross and give our lives to the heart of Jesus.

See, those who seek to take from others make death for themselves, and less of life, and those who make their own rules even have less than life. It is shown by the facts of the outcome and product of what they caused, even logic. God is logical, and he can prove the truth in every position.

Why would.. a person want to take from another? It is not them. It is not their body or spirit .. then it becomes a deformity of death of what they were supposed to be for the person taking or stealing or abusing, and it even murders themselves. See, God did not plan and create their cell makeup in the creation, and hence, it causes death, and it needs to be redeemed if they allow it to be .. in the free will of choice to decide.

Yet, God does force and is a sovereign God who also chooses what will happen to the good and the bad. Yet, he loves the sinner yet hates their sin.

In Revelations, we hear that there is a time that he will stop the time for those who need to make a choice. Even those whom.. have and now ask about the question of the evil they do against the person who guards God's glory and purposes at all levels.

See, there is a mystery, and this answer is endless because God always redeems righteousness, and there are eternal treasures —and we will speak of that. The treasures are eternal, yet they are brought to Earth also and continuously used to help bring God's glory because they become vast and big.

Yet sometimes there is terrible suffering, and many times, this is the case. God will redeem us. Does that take into account the contraindications of the victim that they did evil against?

See, I wrote this before I saw the verse below. I am hearing God's Word. He told me you heard.

Is. 28:14 Hence listen to Yahweh's word, you insolent men, rulers of this people in Jerusalem. 15 Because you have said, 'We have made a treaty with Death and have struck a pact with Sheol. When the scourging flood comes over, it will not touch us, for we have made lies our refuge and hidden under falsehood.' 16 So the Lord Yahweh says, 'Now I shall lay a stone in Zion, a granite stone, a precious corner-stone, a firm foundation-stone: no one who relies on this will stumble. 17 And I will make fair judgement the measure, and uprightness the plumb-line.'

See, I will make a "corner-stone,' God said .. firm foundation-stone .. see the new restoration. See, God has made a weaker stone .. of us the "granite," and redeemed it and made a "precious corner-stone," a firm foundation we give our life..,.. and "no one who relies on this will stumble."

But hail will sweep away the refuge of lies, and floods wash away the hiding place; 18 your treaty with Death will be broken, and your pact with Sheol will not hold. When the scourging flood comes over, you will be trodden down by it; 19 every time it comes over, it will seize on you, for it will come over, morning after morning, day by day, and night by night. Nothing but fear will make you understand the storm and what you hear. 20 The bed is too short to stretch in, and the blanket is too narrow for covering. 21 Yes, as on Mount Perazim, Yahweh will rise, as in the Valley of Gibeon, he will do his work, his mysterious work, to do his deed, his extraordinary deed. 22 Stop scoffing, then, or your bonds will be tightened further, for I have heard it: it has been irrevocably decided by the Lord Yahweh Sabaoth regarding the whole country.

He told me to read Isaiah and comment on it. This would show that what I say is in concordance with His Word of Holy Scriptures.

Is. 28:23 Listen closely to my words, be attentive, understand what I am saying. 24 Does the ploughman plough all day to sow, breaking up and harrowing his ground? 25 Once he has levelled its surface, does he not scatter fennel, sow cummin? Then he puts in wheat, millet, barley and, round the edges, spelt, 26 for his God has taught him this rule and instructed him. 27 Fennel must not be crushed with a sledge, nor cart-wheels driven over cummin; fennel must be beaten with a stick, and cummin with a flail. 28 When you are threshing wheat, you do not waste time crushing it; you get the horse and cart-wheel moving, but you do not grind it fine. 29 All this is a gift from Yahweh Sabaoth, marvelous advice leading to outstanding achievements.

See, all work is a " gift from Yahwe Saboth, marvellous advice leading to great achievements."

This is what the Spirit of God guided me to write and speak prior .. ..That when .. we "sow," "God has taught him this rule and instructed him.. " and a "gift of his sowing is from God ..and it will be "marvelous," look that word up.. "marvelous," to marvel.. like you cannot even imagine of gifts God has for you.

He told me the Spirit of God.. that even if a person has sinned and the time has passed, and they repent and seek righteousness .. will obsolete all the sin and make the time of the person .. that the person lost whether it was the sinner or the person the sinner sinned against. He, God, would even. Make a more fantastic gift if that is choice for the repented sinner.. this is why we should never give up hope and be faithful.. knowing God can redeem all things .. and make a.. more beautiful .. happening.. see because all things He creates are more attractive and more perfect than the other in timing.. even Actually, what is produced before a human seeking on December .. for doing God's glory should be better in January .. .. see crossing over to a more beautiful quintessential life in God. Hence, he can redeem us. A thousand years of Jesus Christ can be one year of .. humans . and 1000 years of humans can be one year of Jesus Christ. However, note that we are supposed to get closer to His perfect, omniscient truth. This is why He will forgive us and give us a better life when we repent and turn away from sin. See, He waits for us .. yet the omniscient life fusion of love is .. waiting and ready to burst in the quintessential life of the omniscient truth of God's most incredible beauty and greatest love. See, you are His greatest love.. and you. He wants to share the Trinity in the highest God, the Highest God in the Father of Abraham, so He wants to give you that love.

Is. 29:5 The horde of your enemies will be like fine dust, the horde of the warriors like flying chaff. And suddenly, in an instant, 6 Yahweh Sabaoth will visit you with thunder, earthquake, mighty din, hurricane, tempest, flame of devouring fire. 7 It will be like a dream, like a vision at night: the horde of all the nations at war with Ariel, all those fighting, besieging and troubling it. 8 It will be like the dream of a hungry man: he eats, then wakes up with an empty belly; or like the dream of a thirsty man: he drinks, then wakes up exhausted with a parched throat. So will it be with the horde of all the nations making war on Mount Zion.

Let us not horde the truth about America… hoarding, trickery, what is due to the people, lies, abuse, and the life a person can give to another. We do not want the beauty of God's purpose stolen and death.

Is. 29:13 The Lord then said: Because this people approaches me only in words, honors me only with lip-service while their hearts are far from me, and reverence for me, as far as they are concerned, is nothing but human commandment, a lesson memorized, 14 very well, I shall have to go on astounding this people with prodigies and wonders: for the wisdom of its wise men is doomed, the understanding of any who understand will vanish.

Let us not vanish the "wisdom of its wise" that God has given us. Let us be His light and eat from only His table of truth. Our heart is His first. Reconcile now to gain and receive and be redeemed of the wisdom…

Is. 30:19 Yes, people of Zion living in Jerusalem, you will weep no more. He will be gracious to you when your cry for help rings out; as soon as he hears it, he will answer you. 20 When the Lord has given you the bread of suffering and the water of distress, he who is your teacher will hide no longer, and you will see your teacher with your own eyes. 21 Your ears will hear these words behind you, 'This is the way, keep to it,' whether you turn right or left. 22 You will hold unclean the silver plating of your idols and the gold plating of your images. You will throw them away like the polluted things they are, shouting after them, 'Good riddance!' 23 He will send rain for the seed you sow in the ground, and the bread the ground provides will be rich and nourishing. That day, your cattle will graze in broad pastures. 24 Oxen and donkeys that work the land will eat for fodder wild sorrel, spread by the shovel-load and fork-load. 25 On every lofty mountain, on every high hill there will be streams and watercourses, on the day of the great slaughter when the strongholds fall. 26 Then moonlight will be bright as sunlight and sunlight itself be seven times brighter—like the light of seven days in one—on the day Yahweh dresses his people's wound and heals the scars of the blows they have received.

See, God protects us .. and will take away the strongholds of the evils.. of those seeking to take away our freedoms. We will not have to hold onto the evil of the leaders and people who trick us. We will now see that only by keeping God's right arm of strength will the moon be brighter at night, bringing light within the heart, and the light of sunlight of the day will bring. See the problem. The work is that we need to get to the truth, the lies.. that hurt us.. and then they will be stopped because those who do evil or abuse against us do it, hiding it. Then, they shall be exposed and will stop. And now the Lord will make the restitution …

Ishiah. 30:27   See, the name of Yahweh comes from afar, blazing his anger and making his threat heavy. His lips are brimming with fury. His tongue is like a devouring fire. 28 His breath is like a river in spate coming up to the neck, to sift the nations with the sieve of destruction, harness the peoples in a bridle that will lead them astray. 29 Your song will be like that on a festal night, and there will be joy in your hearts as when to the sound of the flute people make a pilgrimage to the mountain of Yahweh, the Rock of Israel. 30 Yahweh will make his majestic voice ring out, he will show the weight of his arm in the heat of his anger, with a devouring fire, with thunderbolt, downpour and hailstones. 31 Yes, at Yahweh's voice Assyria will be terrified, he will strike him with his rod; 32 each time he goes by, will fall the punishing rod that Yahweh will lay on him, to the sound of tambourines and harps, in the battles which he will wage against him with uplifted hand. 33 Yes, Topheth has been ready for a long time now, that too is ready for the king, deep and wide his pyre, fire and wood in plenty. Yahweh's breath, like a stream of brimstone, will set fire to it.

See this why I see and speak of the blazing anger and heavy threat .. He tells me when believers say that they are His children .. hurt .. and secretly abuse and trickery of life, open doors.. see God will expose .. those many soon of their .. eating from both tables assimilating from their artificial ideas .. that is not of God. See, they desire more .. they desire life.. and they seek it in the wrong .. places.. .. and seek to take from God's beauty of life and truth.. because they are feeding their emptiness of sin and assimilation of the society of the culture .. of hidden sin and hideous sorrows indeed in their heart they need to seek first loving instead of abusing. This is what they did to America: they made the rules of justice and took to use in a way that is not the best for the people.. now they seek to take.. even the persona, thoughts, and spirit of life.. and it shall not be God will redeem, and many will be exposed.

Help us, Lord. Many do not want to believe the truth of what has happened: It is a human sin against humans. And I seek to bring the foundation of God's love to heal the people.

How can we determine what is correct .. of those leaders who let us down and destroyed our America. Of course, they cannot always deal with the outside international .. happenings with justice perfection .. because the international .. peoples

30 Yahweh will make his majestic voice ring out; he will show the weight of his arm in the heat of his anger, with devouring fire, thunderbolts, downpours, and hailstones. 31 Yes, at Yahweh's voice Assyria will be terrified, he will strike him with his rod; 32 each time he goes by, will fall the punishing rod that Yahweh will lay on him, to the sound of

tambourines and harps, in the battles which he will wage against him with uplifted hand

God sings in a majestic voice in and with and through the people.

Is. 31:1 Woe to those going down to Egypt for help, who put their trust in horses, who rely on the number of chariots, and great strength of cavalrymen, but do not look to the Holy One of Israel or consult Yahweh. 2 Yet he too is wise and can bring disaster and he will not go back on his word; he will rise against the breed of evil-doers and against those who protect wrong-doers. 3 The Egyptian is human, not divine, his horses are flesh, not spirit; Yahweh will stretch out his hand: the protector will stumble, the protected will fall and all will perish together.

We need to consult Yahweh.

The Spirit of the Lord told me .. the Egyptian is human the Hamas and Hezabolla .. "All shall perish. He will rie against the breed of evil doers and against those.. who protect wrong doers

Today I heard the yelp screaming of the Coyotes .. calling..

El Salvador.. took down gangs. We also in America and Hamas Hezabolla and stop the war .. of Russia and Ukraine. And Now the American War with Russia and our War in our Country and the war at the boaders

9 In his terror he will abandon his rock, and his panic-stricken officers desert the standard— declares Yahweh, whose fire is in Zion, whose furnace, in Jerusalem.

This is what Jesus Christ will do for me now those whom are seeking to hurt us.. Help us now Jesus Christ.. now.. immediately..

5 The fool will no longer be called generous, nor the rascal be styled bountiful.

Terrible this is .. Gates and other the toxins foods and science and

Is. 32:6 For the fool speaks folly and his heart is set on villainy; he is godless in his actions and his words ascribe error to Yahweh; he starves the hungry of their food and refuses drink to the thirsty. 7 Everything to do with the rascal is evil, he devises infamous plans to ruin the poor with lying words even when the needy has right on his side; 8 but the noble person plans only noble things, noble his every move. Is. 32:18 My people will live in a peaceful home, in peaceful houses, tranquil dwellings. 19 And should the forest be totally destroyed and the city gravely humiliated, 20 You will be happy to sow wherever there is water and to let the ox and donkey roam free.

Help me Lord.. please .. with our protections..

See "noble," God's kingdom 108 [105] ἀετός, aetos, n. eagle (a noble, powerful bird), vulture (a carrion bird)[105] Look we are eagles of America the symbol of freedom . "wings on an eagle," God's life from heaven to earth. See "the noble person plans only noble things, noble his every move."

Divine Message July 17, 2024

997 [937] βασιλικός, basilikos, a. [995]. royal, noble, kingly; as a noun, royal official (possibly of the Herodian family)

Look the people need to be "kingly," , noble, royal official of all they do.

2302 [2104] εὐγενής, eugenēs, a. [2292 + 1181]. of noble birth, of noble character

Responsibility at birth to bring "of noble birth," bring a "noble character."

4948 [4586] σεμνός, semnos, a. [4936]. worthy of respect, noble

See this is why God will eventually … see those things.. that are against the noble He will judge.. Because, nobles are by fact at God's creation and

[105] NIV GREEK DICTIONARY Greek to English Dictionary and Index to the NIV New Testament (NIV Greek)
from Zondervan NIV Exhaustive Concordance Edward W. Goodrick, John R. Kohlenberger III, and James A. Swanson
Copyright ©1999, 1990 by the Zondervan Corporation Grand Rapids, Michigan 49530
All rights reserved. Electronic text prepared by OakTree Software, Inc. Version 1.3, Noble interesting is eagle that is a .. symbol for Americans.

while they live "worthy of respect." Look at this: Even God showed "worthy of respect," to Nebuchadnezzar when he follow God's command to humble himself and turn from his wicked ways and give to those in need. And God of Abraham multiplied his kingdom. Daniel 4.

When I wrote my second book 'Arise to God's Truth," Restore and Keep America's Freedom. There was a Divine Message.. America needs a "new seed of Seth," to restore America in God's righteousness in truth. 4953 [4589] Σήθ, Sēth, n. pr. Seth, "determined, granted [Ge 4:25]; restitution"

Interesting I found this in the .. dictionary now right below noble … See even in the time when Cain killed Abel and Adam and Eve had a new son Seth, God "granted, restitution," of what was intended at His creation.

Romans 10:2 For I bear them witness that bthey have a zeal for God, cbut not according to knowledge. See according to God.

Romans 13:13 hLet us walk properly as in the daytime, inot in orgies and drunkenness, not in sexual immorality and sensuality, jnot in quarreling and jealousy.[106]

I speak of "noble" because noble is the "kingly" persona authentic being that each person is when he or she is created by God. God hopes and wholeheartedly fiercely and jealously wants His humanity to be in the "kingdom" of the eternal Father in the Trinity, the Virgin Mary, and the Saints and Angels of God.

He is a jealous God .. and the "kingdom of God is on earth, as believers. And even in heavenly when appointed.. And even the prayers sent to the

---

[106] MOUNCE GREEK DICTIONARY Concise Greek-English Dictionary of the New Testament (Mounce Greek Dictionary)
edited by William D. Mounce with Rick D. Bennett, Jr. Copyright © 2011 by William D. Mounce
http://www.billmounce.com/greek-dictionary All rights reserved. Greek Strong's Audio pronunciation, Open Source
Accordance edition hypertexted and formatted by OakTree Software, Inc. Version 4.5
noble

Father in the Trinity. And even the Saints and Angels and Virgin Mary participate in the miracle of restoration."

1Corinthians 15:40 There are heavenly bodies and earthly bodies, but the glory of the heavenly is of one kind, and the glory of the earthly is of another.

Yet, God brings them together in the Holy Spirit.. the mystery of His sovereignty and majesty.

Mark 13:24 "But in those days, after tthat tribulation, uthe sun will be darkened, and the moon will not give its light,

Let us be ready now and begin the "noble," restitution of the glory of God's purpose and even today in the "tribulation," of geopolitical powers and political ideological beliefs and secret powers of 'elite communist," to cause "art of war,"

Pitting the people against each other. 2. Making truth a lie and lie a truth. 3. Cause many major catastrophe for the peoples.

Let us begin now with this very moment each one of us to bring God's truth, justice, peace, and restoration, forward building in love .. before the appointed time of the "tribulation."

Let your light shine in the darkness, even in the moonlight evening. The truth will vacillate in the energy of God's creation and scintillate with the beaming majesty of God's serene love. The day of the brilliant, soothing sunlight in you will be the miracle to bring the quintessential harvest of life of redemption. So all with "taste and see" the beauty of the Lord will have to choose. Righteousness, the redemption to restore America and even the world to God's power, and the tenderness of His mystery, the wisdom of His purpose and mercy. You, America, and the world's peoples can do and be God's love. In, and with, and through you, God's love will bring miracles.,

ἀγαθός [ἄγ], ή, όν: (deriv. uncertain):–good, Lat. bonus :

I. of persons,

1. in early times, good, gentle, noble, in reference to birth, opp. to κακοί, πατρὸς δ᾽ εἴμ᾽ ἀγαθοῖο, θεὰ δέ με γείνατο μήτηρ Il.; ἀγαθοὶ καὶ ἐξ ἀγαθῶν, Lat. boni bonis prognati, Plat.:—with this early sense was associated that of wealth and power, like Lat. optimus quisque in Sallust and Cicero; esp. in the phrase καλοὶ κἀγαθοί (v. καλοκἀγαθός).

2. good, brave, since these qualities were attributed to the Chiefs, Il.:— ἀγαθὸς ἐν ὑσμίνῃ, βοὴν ἀγαθός, πὺξ ἀγαθός etc., Hom.; ἀγ. τὰ πολέμια, τὰ πολιτικά Hdt., etc.;—also c. dat., ἀγ. πολέμῳ Xen.;—and, ἀγ. εἴς τι, περί τι, πρός τι Plat., etc.; lastly, c. inf., ἀγ. μάχεσθαι, ἱππεύεσθαι, good at fighting, etc., Hdt.

3. good, in moral sense, Plat., etc.

4. ἀγαθοῦ δαίμονος, as a toast, 'to the good Genius,' Ar.[107]

Notes of Importance.

Divine Mission May 13, 2023

Paseso Robles, California

The Spirit of the Lord told me .. Do not tempt the Lord, Do not tempt the Lord

Use the Bible I will give you the verses

1.People of Communities, Cities, States.

A. They seek to make peace
B. They seek to take care of each other
C. When someone makes a mistake, they seek to correct it
D. You can feel in the cities there is a quietness of unending prayer of listening to find truth; and even if they do not know the entire truth

---

[107] LIDDELL & SCOTT (INTERMEDIATE) An Intermediate Greek-English Lexicon (Liddell & Scott) founded upon The Seventh Edition of Liddell and Scott's Greek-English Lexicon. Oxford, At the Clarendon Press, 1889. The print form is in the Public Domain. This electronic version of Liddell-Scott Greek-English Lexicon copyright the President and Fellows of Harvard College and the Corporation for Public Broadcasting, 1996. Used by permission of Yale University Press. Accordance edition hypertexted and formatted by OakTree Software, Inc. Version 2.3

or the entire information to access the truth they are faithful it is absolutely evident when these people have picked up the and all is in line the nature and God seeks to deliver what is needed for the people and His all creations.

E. Even though there has been division I heard and feel there is an awareness peaking through the beautiful hearts of the Americans; because, now all things are now being revealed and shall be revealed.

2.The Government

A. The government has shown that they have not addressed the people's first needs and the most beneficial way.

B. We of course know intentions of leaders have all different reasons and truly justice of intentions and others are decisions that have to be accepted by many or the most powerful?

C. The thick walls of deceit the Communist Elite attempted to bring against the Americans. Hidden in almost every hall way of each governmental branch. However, not hidden by the eyes of God. All the technological powers in the universe is one finger pointing of the great creator. See cannot you see all is being revealed.

Now American we need now to chose leaders in our Communities and States and Nation that our justice, truth, ethical, integrity, and first protecting the eyes and minds and life of the children borned and unborned and the humanity of the God's intentions what is it to be human nothing in between God created Man and Woman.

D. What are these hidden powers in our own government that we need now to swiftly forgive and tell the children we will seek and live for justice?; Yes, now they are being revealed. Since, centuries of times there has been crimes in our own America; however, we have to continued to lift America up in pray powerful wisdom of miracle to God and serve our country in the foundation of the civil liberties and Constitutional Rights with the covenantal platinum heavenly pin written by the forefathers in the light of the

Declaration of Independence in the "God Most Highest" table of truth of the 10 Commandments.

Oh we cannot deny our first President George Washington knelled in humble honor and powerful pray to the God Most Highest of the everlasting covenant of God and His people to save America and give her freedom of justice and liberty for all.

Arise America Arise America the Covenant of the God Most Highest is hear take up the heart of His justice in the power of the right arm of His strength He carries the nations on His shoulders.

3. Examples, Boarders

A. The boarders have to have protections because of the life threatening magnitude ever in the history of America or the world. What are these life threatening magnitudes? Listen it is not just a simple crime it has more than one crime and could destroy an entire country.

B. There is significant variables that cause effects to every part of life and that are the differences of injustice and justice and evil and truth and controls and freedoms.

C. We asks what has caused this finding and the variables of the greatest dangers of our country

4. Immigrants from Countries that use their people and do not

A. Country uses the peoples.. and takes all the productions whether in the country or within monies brought back from investments for other countries. See they

B. The Countries sent their peoples to USA and their leaders of their countries and business peoples are keeping all the funds and monies and benefits.

5. When the Billionaires when they make things and create they have to think

A. Of the contraindications of things such as the sky scrapers now cannot be used to the fullest access.. many peoples are working at home. See they build for quantity and mass. They need to build for quality and life intensity of creations for others. Otherwise, what they created they will not even be able to enjoy it because it will die because it is only used by a few and the few may not be in agreement and there is not enough allies and friends to keep the great creation that some other group enters and takes or destroys the great creations. This is evident in the power of the geopolitical controls and the plan of the holocaust of the humanity of the inside job of the CCP VIRUS. ..

B. Because the evolution of different human populations and cultures and belief systems and traditions and even identifying injustice or evil as justice or truth. Has caused what men build for the intention of good to be destroyed or wounded because of the identification of what is justice and truth.

6. Geopolitical powers

A. the thick walls of deceit the Communist Elite attempted to bring against the Americans.
B. All wanting of power in turn wound and destroy and bring death
C. This is evident in all treacherous stratigeic ways of
D. Vote taken away President Trump
E. Silencing or crimes against advocates and consultants for the freedom of America
F. Conspiracies and Crimes against President Trump and his supporters

CHAPTER THIRTEEN

Aristotle's Metaphysics Book 1 Chapter 1-3

I want to state that I am wholeheartedly grateful for the opportunity to study and write on the wisdom of the soul. Metaphysics is infinitely vast, and we can only touch upon it in a childlike faith since we are speaking of God's possessions and divine things. Also, I will integrate the Holy Scriptures briefly in our Catholic understanding of poverty and the social issues of today.

Metaphysics of God as Believers Brief Explanation

The Most Holiness Pope Benedict said, "that in any case, the Christian faith will always be "a scandal" because it will always be a "daring" to think that God has left to give the resurrection crucified men." 1

To be Intelligent; To be Truly Sincere; To believe in God 2

Yes, it is a "scandal" when we believe our Redeemer lives, the Resurrected Christ He shines right through us the love of the Lord our God with all our heart, all our soul, and all our mind. Giving us courage and strength and miracles. Mat. 22:34 Yes, God has entrusted in us His redeeming Love through the Holy Spirit in the power of truth and justice. Yes, it is a "scandal" to the world to be "daring" [faithfulness] enough to believe in our Resurrected Lord Jesus Christ. This "daring scandal" is the true wisdom: first accepting the life of Christ [all His precepts-seeking to follow them]; secondly, accepting His death on the cross[redeeming our human frailties and sin and living in this world to be His people of love toward humanity]; thirdly, believing in His resurrection[being sanctified in Jesu's cross giving to Him our life toward heaven and faithfully knowing we have life on earth and life in [aeterna]. We will find and be fulfilled in wisdom "on earth as it is in heaven." Aristotle tells us that "all men desire knowledge", this knowledge is all the different aspects of Metaphysics of: 1. First cause and the ultimate principles of reality. 2. Being as such. 3. Nature of substance 4. God and the divine

things3: Ezekiel the prophet tells us in 11:4"The spirit רוּחַ of Yahweh fell on me." We will as

believers in Christ have this ongoing spirit of Yahweh in His sovereignty over humans.

Creation of Humans the ruah, breath of life, wisdom, mind, life force:

"Yahweh God shaped man from the soil of the ground and blew the breath of life וַיִּפַּח4

(8); וַיִּפַּח into his nostrils, and man became a living being." Genesis 2:7. וַיִּפַּח The word meaning a being animated by the breath of life manifested also by the 'spirit', [ruah] the life force Genesis 6:17f .5 Gen. 6:18 And I will establish my covenant with thee, is singular first common singular noun receiving the action of the verb and בְּרִיתִי is the particle

meaning direct object. This is a covenant בְּרִיתִי covenant, one covenant, one promise, with our Lord God and no other gods. Keeping the covenant with our Lord we are transformed into all that God desires in our life from the knowledge of the world to the wisdom of His purpose.

Through history God and humanity have had a living covenantal relationship: "He will be our God and we will be His people." Here we clearly see and are in Genesis 6:17 speaks of God destroying "all living things having the breath of life under heaven; everything is to perish." This shows the sovereignty and omnipotence of the Lord "that the Most High rules over human sovereignty and gives it to whom he pleases."

God made human individually

Psalms 139:13   You created my inmost self, knit me together in my mother's womb.

14 For so many marvels I thank you; a wonder am I, and all your works are wonders.

You knew me through and through, 15 my being held no secrets from you, when I was being formed in secret, textured in the depths of the earth.

Psalms 139:16   Your eyes could see my embryo. In your book all my days were inscribed, every one that was fixed is there.

Note: Abortion is killing the "embryo" of the breath of God.

Each person is perfectly made. Each is an individual. Each has the ability for his or her particular knowledge and wisdom that they "naturally desire". We as believers know our Dominum gives us the "life force" רוּחַ(ruah) to live as His children and

His people. In Isaiah 11:2C, it was prophesied that "On him[Jesus Christ] will rest the spirit [ruah] רוּחַof Yahweh, the spirit (ruah) of wisdom and insight, the spiritרוּחַ רוּחַ (ruah) of counsel and power, the spirit (ruah) of knowledge and fear of Yahweh." Spirit translated as (ruah)רוּחַ. Jesus Christ is human and divine in His humanness He is perfect without sin. Jesus Christ is human and Divine He gave us an example. But not one human is good. We are children of Christ and in Him we have His promise that He would send the advocate the Holy Spirit to teach us all the things we should know.

Out of Love the Foremost of all Things:

Out of love God has given us life. Out of love God has given us His "only begotten son" that whosoever believe in Him shall have life and life abundant and life everlasting. Our love Jesus Christ gave us His life Out of love God created love from love which true wisdom is truly love. Live, "Love is considered the foremost of immortal beings." Because giving us life through His breath, His ruah, His breath of life, is that immortal being He gave. Wisdom is that all men desire to know. All men desire to know God, knowing(comprehending) God is knowing wisdom.

Our Catholic Teachings in The Catechism of the Catholic Church Love and Wisdom:

THE DESIRE FOR GOD

27 The desire for God is written in the human heart, because man is created by God and for God; God never ceases to draw man to himself. Only in God will he find the truth and happiness he never stops searching for: The dignity of man rests above all on the fact that he is called to communion with God. This invitation to converse with God is addressed to man as soon as he comes into being. For if man exists it is because God has created him through love, and love continues to hold him in existence. He cannot live fully

according to truth unless he freely acknowledges that love and entrusts himself to his creator.[108]

Professor Bauzon, speaks of the "contingency" we must realize in our world. We as citizens are contingent on "Natural Law, Politik, Natural Right, Positive Right." Even though we are in a contingent society, as Professor Bauzon says, we still have our "Faith" paradigm of life in God. As the people of God, we need a steadfast "heart," as Apostle Paul tells us in a "political" aspect with God's "insight".[109] We need to take hold of that knowledge the Lord has allowed us to have of concepts of the world and dynamically with wise action and powerful transformation use for the better of humanity in the world. Christians are more educated than ever in history. When people see the truth, they will want to take hold of it and follow even if it is one small step toward God. We know there is a continuous change in that one small step for good. We need to offer them

---

[108] The Catechism of the Catholic Church, Libreria Editrice Vatican, Vatican City Used by permission of Amministrazione del Patrimonio Della Sede Apostolica, Vatican City, Electronic text hypertexted and prepared and prepared by Oak Tree Software, Inc. Version 1.2 The Desire to for God. under wisdom.

[109] Bauzon, Political Science, Pontificia San Tommaso D' Aquino, Fall Semester 2011. This is truly living in God's wisdom for His humanity when we are able to live effectively in a contingent society as believers of God. Nicodemachean Ethics by Aristotle is the foundation of Justice in a Political Society, Refer to Book V. Refer also to Aristotle's Politics.

truth and life in our daily actions; then they will question who, what, and why. Professor Senner teaches us with strength and faithfulness: 1. First is the wellbeing of Humanity. 2. Prepare oneself and others to be debaters of the truth of Political views in our world.[110]

What does it mean to be a human being?[111]

We need to ask ourselves: What is the correct ethical Political System? Political system that has Constitutional Patriotism. The Constitution is the rule of the land. Patriotism is the culture of the land. Constitutional patriotism seeks what is fair: the constitution of morality, laws and Proceedings for public life, and regulations of degrees. Other paramount aspects are essential for a political system of Constitutional Patriotism, such as family values, the "veil of ignorance" [when one does not speak about their convictions], aspects of the needs of the minority, citizens having a voice and seeking to protect humanity's welfare. Remember the basic foundation of ethics mapped out for us in Nicomachean Ethics. In particular Book V of Nicomachean Ethics speaks of the Political life.[112] Saint Peter was given the keys to the Church. We have these keys from the Catholic Christianity and the kleis(key) of ancient philosophical genius to support the best for the care of humanity in our Lord's eyes. Today we can have the power of intelligence and the pristine wisdom from on high to have rectification of an act of injustice (dikaioma)[113] through our continuous fight against injustices for justice bringing peace to the world.

ARTICULUS 1

---

[110] Senner, Walter Father, Dr. O.P. Epistemology, Pontificia San Tommaso D' Aquino, Fall Semester 2011

[111] Bauzon Political Science. We need to at least mention this aspect.

[112] Ibid, Political Science. This is such a vast subject that I can only mention it briefly.

[113] Nicomachean Ethics, V. vii. 3-7, 1135 a ." Acknowledge reason and nature in their [Chritian theologian] interrelation as the universally valid source of law." Most Holiness Benedict XVI Reichstag Building, Berlin Thursday, 22 September 2011.

DE REVELATIONE DEI

I. Deus Suum revelat «benevolum consilium»

51 «Placuit Deo pro Sua bonitate et sapientia Seipsum revelare et notum facere sacramentum voluntatis Suae, quo homines per Christum, Verbum carnem factum, in Spiritu Sancto accessum habent ad Patrem et divinae naturae consortes efficiuntur».[114]

Through the love of God we are given life and bestowed upon us in the Holy Spirit of wisdom and sharing in the beauties of life and even "becoming [sharers] in the divine nature."

Our bodies are the temple of the Holy Spirit.[115] The Holy Spirit flows through without measure when our bodies our the temple of the Holy Spirit. As faithful believers in Christ 'the temple of the Holy Spirit within [us]you. pneuvma, pneuma is from the Holy Spirit is defined as "Christ

---

[114] C. Catechism-E, I I. GOD REVEALS HIS "PLAN OF LOVING GOODNESS"51"It pleased God, in his goodness and wisdom, to reveal himself and to make known the mystery of his will. His will was that men should have access to the Father, through Christ, the Word made flesh, in the Holy Spirit, and thus become sharers in the divine nature.

[115] The New Jerusalem Bible, Copyright 1990. by Darton, Longman & Todd Limited, and Doubleday, a division of Bantam Doubleday Dell Publishing Group. All rights reserved. Published by arrangement with Doubleday, a division of Bantam Doubleday Dell Publishing Group, Inc. Version 2.2. 1Cor. 6:19 Do you not know that your body is the temple of the Holy Spirit, who is in you and whom you received from God? We need to take into consideration that the unclean spirit also exists. This spirit is used sinfully as it kills, steals, and destroys. Seemingly, it is good, but a deceiving master's mind is eventually revealed. This is why, as Christians, we need to be shrewd and wise at the same time. I know we hear this all the time, but we need to protect our little ones, our loved ones, our Priests, and our Nuns. Education is the most precious beginning with Ethics, and adults must also be cognizant of the latest drugs. Especially young mothers who are alone in raising their children. Single mothers do not know what indications of substance abuse are. Something to consider and question. ***** We have continuously changed, changed, and grown in the understanding of knowledge since the Ancient period of Aristotle of the sciences until now. Would you not think that there is also a continuous change in the spiritual realm? The Holy Scriptures monent (they warn) "It is not the flesh and blood that cause sin" but the powers and principalities of satan.

spirit, the Holy Spirit; [also] life, spirit(-ual, -ually), mind."[116] Then believers may also have a "special endowment ("chrism") of the Holy Spirit:[but] anointing, unction. The Holy Spirit en pneumati hagiœ imbued with the Holy Spirit, the divine source of holiness) Rom. 15:16.[117] The Holy Spirit is a guide, helper, intercessor in Greek para¿klhton masculine singular accusative[expressing the goal of motion]; the Holy Spirit is one Spirit as we know part of the Trinity . 1 John 2:1. Also, 1John 2:1 speaks of Jesus being the advocate: "My children, I am writing this to prevent you from sinning; but if anyone does sin, we have an advocate with the Father, Jesus Christ, the upright." Of course, we need to seek with all our heart, mind, and soul to be in the right relationship with Jesus Christ, but He guides us even when we do not realize truth and sin. Also, the Eucharist and all the sacraments and Christian precepts will sanctify us in the mystery of the Spirit. This is that ongoing love that the Lord freely gives to us, and if we search for things of beauty, beauty of knowledge, it is good, in love, justice, hope, faith, and forgiveness, and all good things come from the Lord. The pneuvma is considered breath also "a current of air i.e. of breath. . . or human rational soul"[118] just as when God created humans He continually gives the Spirit when we ask "in His sovereign will" without measure.

Hesiod Ancient Philosopher writing in Theogony:

First of all things was Chaos,[119] made, and then Broad-bosomed Earth ...

---

[116] Strong's Greek Dictionary of the New Testament Public Domain Electronic text downloaded from the Bible Foundation e-Text Library <http://www.bf.org/bfetexts.htm.> Hypertexted and formatted by Oaktree Software, Inc. Greek text added by Oak Tree Software, Inc. Version 2.4

[117] Thayer's Greek- English Lexicon of the New Testament by Joseph Henry Thayer, D.D. Public Domain Formatted and hypertexted by Oak Tree Software, Inc. Holy Spirit.

[118] Strong's Greek Dictionary of the New Testament , Holy Spirit.

[119] Liddel &Scott Nu/x as prop. n., the goddess of Night, daughter of Chaos, Il., Hes.IV. the quarter of night, i.e. the West, Hes.CAáOS, eoß, Att. ouß, to/, chaos, the first state of the universe, Hes., etc.2. infinite space, the expanse, Ar.3. the nether abyss, infinite darkness, Anth.

And Love, the foremost of immortal beings.[120]

Hugh G. Evelyn-White in 1914 translation of Hesiod's writing on Theogony expresses "Love" as: "And Eros (Love), fairest among the deathless gods, who unnerves [make someone lose courage or confidence] the limbs and overcomes the mind and wise counsels of all gods and all men within them."[121] If I am without love, I have nothing, I am nothing. Love finds its joy in the truth. Love never comes to an end. God gives His resurrected Son so that we have a life of love on earth and as it is in heaven. Love is before knowledge, prophecy, words, and the body.

But if there are prophecies, they will be done away with; if tongues, they will fall silent; and if knowledge, it will be done away with. As it is, these remain faith, hope and love, the three and the greatest of them is love. **1Cor. 13:3-13** Do everything in love. 1Cor. 16:14 When you have the love of God you will have the greatest wisdom. It is also foremost to have knowledge of the world in the wisdom of God with this vestibule of love to be affectively dynamic people of God in the contingency of the world's views as Professor Bauzon monet us as stated above. When you have God's love, never forsaking, your actions will come from the heart and

---

[120] Aristotle Metaphysics, 984 b 29 Theogony 116-20. Quotation is slightly inaccurate. Hesiod 750 and 650 BC.Hesiod and Homer have generally been considered the earliest Greek poets whose work has survived, and they are often paired. Hesiod's writings serve as a major source on Greek mythology, farming techniques, early economic thought (he is sometimes identified as the first economist),[6][7][8] archaic Greek astronomy and ancient time- keeping.

[121] Theogony of Hesiod, translation by Hugh G. Evelyn-White [1914] Agape,[Unconditional Love-God has only this love] Eros, Phial. The subject of love is intrinsically extensive.What is evident in Soble's description of eros is a shift away from the sexual: to love something in the "erosic" sense (to use the term Soble coins) is to love it in a way that, by being responsive to its merits, is dependent on reasons. Such an understanding of eros is encouraged by Plato's discussion in the Symposium, in which Socrates understands sexual desire to be a deficient response to physical beauty in particular, a response which ought to be developed into a response to the beauty of a person's soul and, ultimately, into a response to the form, Beauty. Helm, Bennett, "Love", The Stanford Encyclopedia of Philosophy (Fall 2009 Edition), Edward N. Zalta (ed.), URL = <http://plato.stanford.edu/archives/fall2009/entries/ love/>.

guided, and transforming reason. Those precepts God teaches us all throughout history of His relationship with His people will bring justice, and truth and power to change for the better of humanity.

"To love something in the "erosic" sense (to use the term Soble coins) is to love it in a way that, by being responsive to its merits, is dependent on reasons."

"Love the foremost of all things."

We know as Christians that when we love it brings the foremost of all things. The foremost of all things is love and from love comes wisdom. When we love bringing the foremost of all things it is God within us. Love is seeking and desiring wisdom. Humans are the foremost of all immortal beings God and His people have an everlasting eternal covenant. This October 27, 2011 Pope Benedicto came together with all the representatives and people of all the Religions of the world for peace and justice. Giving oneself without a hidden motive is giving a miracle to the world. This is what the master craftsman, artist, and man of experience should live for giving oneself is loving the Lord with all your heart, soul, and mind and in turn giving this love to your neighbor.[122] This love in turn will exercise the reason for the good of humanity.

Even in Aristotle's period of History of the Greco-Roman culture of the belief the Poli, the city of community is foremost. And putting God first in thy life one will come to know thyself the authentic being God created as stated above in our Catholic Catechism. In coming to know thyself one gives thyself to others. But, when one puts God first in thy life one abides in God and then God abides in that one human. Then that one individual

---

[122] Israel as a people is servant of : as having a mission to the nations; and chosen as witness of . But there is also an ideal servant chosen and endowed with the divine Spirit to be a covenant of Israel and a light of the nations; formed to bring back Jacob, raise up the tribes, and become salvation to the end of the earth; bearing the sins of all as a lamb and a trespass-offering, and yet prospering and justifying many as interposing martyr.[Jesus Christ for Christians.. Jews are waiting for their Davidinic King!] 6. In polite address of equals or superiors the Hebrews used servants = we; also his servant = I; also in addressing God, esp. in prayer. 7. Phrases are: (hyh), c. VI pers., become servant to; pers.

will live closer to that 'final end' in 'happiness'in seeking the 'natural desire for knowledge' as Aristotle states.

Our Pope Benedicto proclaims of this happiness in love: "For us the Cross of Christ is the sign of the God who put "suffering-with" (compassion) and "loving-with" in place of force. His name is "God of love and peace" (2 Cor 13:11). It is the task of all who bear responsibility for the Christian faith to purify the religion of Christians again and again from its very heart, so that it truly serves as an instrument of God's peace in the world, despite the fallibility of humans."[123]

Creation Christian view and the First Principles of Ancient Philosophers:

In the beginning God created heaven, and earth. Genesis 1:1 "The spirit of God moved over the waters." With the spirit[124] of God moving over the waters with His command He created. When God spoke He created. And the earth was void and Chaos ‹ …Genesis 1:2

And God called the dry land, earth and green, water, seed, fruit, and creatures existed upon it day and night. Yes, Hesiod's "broad- bosomed earth" holds all things God made. Genesis 1:10. And the Lord God formed man of the slime of the earth: and breathed into his face the breath of life, and man became a living soul. Genesis 2:7 And man that part of God is Love the foremost of all immortal beings. "[God's]Love is the cause of good."[125] It is almost as this "broad bosomed earth" is the Mother that

---

[123] Day of Reflection, Dialogue and Prayer For Peace and Justice in the World "Pilgrims of Truth, Pilgrims of Peace." Address of His Holiness Benedict XVI at the Meeting for Peace in Assisi, Basilica of Sain Mary of the Angels Thursday, 27 October 2011. www.vatican.va/holy_father/benedict_xvi/speeches/2011/october/documents

[124] TWOT Wind, breath, mind, spirit.Hiphil, "perceive by breathing an aeriform thing," KB, p. 877, see below), it is best considered a primitive noun, related to an -vowel root j…wr, "to breathe" (BDB, p. 924); cf"odor"; Ugaritic n.f. (less oft. m.) breath, wind, spirit —1. breath of mouth or nostrils a. breath.b. as mere breath: cf. 2 e. c. as word of command: (1) of God; (2) of Messianic king. d. as hard breathing through the nostrils (1) of God; (2) of man.e. as sign and symbol of life: breath of life.

[125] Aristotle, Metaphysics Books I-X Translated by Tredennick Hugh, Loeb Classical Library, Harvard University Press Cambridge Massachusetts London England, 1933. 985 a 5s,

takes care of all things on earth.[126] We need to give to the Mother earth so she can feed and give life to the earth. Yes, we are responsible as humans in that we were given the earth to take care of the earth in a philosophical view. In the omniscient hands of a Christian view, God's kingdom on earth, believers need to care for all the earth and its beauty. The Catholic Catechism states that Mary is the mother of our Redeemer Christ, and has "undoubted faithfulness" that we need to follow in taking care of the world.

"Mary she shines forth on earth until the day of the Lord shall come, a sign of certain hope and comfort to the pilgrim People of God."

Interesting to note the first philosophers believed the first principles were: Thales believed the first principle was water; Empedocles believing earth, the elements as the first principle; Anaxoragas believed the first principle was intellect, the mind nouvß (nous).[127] " The intelligence is the most subtle and pure of beings it knows everything completely and has

---

[126] Mary to the Catholic Church: C. Catechism-E. Mary.[1. Mary's divine motherhood]495 Called in the Gospels "the mother of Jesus", Mary is acclaimed by Elizabeth, at the prompting of the Spirit and even before the birth of her son, as "the mother of my Lord."144 In fact, the One whom she conceived as man by the Holy Spirit, who truly became her Son according to the flesh, was none other than the Father's eternal Son, the second person of the Holy Trinity. ARTICLE 3: "HE WAS CONCEIVED BY THE POWER OF THE HOLY SPIRIT, AND BORN OF THE VIRGIN MARY" Paragraph 2. "Conceived by the Power of the Holy Spirit and Born of the Virgin Mary"

1. BORN OF THE VIRGINMARY Paragraph 6.[2. Mary-- Mother of Christ, mother of the Church.] Mary is truly 2[3"Mother of God" (Theotokos)]145 "The Virgin Mary . . . is acknowledged and honored as being truly the Mother of God and of the redeemer. . . . She is 'clearly the mother of the members of Christ' . . . since she has by her charity joined in bringing about the birth of believers in the Church, who are members of its head."502 "Mary, Mother of Christ, Mother of the Church."503. Please, note Professor I know you know all this it is just that I learn.

2. MARY — ESCHATOLOGICAL ICON OF THE CHURCH 972 In the meantime the Mother of Jesus, in the glory which she possesses in body and soul in heaven,[4. is the image and beginning of the Church as it is to be perfected in the world to come. Likewise she shines forth on earth until the day of the Lord shall come, a sign of certain hope and comfort to the pilgrim People of God.]519

[127] Aristotles, Metaphysics 983 b 7-984 b

maximum power."[128] When God created us He gave us a "mind, wisdom, breathe," the (ruah). In Him He is the joy of our strength. Phil. 4:13. These substances were thought of the first principle this is God's creation. These are the entities that we desire to know about innately because we are given dominion to take care of these beauties and seek to understand them in the best, most righteous, and wisest truth, as a master craftsman, man of experience, and artisan.

Out of Chaos, or "infinite space" God creates "Love". Love is determined as love when it loves something pouring out love upon it as did God, making the earth, and Love from "void" and "chaos" of His infinite space. As we know this infinite space the atoms in substances have continuous change and continuous change in space. The freedom of God's love allows us to have continuous change of transformation, forgiveness, and truth; but the essence of the substance of His love never changes.

God created the universe, "broad-bosomed earth" and all things in it. Love is immortal. Love of giving His life to us; giving us His breath: "ruah" My^¥yAj Aj…wr breath of life. "And love, the foremost of immortal beings." God created us as beings with His breath the ruah, Genesis 2:7 Throughout that broad-bosomed earth we can enjoy that searching of wisdom that God allows marking time for humanity. The Aj…wr (ruah) (the air in motion) is the breath or the mind or that wisdom that we as humans naturally desire that Aristotle speaks of in his first sentence of the Metaphysics. We naturally desire it because it is part of us and it forms and transforms us as the authentic being God created; He had us in 'mind'. We are wonderfully and beautifully made by Christ.

"HALLOWED BE THY NAME"

2813 "he is the source of [our] life in Christ Jesus, who became for us wisdom from God, and . . .sanctification,"80 both his glory and our life depend on the hallowing of his name in us and by us. Such is the urgency of our first petition."[129]

---

[128] Ibid 983 b 7 984 b and Simplicious, In Arist., Phys., DK 59 B 12 Found in Yarza p., 52.
[129] The Catechism of the Catholic Church Article 3: Seven Petitions.

Our burning desire to know and love the Lord is hallowing His name. His holiness, His body, and blood He has given us freely so that we may have life and life abundant receiving all good things, knowledge, wisdom in His name. In Christ we have the "Power of Truth." For the philosophers they did not know the Lord Jesus Christ. Their reverence and belief was in the "knowledge" of knowing. "Knowledge" was their first god. Their intentions were noble and searching for and to be the best, most righteous, and most wise as Socrates was their life endeavor and hoping to meet there fellow believers in after life. Logically one would want to know first where we can seek the purest knowledge the closest understand of truth and wisdom. In God in Christ through the mystery of the Holy Spirit is for us as Christians. We today have the truth by the history that the Lord has given with his people that ancient living covenant sign, pledge of covenant, הַבְּרִית א׳ (v. ברית) covenant; circumcision, of Abrahamic covenant; the sabbath. is reality today in the hearts and souls and life of God's people on earth and in heaven. Covenant .. the Sabbath… also reflection of Jesus Christ the Savior.. . gave His life to us the New Covenant. We have the New Covenant America in the Prayer of Continental of Congress 1774, Constitution, Declaration independence. Please see Book "God First, America our Miracle," Lisa Lucia Arden.

Aristotle's Metaphysics Book I Chapters I - III Purpose of Paper:

I. We will briefly discuss the main characteristics in Aristotle's Metaphysics Book I Chapter 1-3

Truly as a new student being immersed in infinite subject of ancient philosophy I am honored to have the audience of my Professor Seidl to read this paper. I will briefly discuss the main characteristics of Aristotle's Metaphysics Book I Chapter 1-3.

Professor Seidl in his book Metaphysics and Realism

"The first philosophy" that Aristotle is illuminated by is that his genius works is the highest level of thought and profound depth of reality.

Professor Seidl in his book Metaphysics and Realism uncovers a scintillating jewel of ancient fragment 35 of HERACLITUS:

"Of quite man things philosophical men must be investigators, according to the word of

Heraclitus, vast in human knowledge.[130]

Metaphysics the Term

We as humans are searching for that evening star, vesperi, prayer of desire of luminosity of knowledge. In our present dimness we are looking for that new star of light of knowledge.

Metaphysics for Aristotle is the most noble of the speculative sciences. The term 'metaphysics' is a term that "was probably Andronicus of Rhodes (1st Century B.C.) who used this term for the first time in the edition of Aristotle's works that he published."[131] Metaphysics also has a meaning of "after the Physics." Metaphysics to Aristotle or the primary philosophy are objects consisting of realities that lie beyond the knowledge of our sense immaterial realities; in other words, at least realities which intellect and which in themselves depend in no way on sensible things for their existence.

Aristotle's Metaphysics of science structure in a tetralogy:[132]

Metaphysics is the first Cause and the ultimate principles of reality- are looking into causes which affect the whole universe. Why does something happen? Studying the the first principles in all reality looking for the

---

[130] Seidl, p. 15 Note: Because Aristotle's Metaphysics Book 1 Chapters 1-3 is vast in human investigation for knowledge, I will only briefly outline and then choose specific topics to discuss. Note: I am reviewing a brief outline for the study of my understanding and then I will focus on certain topics to compare with Phaedo.

[131] Yarza , p. 141 Aristotle most of the time he used the expression primary philosophy.

[132] Seidl, Lectures History of Ancient Philosophy Spring 2011 Metaphysics is the 'first philosophy', or 'the study of being qua being', or 'wisdom', or 'theology'. Metaphysics has two main strands: that which holds that what exists lies beyond experience (as argued by Plato), and that which holds that objects of experience constitute the only reality (as argued by Kant, the logical positivists, and Hume). Metaphysics has also concerned itself with a discussion of whether what exists is made of one substance or many, and whether what exists is inevitable or driven by chance.

causes in the reality. Not studying causes of particulars such causes of earth, water, or various investigation of fish in the ocean; but what is affecting or changing the entirety of the universe. Metaphysics taking in position all things in the entirety of Metaphysics "in so far as" the first principles in reality. The primary cause of principals of all things is called Wisdom.[133]

Metaphysics Being as Such[134] - Being qua Being "The most basic feature of all things is they are: being is the most universal aspect of real things. Metaphysics studies the nature of being as such, the properties that flow from it and the different modalities of being as such (potential and actual being, being in itself and being in another, etc.)"[135]

Aristotle himself described his subject matter in a variety of ways: as 'first philosophy', or 'the study of being qua being', or 'wisdom', or 'theology'. Aristotle views the metaphysics of being as: one for a study, two as a subject matter being, and three as a manner in which the subject matter is studied qua being.

Aristotle's Greek word that has been Latinized as 'qua' means roughly 'in so far as' or 'under the aspect'. Aristotle's study does not concern some recondite subject matter known as 'being qua being'. Rather it is a study of being, or better, of beings — of things that can be said to be — that studies them in a particular way: as beings, in so far as they are beings.

Professor Seidl points out in meticulously pristine Thomas Aquinas' Aristotelian canon of "being qua being":[136]

---

[133] Aristotle, Metaphysics 981 b 27.

[134] Univocal - adjective of a word or term having only one possible meaning; unambiguous; a univocal set of instructions.Analogical- Seidl, Horst History of Ancient Philosophy I Being is not univocal but analogical.

[135] Yarza, p. 142 "Hence the study of all species of Being qua Being study of the several species of Being belongs to the specific parts of that science. . . Since Being and Unity are the same as predicates are always associated with Metaphysics."
[136] Seidl, Horst, Metaphysics and Realism: Discussion on Modern Criticism of Traditional Roma: Angelicum University Press, 2008. p. 23-25.

"Being (to ovn, enß) the primary object of intellect which comprehends it as most evidently known. Thomas calls it ens commune everything whatsoever."

Initial entity of intellect is genuine qua(in so far as) being- The initial object is intellect as a substantial qua being. From the being flows the intellect to the exploration of the essence.

Intellect investigative open-minded behavior - The being is understood by the exploring using the intellect's receiving behavior by way of the intellect's process of abstraction.

Ad modum cognoscentis- " by the mode of the knowing". The intellect actively abstracts intelligible information from the being and in doing so finds the essence in the being.

1. Adaequatio intellectus et rei- "adequacy of intellect and thing" represents truth. The judgement of the intellect determines truth or non truth insofar as it represents what is knowable (remember as Professor reminds us Holzer reminds us we have never reach the full truth yet). The soul and the object come into contact there is almost a tension because there is unequalness; however, there is some likeness or purpose because the, soul and the object are attracted. This is the aspect of Aristotle 'all men desire to know." Possibly, this is the "God-Particle" that one particle that God made everything out of that scientist are looking for today.
2. Conversio ad phantasmata-The cognitive process in Intellectus de Anima, John Philoponus is the senses are used as a tool for repeated experiences becoming images in the intellect to from the intellect this would be the soul coming into understanding of the object. The essences of the objects are known by the intellect as known as conversio ad phantasmata in the process of abstraction. Plato's belief of "reminiscence" intellect from the past life of the soul is what Aristotle replaces with conversio ad phanasmata.
3. Intellect inters into the contact with the being immediately prior to all abstraction or understanding. Yes, as Democritis states everything is atoms, the smallest of atoms we do not know yet it all mixes together

with each other the atoms: accepting, changing, destroying forming.. etc. Are intellect is not cognizant of the smallest part of the being of the object prior to realizing its adaequiatio intellectus et rei. This it is why it is paramount to harvest in each season stagnet or flourishing in pursing bringing the good to others if we have hope in our faith and are wise of the contingencies of the world we can be a true vessel in Christ's light to bring about change for God's purpose.

4. Consciousness or self-consciousness is the understanding or intuitive change of awareness that the intellect is enlightened with. It is the coming to know the object or being and even itself. The intuitive act of what consciousness has, the intellect, or even the characteristics of the senses used prior to stepping into the object of desiring to understand has all a determination to grasp the being.

Haibtualem se esse the intellect has a habitual notice of its being. By experience, abstraction, and " discursive" [archaic Philosophy proceeding by argument or reasoning rather than by intuition] investigation, the intellect knows itself as its essence. I would say intellect needs to "grasp its being/ existence immediately" because it is needed to carry on to exist. Existing and coming to know objects requires the intellect to know the essence of oneself. Therefore, the intellect knows its essence, the "immaterial substance," through the process of living. This is the authentic being of our essence God created that we are all seeking to find. This is what we can say to young teenagers who do not want to study or educate themselves. Experience, attending school and being exposed to knowledge, abstracting what you learn, and discursively questioning it by argument and reasoning they will understand who they are. But as we know, abuse of social issues, technology, and drugs causes experiences without even abstracting and questioning and not even requiring imagination.(imposed experience and imagination and formulated abstraction). Logically, this impedes and blocks and even kills, the awareness of the intellects essence, steals the life of the essence, could destroy the beauty to be covering it with imposed objects.

Continuation of Metaphysics Definition:

Metaphysics Nature of Substance - Substance is the ultimate essential being. Aristotle explains his philosophy of substance by connecting contrast, integrating form and matter, and integrating potentiality and actuality. All entities are substances or are contingent on in some way on substance. Parmenides believed that there was only one concept of being that is univocal in aspect. But we know there are various ways of being the most basic, of which is to be substance. How do you know you are a substance? You are not in something. " An accident is that which is in a subject, but a substance is that which is not in a subject."[137] Substance has three principal meanings (characteristics): substrate, essence, and subsistence.[138]

Metaphysics of God - the science of things that transcend the physical world and reality. God's thoughts are not our thoughts. The Metaphysics of God is the prima and the pinnacle the alpha and omega. The Metaphysics of God is God's relationship with His people. The Metaphysics of God is our personal experience. This is what Aristotle said: " And if there is such a kind of thing in the world, here must surely be the divine, and this must be the first and the most dominant principle."[139] As we know Aristotle was placed in history at a time when he, did not experience Jesus Christ, His life, death, and resurrection and the realization of the sending of the Holy Spirit and the realization of the perspective of the understanding of the gospel and in retrospect of all the sacraments and History of all the Saints and the people of the Church. I know Aristotle would discursively question as Professor Seidl uses that

---

[137] De Spirit. Creation., a. 11

[138] Refer to Terms: Principal Meanings Substrate-(subiectum, hpokeimenon) The subject, matter , for or composite. Essence-(quidditas, ousia detuera) The essence is that which makes the thing to be what it is. Composed of the matter not the flesh and bones but includes the flesh and bones. The essence is the subject of being, through which it is in potency for the act of being through it and in it that which it ahs being.2 A substance is " that which has a quiddity [essence] to which it belongs to exist not in another [subject]. Subsistence (hypostasis)- it exist in it itself per se and for itself and not in another.

[139] Aristotle, Metaphysics, I, 1 981 b 27.

salient word. Indeed, I know that Aristotle would deduct logically and divinely. Because Aristotle's intellect comprehended the difference between the "science different from physics and mathematics" and the metaphysics of God Divine, he pointed it out himself. Now I can see, as an elementary student, why San Tommaso D'Aquino lifted Aristotle up as a believer as Torrell formally avers, averrer, [declare or confirm to be true] us in his Book that we discussed earlier.

Metaphysics is the universal desire for knowledge.

"All men naturally desire knowledge."[140]

In Metaphysics A.1, Aristotle says that "all men suppose what is called wisdom (sophia) to deal with the first causes (aitia) and the principles (archai) of things" (981b28), and it is these causes and principles that he proposes to study in this work. Since God created humans to have dominion over creation, humans would have the natural desire for knowledge of what is given one seeks to understand it. The theory of universal science, as sketched by Plato in the Republic, was unsatisfactory to Aristotle's analytical mind. Aristotle believed that there was a regular system of sciences, each concerned with different aspects of reality. Aristotle tells us their is a supreme science which is more ultimate, more exact, more truly wisdom than any of the others. The discussion of this science wisdom, primary philosophy or Theology, as it is variously called, and of its scope, forms the subject of Metaphysics.

Professor Seidl explicitly teaches us: in all cases, Aristotle was looking for reasons. He wanted to find out what things are or what is going on at the roots of things (definition) so that he may then explain the effects by an appeal to these reasons (demonstration).[141]

---

[140] Aristotle, Metaphysics Books I-X Translated by Tredennick Hugh, Loeb Classical Library, Harvard University Press Cambridge Massachusetts London England, 1933. 980 a 22.

[141] Seidl, Horst History of Ancient Philosophy, Lectures. The peculiar principle that Aristotle invoked to explain living phenomena may be called 'soul', translating his word psyche. His teaching on this topic is found in his work On the Soul where he shows that things are either 'with soul' or 'without soul'.

"Sight is the most esteemed of all the senses."[142]

Aristotle's first statement in The Metaphysics Book 1, all men naturally desire knowledge, is characteristic of Aristotle as the master philosopher who breathes and lives and appreciates others who desire knowledge and also sees with a genus pristine eye of wisdom. When humans are desiring knowledge, sight of all the senses is the most "esteem". Sight, the most powerful of the human senses, guides us to know things. In Aristotle's Intellect de anima he tells us that we build our intellect, or our knowledge, of (with) repeated imprints that are stimulated by our senses. Our sight would give the photographic images and imprints in our mind, which emerge as sight most salient. Reading, observing, and seeing the characteristics of sight, the most "esteem" of the senses, works hand in hand with all the other senses. When you hear something, you seek to see what it looks like. When you taste something, you want to know what it is and see it. When you touch something, you see it. When you smell something you see it or want to know where the smell is coming from. These processes are also from the memory of sight integrated with all the senses.

"Animals are by nature born with the power of sensation."[143]

As we know Aristotle while working for King Philip as a tutor for his son Alexander the Great, and he and his specialized assistants studied and investigated biology and classified a vast number of species of animals and plants. This "desire for knowledge" that Aristotle had as a biologist seemed to manifested into his deduction that different animals have different magnitudes of intelligence. Some animals have the capability for learning; others do not. Animals that have the ability to learn need to have the sense of auditory and also the faculty of memory. Though it is rare, however, with extreme stimulating and healthy human contact and proper training and environment and having an above intelligent animal one can see glimpses of exceptional learning and reasoning.

---

[142] Aristotle Metaphysics Book I 980 a 23,24
[143] Aristotle's Metaphysics, 980 b 22

"Animals are by nature born with the power of sensation."[144]

Aristotle's intense investigation of the differences and similarities of animals and the human race made it clear for him to understand each more comprehensively. Some animals live by impressions and memories, having an infinitesimal or small related experience. Humans live by the art of reasoning. Repeated multitudinous experiences of the corresponding entity generate art and science. As we know, this is how the human develops intellect potentiality. Intellect actuality is from the repeated experiences the senses have, and then the senses form imprints into the mind developing intellect. Intellect, being art and science. Inexperience produces change. Universal judgement accepted from numerous notions of experiences is considered art. Identifying same commonalities of symptoms for a group of people having the same disease is judgement considered arts.

"Three types of men: Master craftsmen, Artisan, and Experience."[145]

There are three types of men: first, the artist that knows the causes of things; second, the man of experience has knowledge of particulars; thirdly, the master craftsmen withhold the understanding of the art of universals actions and effects carried out are the experiences and know the reasons why entities are executed and fulfilled. Aristotle then ranks these there types of men: the master craftsmen being the pinnacle in wisdom because they withhold in their intellect the theory and understand the causes. The artisans are superior to men with experience because of their knowledge of the cause of the world's processes and proficiency. The master craftsmen know the theory, and universal judgement. For example, to identify a disease in humans there has to be recognition and agreed universal judgement. The master craftsman understands how to treat the disease: identifying the universal, theorizing the treatment, knowing the cause in order to target the cause to stop the disease.

---

[144] Ibid., 980 b 28
[145] Aristotle, Metaphysics., 981 a 27.

"One who has Knowledge has the ability to teach."[146]

TWOT Theological Wordbook of the Old Testament

In the first three chapters of Gen there is a wordplay on man, mankind, and the first man "Adam." אָדָם connotes man in the image of God as to: soul or spirit (indicating man's essential simplicity, spirituality, invisibility, immortality), physical powers or faculties (the intellect and will with their functions), intellectual and moral integrity (true knowledge, righteousness, and holiness), body (as a fit organ of the soul sharing its immortality, and as the means through which man exercises his dominion), and dominion over the lower creation.[147]

In order for one to teach they have to possess knowledge of the subject. Aristotle considers scientific knowledge as the ability to teach as art instead of experience. Our cardinal

The provenance of our knowledge is our senses laying down the particulars, but the senses do not tell us the reason for things. Our intellect gives us our reason. Human senses are tools to take off veils in our minds to receive knowledge. didaskein (didaskein) to teach, is meant to change one's mind by having a prolonged position as a causative verb form.[148] Therefore, the teacher has to also support the subject with a moving understanding for the student. Knowledge tells us the reason for things. It is beauty forming beauty when the teacher pours out his or her intellect that is stored information and also uses objects as aides to teach others.

---

[146] Ibid., 981b 10 TWOT (manda{) knowledge. Derived from the this Aramaic noun develops the noun by dissimilation from the form This noun was later used as the equivalent of the Greek The Aramaic Gnostics were called Mandaeans. Hebrew strongs: ; wisdom or intelligence:—knowledge, reason, understanding. When one has understanding they are able to teach another.

[148] Greek Strongs, didaska Prolonged position as a causative form of a verb is an ongoing action making a cause a reason for the action. It is also a time period of prolonged action. To teach is to have an action prolong: the teacher has the information transposes it to the student and then the student holds or accepts the information.

Teaching is creating the ongoing life of ancient, present, and the catalyst of the futuristic enlightened human history of knowledge.

"Wisdom is concerned with the primary causes and principles."[149]

During the natural inquiry of the earliest philosophers, secrets of life became unveiled to illumination: inventors of arts and science developed throughout antiquity. Inventors were thought to be superior, wise men. Those inventors who discovered mathematical sciences were men of leisure of the priestly class. Wisdom is the primary cause and principle. Wisdom is knowledge of certain principles and causes. "Man of experience is held to be wiser than the mere possessors of any power of sensation, the artist the man of experience, the master craftsman than the artisan; and the speculative sciences to be more learned than the productive."[150] It is paramount to recognize the different levels of wisdom between each. They also realize that one may develop into one or the other, such as an artisan becoming a master craftsman and a man of experience becoming an artisan. The wise man must have universal knowledge of complex entities, which are highly complicated for standard human cognizance.

Humans have a mainspring or the realization of the origin of understanding and fundamental principles which is the specialty of knowledge and even future 'intellectual actuality'. If men of the highest knowledge or the master craftsman utilizes the other man's knowledge of experience, and the man as the artisan for there selfish motive, this is not truth. Furthermore, in manipulating the artisan and man of experience this form of development will impede the natural knowledge and formation to manifest. Not only will this manipulation obstruct the flow of human knowledge but it will eventually cripple the master craftsman if he does not work for justice in love. Man of experience and or man of art should have the opportunity to have fecundity of their knowledge into the knowledge of a master craftsman this will make them a wiser master

---

[149] Ibid, 981b 30-31
[150] Aristotle Metaphysics, 982 b a 30-33

craftsman. Also, especially in these times of information rapidly changing in technological systems, it is vast and influential and needs to be scrutinized and observed to find and prove the truth, as Christians, God's truth. For example, when does an embryo or fetus become human? How do we help stop poverty and social problems?

"Wisest man has universal knowledge with precise understanding."[151]

The wisest of men has universal knowledge of the magnitude of elucidating the causes in a precise and elaborate method. Aristotle tells us again that the sciences are used for a desirable purpose in itself, for knowledge's sake, not for results.[152] However, today, in modernity, we use science for results of world issues, universal knowledge, and directed missions depending on the purpose. For example, to investigate nuclear science and understand the concepts, we need to ask ourselves how we are using them. Some countries are using it and want to use it for warfare to take power over other nations. I have a nephew who is a student of nuclear science.

He is part of a country and team seeking an innovative paradigm as a scientific mission to help humanity conserve energy for a better and more efficient world, saving our precious resources.

" Wise man should give directions, and others should implement his directions, not the inverse." "Wise men seek after justice."[153]

"The wise man should give orders and not receive them; nor should he obey others, but the less wise should obey him."[154] This argument is valid if the wise man is the most righteous and seeks justice, peace, and truth. For Aristotle, we know that the wisest man seeks justice, for Plato's soul should be judged with justice. Socrates tells us we should seek after the truth. The wisest men should contemplate all areas of suggestions,

---

[151] Ibid., 982 a 6-7.

[152] Ibid., 982 a 33-34.
[153] Ibid., 982 a 19-20.

[154] Ibid., 982 a 19-20.

seeking and proving the truth. Because, with the experienced and artesian men, new causes and principles may be developed. For example, new scientific paradigms may seem more practical and emerge since everything changes. For instance, I talked with a scientist who works on NASA projects and government contracts. The scientist said, " The chief scientist needs to listen to our ideas. They are outdated. What they are proposing to NASA for contracts is not important. We as scientists can see and know a better plan to help humanity in this era." During Aristotle's time, few could read and write. Seemingly, there may be a crossing over of experience and or the artesian scientist into the master craftsman scientist of superior knowledge because of the vast information systems available at the speed of light. Chief scientists and policymakers must be allowed to prove their new and effective paradigms.

"Wisdom has a myriad of opinions."[155]

Wisdom also has numerous opinions withheld for the wise. The supreme quality of wisdom is needed for men to grasp the particulars of the universe, which has a degree that is polar opposite to that of the senses. The 'first principle' is based on fewer principles and is more exact than aspects of knowledge with various principles. Aspects of the 'first principles' are sciences instructing us and telling us the causes. In addition, knowledge for their own sake is a science of the first principle. The 'first principle' is "through [the first principle] other things come to be known."[156] The science of the 'first principle' that is the pinnacle of all sciences is the one that knows what the end is for 'the highest Good of the whole of nature."[157] Apostle Paul, the man who sought knowledge, tells us in the Sacred Holy Scriptures that all things work together for good for those who love God (Romans 8:28). What we do has a stream effect on

---

[155] Aristotle, Metaphysics I, 982 20-21

[156] Ibid 982 b 1-4

[157] Ibid, 982 b 6-8

everything. Everything works together in nature. Things in nature all depend on or affect each other.

"Wisdom is the knowledge of the first principle."[158]

"Wisdom is the knowledge of the first principle."[159] This is a speculative science because it involves entering the unknown, the metaphysical, and the Divine. Aristotle tells us that man should seek only the knowledge that is in front of him. For me, this excludes faithfulness in a way.

Faithfulness is things not seen or given yet but hope for. Even Aristotle did not realize the aspects of his genius had more things beyond his present reach. God marks time and pours out wisdom to His humanity at His time. Wisdom in the reflection of human scintillating light is the being of humans coming to the Divine. The wonderment of the philosophers is the innate desire for all humans to seek after God, which is what they are trying to find in their investigation of life. This wonderment is connected with faith and hoping that something will come. For Plato, in Phaedo, it is reminiscent of our past soul, where our wonderment comes from, and wisdom. In Hebrews 11:1,3, "Only faith can guarantee the blessings that we hope for, or prove the existence of unseen realities. . . It is by faith that we understand that the ages were created by a word from God so that from the invisible the visible [from all that is seen and unseen visibílium ómnium et invisibílium]world came to be[and continuously come to be]."

"The Divine Science of God is the most quintessential."[160]

Science of the divine is a science of possession of God and is concerned with sacred matters. The holy science has a two-winged chariot, fulfilling these conditions: all believe God is one of the causes and a principle, and God is the sole or King possessor of this knowledge. This is evident if there were different chief or sole possessors of the knowledge of the

---

[158] Ibid, 982 b 11-13

[159] Ibid., 982 b 9-10
[160] Aristotle Metaphysic, 983 a 34 1-11

universals. Possibly, there would be other views, with various apparent unpredictable changes happening in humans and nature completely controlling humanity and nature itself. The Divine science of God is the pinnacle of omniscience. What is the closest to the reflection of the Divine is the most purely precious. Jesus tells us to come as little children.

"Modern civilization itself often complicates the approach to God not for any essential reason but because it is so heavily engrossed in earthly affairs."[161] Jesus wants us to spend time with Him, Mary, and the Saints. They yearn for our love. Jesus tells us to come as little children. This means spending time with Him in all aspects of our lives and putting Him first.

" When investigating, we seek to find the contrary to what we know."[162]

The whole investigation that we are seeking is contrary to what we know.

At first, I think we have something to connect with from the previous understanding. Then, we take our present thought as a catalyst, a touch of illumination of wisdom and wonderment of faith, and receive that second thought of the new paradigm supreme: "Second thoughts are better."[163] The investigation is traveling into the unknown thoughts that have never been a reality, but in the investigation, reality enters into the second thoughts. As we know, seeking to find knowledge and the wisdom of God, we do not always have it at hand in our vision and understanding of our mind. Our thoughts are not God's thoughts. Aristotle tells us in Intellectus de Anima we need intellectual potentiality to be stimulated by the actions

---

[161] Vatican II Council 1962-1965(English) Libreria Editrice Vatican, City Used by permission of Amministrazione del Patrimony Della Seed Apostolic, Vatican City, Electronic text huyhertexteed and prepared by OakTree Software, Inc. Version 1.1.Vatican II Gaudier et Spes Part 1 Chapter 1 Jesus wants us to spend time with Him and Mary and the Saints. They yearn for our love. Jesus tells us to come as little children this means spend time with Him in all aspects of our life; putting Him first.

[162] Ibid., 983 a 12-15

[163] Ibid., 983a 17-20

of our senses. As stated above, we know that repeated imprints form our intellect, and our senses stimulate our mind. Then, we also have intellect actuality as part of our intellect itself. Plato believes that our soul at birth carries all knowledge and wisdom. It just has to be recollected, or reminiscence needs to occur.

" Ancient Masters of Philosophy investigates to find Truth." [164]

Aristotle tells us that the ancient masters of philosophy investigated the Truth, stepping into reality. The philosophers before us 'Truth "will assist our present inquiry[of course] if we study their teachings."[165] This point is paramount for receiving new Truths. With flowing wisdom, we can come into those second thoughts of the unknown that become known. We use what we have learned in all sciences, and when we understand the most significant point(at a particular time) and are aware of the paradigm of the primary causes of something, we claim to know each entity. These are the causes that are paramount to understanding a specific entity. Furthermore, throughout modernity, we have tools or technology that develop. Our old paradigms become obsolete, and new paradigms become new "Truths." (altho) defined in antiquity as doing truth and speaking the truth. "Truth" is such a vast subject we cannot talk about it in this subject matter. Realizing no one, not one human, comes into the whole truth. The truth of the metaphysical sciences of Productive, Practical, and Theoretical truth differs from the Metaphysical science of God. But we know the absolute "Truth," and finding all "Truth" only comes from the Father's hands in Jesus Christ. Father Dr. Dean Holzer and the Pontifical of San Tommaso D' Aquino proclaim the Truth "The Power of Truth" is essentially trusting in that "Power of God." We trust in God in prayer, worship, and faithfulness daily. Yes, God created us. He wants us to trust "The Power of Truth" and His love.[166] Yes, our God is the Most High Patrem

---

164Aristotle, Metaphysics, 983 b 36-39

165 Ibid., 983 b 1

166 Holzer, Phillipe Andre Dean Fr.Dr.O.P. You tube..Pontificia San Tommaso D'Aquino Rome Italy

Altíssimus. Yes, our God is the Father, the Almighty, Patrem omnipoténtem.

"Aristotle's four causes."[167]

Formal Cause- Essence- Essential nature of the thing (since the "reason why" is a cause and principle of the substance) Structure- exterior the form or the shape of something. It is what dictates its essence to be what it is. For example, the shape of David by Michaelangelo

Material Cause-Matter or Substrate - that of which entity is created. It is the intrinsic constitutive element of something—for instance, the marble of Michelangelo's David.

Efficient Cause -Source of Motion source of change. Michelangelo is the efficient cause; he is the being that changes the sculpture of David.

Final Cause—Final End for Good. The end is an excellent final architectural end. It is the purpose of good for every generative or motive process. It is the perfection of the being (in the case of the statue, this is the purpose for which it was made).[168]

The four causes, or four senses of causes, will be Wisdom's architectonic [end].

"Ancient Master Philosopher's First Principle."[169]

God is so transcendent. To know God is impossible to comprehend Him and to understand the things He created is the investigation of the 'first principle.' The ancient master philosophers "conceived only of material principle or substrate as underlying all things."[170] They also believed

---

[167] Aristotle, Metaphysics , 983 a 24- 39 Note: due to the vast scope of this subject I was just able to mention these salient concepts briefly. I did a report on substance with Father Bagood if you would like me to refer you to this subject I would be happy to.

[168] Aristotle, Metaphysics 983 a 24- 30; Seidl Lectures History of Ancient Philosophy 2011

[169] Ibid., 983 b 1-3

[170] Ibid., 983b 7-9 Also, we realize not until Galileo was science tested in the laboratory results. I spoke to a fresh new scientist coming out of Cal Tech consider the best school

nothing is generated or destroyed because this genus of primary entity continually endures. Aristotle tells us the philosophers believed that there "is someone entity (or more than one) which always persists and from which all other things are generated."[171] Aristotle tells us that we do not agree with the number or type of the first principle. Thales believes water is the first principle. Other ancient philosophers also thought water was the first principle because everything in nature was moist. The seeds of everything have a moist nature. Next, Anaximenes and Diogenes believed air "of all corporeal elements most truly the first principle." Hippasus of Metapontum and Heraclitus of Ephesus sought to feel that fire is the 'first principle.' Empedocles included earth as with all the other three: 1. water. 2. air 3. fire.

4. Earth. The four elements combine in unity or differentiation. Anaxagoras of Clazomenae believed the first principles were infinite in number. They are neither generated nor destroyed; they persist eternally.

"Philosophers realized there was more than just a Material Cause."[172]

Remember, all men, by nature, seek wisdom. God gives secrets to humanity at His timing. Seeking to know more men, ask why this happens and the cause. There was a need for an efficient cause. It is not the substrate itself that causes the change of the wood to become a table. The source of motion was beginning to be understood, and the first thought of the first principle became another second thought. Others believed there was no change in maintaining "the substrate is one thing."

---

in the world. When I mentioned some of the philosophers and their concepts. He said we donot study those Philosophers that do not do testing their results . Possibly, this is what is has caused the scientific paradigms that we have used for industry and have destroy many of our eco-systems because we have not considered the basic ethics of "Truth".

[171] Ibid., 983 b 19-21

[172] Ibid., 983 b 19-21

" Mind in Nature the cause of all order and arrangement."[173]

Anaxagoras said there is a "Mind in nature," just as animals possess, and this is the cause of all order and arrangement. Hermotimus of Clazomenae is credited with having principles in things, which is the cause of beauty and the sort of cause by which motion is communicated of things. In nature, it shows how everything is in unison, and predictable nature has a mind. Anaxagoras believed that the mind is likened to animals in nature's heart. The cause of beauty to beauty is the motion of communication of nature.[174]

Brief comments on San Tommaso D'Aquino

Commentators' opinions about San Tommaso's position on Aristotle: "the notion of scientia to theology."

First groups: San Tommaso's view was reserved, and he rarely disagreed with Aristotle.

Second group: Believes that San Tommaso is poignantly arguing with his personal opinion.

Third groups: The intermediary position San Tommaso was dedicated to Aristotle with a trueheartedness.

Also, Torrell finds that, in general, San Tommaso's commentary on the "Metaphysics is oriented toward a metaphysics of being, which would have been entirely foreign to Aristotle." San Tommaso found the Christian aspects in Aristotle's work and lifted him to the Lord in the beauty of Aristotle's divine work.[175]

---

[173] Aristotle Metaphysics, 984 b 15-18 Footnote: f-Hermotimus of Clazomenae is a semi-mythical person supposed to have been a pre incarnation of Pythagoras.
[174] Aristotle, Metaphysics 984 b 15-23

[175] Torrell, Jean-Pierre, O.P. Saint Thomas Aquinas, Volume 1 The Person and His Work: Translated by Robert Royal. Revised Edition. The Catholic University of American Press, Washington, D.C.1993. p. 236-238 This subject vast we are only able to give a generalization. I am a beginning student on St. Thomas. However, I would agree that San

San Tommaso Aquino illuminates what "incites man to do the good" in Romans 8:2: "The law of the Spirit, who gives life in Jesus Christ." Likened to Aristotle's philosophy, the community's paramount endeavor is to live as the best, most righteous, wise, and just citizens:

> "The Holy Spirit, Himself, who abides in the soul, not only teaches what it is necessary to do by illuminating intelligence but also inclines the affections toward acting rightly. In the second sense, this law can be understood as the proper effect of the Holy Spirit, saying that the faith first operates through charity. It, too, teaches interiorly what it is necessary to do according to the verse from 1 John 2: "His unction teaches you all things, but it also spurs the will toward action. . . The new law . .. is identified with the Holy Spirit . . . carries it out within us... Spirit is given only to those who are in Jesus Christ. . . The Holy Spirit does not come to members not linked to their chief, Christ."[176]

The Lord promises He will teach us what we should know and is watching us with His eyes. Furthermore, we have the spiritual gifts the Lord freely gives us, namely the illuminating intelligence San Tommaso speaks of. Using these spiritual gifts in justice and God's purpose in His precepts, we allow others to live freely, and then they will wonder and ask why. Then, they will see peace conquering poverty, the power to overcome weakness, the love to leave hatred, the joy to heal sadness, the justice to champion injustice, courage in fear, and life over death.

Saint Thomas Aquinas approaches his commentaries on Scripture:

Tommaso lifts up Aristotle in a redeeming way. San Tommaso relates Christianity to Aristotle's concepts in a creative and philosophical supporting His ideas.

[176] Torrell p.257 As believers in Christ this is where we receive our wisdom in the Holy Spirit. This is being in right relationship with Christ. In the Holy Spirit we find true authentic being. If you abide in Me(Christ) I will abide in You and anything you ask it will be given. When one is abiding in Christ one does the will of Christ and they will desire the knowledge of Christ.

Emphasizing: Causa Thomas Aquinas, the Master craftsman, understands the cause.

Matter-Material universal " Above all concerning the work of salvation carried out by Christ."

Form- Modus "The mode of the sacred Scripture is in effect multiple." Living waters. "The soliloquy is the personal colloquy of man with God or, indeed, only with himself; and this is necessary for whoever praises or prays."[177]

End- Finis " The elevation of the soul, toward God..." 1. Faith. 2 Hope. 3. Charity.4. Justice.

Agent- Agnes: " The author of this work is God Himself since the sacred Scriptures are not the fruit of a human will but indeed of divine inspiration.[178]

Conclusions:[179]

The Prime Mover:

For Aristotle, the Stagerite,[Word from an Encyclopedia] of the ancient history of humanity before Christ 384- 322, the Prime Mover is 'Whom all understand to be God.' If we as humans could come closer to understanding the Prime Mover, we could come closer to helping humanity and recognizing that pure essence, substance, and creation that the Creator has made. The four causes will be pure. The causes of the matter. Is this what we need to consider as to how our human actions

---

[177] Ibid, p. 260 dictionary soliloquy noun (pl.-quies) an act of speaking one's thoughts aloud when by oneself or regardless of any hearers, esp. by a character in a play. A part of a play involving such an act. Colloquy noun (pl.-quies) formal a conversation: they broke off their colloquy at once | an evening of sophisticated colloquy. See note at conversation . a gathering for discussion of theological questions. ORIGIN late Middle English: from Latin colloquium 'conversation.'

[178] Torrell p. 259-260

[179] Professor Seidl, Due to my elementary level of understanding. My conclusion will only be a microscopic particle review.

stimulate the causes forming the substance in its changes? If we are made in the same species, with the same elements and exact likeness as humans, we profoundly affect each other. Are our actions forming these changes of motions form secondary substances of each human being? We bring life, or we get death. As Christians, the Lord our God is the Prime Mover, the alpha and omega. Would not one desire to take up that innate beauty the God of that knowledge that (All men naturally desire knowledge.). Live in the fullest of truth for justice, for humanity, bringing, sustaining, and regaining beauty in the world—beauty for beauty. Beauty is made from beauty, as Plato reveals in Phaedo.

In Aristotle's Metaphysics, Mr. Hugh Tredennick writes in the introduction the view of Aristotle as the Prime Mover:

"It is from considering change and motion that Aristotle proceeds to develop his theology. The continuity of the processes in the universe presupposes a moving cause by which they are eternally maintained.

This cause, or Primer Mover, must be eternal and immutable, therefore entirely immaterial. It is a pure form and actuality, and this is Mind or God."[180]

Shama {, shaw-mah´is a primitive root to hear intelligently.

Even though sight is the most "esteemed" of all the senses, we need to take fecund action using what we see, directing it to the closest truth we know in our intelligence. Men realize that in obedience to the nature of life, they will gain knowledge, the knowledge of God.

Obedience shama{,(shaw-mah´) is a primitive root to hear intelligently.[181] Hearing

---

[180] Aristotle, Introduction p. xxix by Hugh Tredennick to Aristotle's Metaphysics In Book

[181] Hebrew Strongs (often with implication of attention, obedience, etc.; causatively, to tell, etc.):—x attentively, call (gather) together, x carefully, x certainly, consent, consider, be content, declare, x diligently, discern, give ear, (cause to, let, make to) hear(-ken, tell), x indeed, listen, make (a) noise, (be) obedient, obey, perceive, (make a) proclaim(-ation),

intelligently is then receiving knowledge. Hearing intelligently, shama{, is coming into that pure knowledge of our Lord God. As stated above, even today, scientists have thought one paradigm is the best until one is discovered to be better. For example, atmospheric pollution causes the ozone layer to have holes. Today, we as humans need to have retribution and repair the ozone layer. First, we did not choose the best way to produce industry or develop modernity in a technological society. There was a better way to do this at the onset of the industry.

But we did not oshama{, we did not hear intelligently in the most accurate knowledge. Wisdom is

given and marked by God. "The Most High rules over human sovereignty and gives it to whom he pleases." Dan. 4:29[182]

There is a natural reward that the spirit and the body feel and experience when one gains knowledge. The light of life interlocutors are people who take part in a dialogue or conversation. Taking part in the light of life and bringing wisdom and knowledge to others is intellectual actuality actively changing in the process of constant movement from beauty to beauty. This is the "True Light". As we know, Jesus Christ is the True light. He tells us to walk in the light as He walks in the light. The happiness and blessedness of others giving to others is God's beauty (}esher), the light of joy and happiness, and also the intensity light of life.[183] You know, when a starving child bites in a piece of bread and is ravishingly hungry, the smile that comes from their hungry soul upon their face sends joy and happiness. You have given love when you have given that mere piece of bread. The burning land of starvation and killing thirst is death for many. When water moistens the child, burning, parched lips and dry mouth that you have given refreshment of hope arise in the human spirit and body. Why can we

---

publish, regard, report, show (forth), (make a) sound, x surely, tell, understand, whosoever (heareth), witness.
[182] The New Jerusalem Bible, Daniel 4:29

[183] Hebrew Strongs, n.f. light (late)1. light. 2. light of joy & happiness; pl. intens.light of life
183a † (}aœshaœr) happiness, blessedness.

not use our wisdom and lay a water line upon the oil line to Africa from Switzerland? We can do it. This is the best wisdom. Let's hear intelligently and do our best. "Second thoughts are always better thoughts." Switzerland is the land of water.[184] Swiss-based Vestergaard Frandsen makes a water filter for Kenyan households for drinking water. Vestergaard has created individual water containers for each household or individual with a filter inside to clean the African water. Kenyans and African people throughout the nation need water for agriculture.[185] There is enough food for all in the world. We need to share.[186]

---

[184] www.swissworld.org

[185] Fighting Water-Borne Disease In Africa, And Making Millions In The Process BY KATAYAMA Fri Fri Apr 22, 2011www.fastcompany.comThe model isn't the perfect solution the issues plaguing water in the developing world: while not having to collect firewood to boil water helps preserve safety and time of the women and children who typically bear the burden of these tasks, they still have to make trips to the water source. And carbon trade is inherently controversial, and as of now no plans have been announced for what happens to carbon offsets after the Kyoto agreement expires in 2012.the company's LifeStraw water filters to 900,000 households in Western Province--nearly 90% of the entire population--providing 4 million people with clean, safe drinking water. The filters will be provided to the end users for free, and company founder and CEO Mikkel Vestergaard Frandsen has invested $30 million of his own money into the project. Over the next five weeks, 4,000 temporary employees will distribute the company's Life Straw water filters to 900,000 households in Western Province--nearly 90% of the entire population--providing 4 million people with clean, safe drinking water. The filters will be provided to the end users for free.

[186] Dan. 4:17 The tree you saw, so large and strong and tall that it reached the sky and could be seen throughout the world, Dan. 4:18 the tree with beautiful foliage and abundant fruit, [with food for all in it], providing shade for the wild animals, with the birds of heaven nesting in its branches: Dan. 4:19 that tree is yourself, Your Majesty, for you have grown great and strong; your stature is now so great that it reaches the sky, and your empire extends to the ends of the earth. The life of the wealthy mind, heart, and money is enough in the world "with food for all in it". Those who have more need truth in others to give. If we can be trustworthy and knowledgeable friend. ds, business partners, and working together for the help of humanity, those who have more will give. Even as Father Senner said: be debators in truth of Judeo-Christian precepts in Political issues of the world.

There is enough food for all in the world. We need to share.[187]

Daniel, the great prophet of the Old Testament, was given a gift from God to interpret dreams. Daniel interpreted King Nebuchadnezzar's dream: The tree is yourself, Your Majesty, for you have grown great and strong; your stature is now so great that it reaches the sky; and your empire extends to the ends of the earth. Your empire has enough food for the entire world. You will be taken from society and become like a beast. Not until you realize that the Most High God rules over human sovereignty and gives it to whom he pleases will your kingdom return to you and become even greater.[188] Today, as we have seen, many individuals and even groups of people have denied the precepts of Judeo-Christian values and of Jesus' works that manifest the truth of the existence of humanity. His Holiness Pope Benedetto speaks in truth:

" The denial of God corrupts man, robs him of his criteria, and leads him to violence."[189]

Retribution of Humanity toward God:[190]

King Nebuchadnezzar did have(has) retribution גּוֹרָל (gôrāl) lot, portion.

The[present tense always in the present of his life]: "Praise, extol and glorify the King of heaven, all of whose deeds are true." Also, in retribution, Nebuchadnezzar takes the advice of Daniel: "By upright actions, break with your sins, break with your crimes by showing mercy

---

¹⁸⁷ NJB Daniel 4:9

¹⁸⁸ NJB Daniel 4

¹⁸⁹ Day of Reflection, Dialogue and Prayer For Peace and Justice in the World "Pilgrims of Truth, Pilgrims of Peace." Address of His Holiness Benedict XVI at the Meeting for Peace in Assisi Assi, Basilica of Sain Mary of the Angels Thursday, 27 October 2011. www.vatican.va/holy_father/benedict_xvi/speeches/2011/october/documents

¹⁹⁰ BDB גּוֹרָל (gôrāl) lot, portion. = recompence, retribution, both implying divine agency. Faith is a vast subject and most salient in accepting the knowledge and wisdom go God and even the knowledge that the Lord allows you to have as an individual.

to the poor, and so live long and peacefully."[191] In retribution, one steps into faith. This faith reflects the sovereignty of the Most High, realizing one will be forgiven if one gives retribution. Nebuchadnezzar learned the power of God. King Nebuchadnezzar acknowledged that the "Most High is sovereign," and he now desired to be "best and wisest and most righteous." Being that "best, wisest, and most righteous" means giving oneself, by upright actions, as being a created being of love: "love the foremost of all immortal beings." Yes, as we realize in faithfulness as believers as Christians

being an immortal being is only from the breath[192] רוּחַ (rûaḥ), of God at creation is His love to us.

Retribution of the Eco-System

There are various extremely detrimental issues existing in our eco-system today. One example, today scientist are seeking to repair and sustain the ozone layer because the human consumption of energy has gone beyond the resources. Nasa : The NPOESS Preparatory Project (NPP) represents a critical first step in building the next-generation Earth-observing satellite system that will collect data on both long-term climate change and short-term weather conditions.NPP will extend and improve upon the Earth system data records established by NASA's Earth Observing System (EOS) fleet of satellites that have provided critical insights into the dynamics of the entire Earth system: clouds, oceans, vegetation, ice, solid Earth and atmosphere.The mission is scheduled to launch on Oct. 28, 2011 at 2:48 a.m. PDT/ 5:48 a.m.

---

191 NJB Daniel 4: 24,34

192 רוח (rāwaḥ), רוח A, q. become wide or spacious; pu. be spacious (HALAT 1116; H8118); der. nom. רוח (rewaḥ), space, liberation (only in Gen 32:16 [17]; Esth 4:14; H8119); רוח (rûaḥ), air, breath, temper, spirit, Spirit (H8120)

EDT, from Vandenberg Air Force Base in California. NASA's Goddard Space Flight Center, Greenbelt, Md., is managing NPP for the Earth Science Division in NASA's Science Mission Directorate, Washington.[193]

Lord's Prayer is the essence to all Wisdom

ARTICLE 1: "THE SUMMARY OF THE WHOLE GOSPEL"

2761 The Lord's Prayer "is truly the summary of the whole gospel."7 "Since the Lord . . . after handing over the practice of prayer, said elsewhere, 'Ask and you will receive,' and since everyone has petitions which are peculiar to his circumstances, the regular and appropriate prayer [the Lord's Prayer] is said first, as the foundation of further desires."[194]

When we "hallowed" the name of God we are honoring Him as "Most High God".

We ask ourselves were do we get our true wisdom as humans? From the one who created us. From what we came from? We as believers seek in unity in our Lord we come to know wisdom, wisdom not of this world but the wisdom of Christian precepts: love, faith, justice, truth, mercy, hope, faith, and beauty. Beauty of not only to sustain us in the imperfections and but to heal us from our sins of our humanity by the the cross of Christ by the resurrected Lord.

Kneeling: Together for the Church: In the Father, In the Son, In the Holy Spirit

Humbling oneself is coming into the Spirit of the Lord; Humbling oneself kneeling in the Church.. all in unison. First, next, last or all together in unity. The energy of movement, energy of the soul, movement of the soul mixed in the infiniteness of God and the unity of each individual believer together in the Church of our Lord Jesus Christ. The sound I heard in the

---

[193] http://www.nasa.gov/topics/earth/features/ozone-2011.html

[194] C. CathecismPART FOUR: CHRISTIAN PRAYER SECTION TWO: THE LORD'S PRAYER "OUR FATHER!" ARTICLE 1: "THE SUMMARY OF THE WHOLE GOSPEL" II. THE LORD'S PRAYER. Hallowing the Lord's name is showing respect and loving the Lord with all your heart and soul and mind; then everything in your life shall follow, follow in right relationship and ongoing sanctification in Him.

Church when all bowed down the sound was like rolling pure wind for all going together to show reverence. This is like wisdom when one believes and carries out the actions then another follows, then another follows, then another. Realizing announced by the holy ones— so that every living thing may learn that the Highest rules over human sovereignty.

The tree of our Catholic Church of God in Christ be so large and strong and tall that it reaches the sky and could be seen throughout the world and this begins with each one of us believers.

We have all we need in Gratia Domini nostri Jesu Christi, et caritas omnipotentis Dei , et communicato Sancti Spiritus, (The grace our Lord Jesus Christ, and the love of omnipotent God and the fellowship of the Holy Spirit. His love and the ruah, life- power of the mystery of the Trinity,[195] and life eternal - from the resurrected Lord.

Jesus Christ our Omniscient Lord promises us: I myself shall give you a wisdom in speaking that all your adversaries will be powerless to resist or refute. Luke 21:15

Retribution for the modern world and the drug and other problems of post modernity How Wisdom should be used Pope Benedicto

Most Holiness Pope Benedetto:

"Yet I do not intend to speak further here about state-imposed atheism, but rather about the decline of man, which is accompanied by a change in the spiritual climate that occurs imperceptibly and hence is all the more dangerous. The worship of mammon, possessions and power is proving to be a counter-religion, in which it is no longer man who counts but only personal advantage. The desire for happiness degenerates, for example, into an unbridled, inhuman craving, such as appears in the different forms of drug dependency. There are the powerful who trade in drugs and then

---

[195] Trinity- Father, Son, Holy Spirit is subject that is vast and this is not the scope of our subject.

the many who are seduced and destroyed by them, physically and spiritually." [196]

Father's and Mother's Child:

I search constantly in the memory of my heart to find where did I go wrong. What did I do and not do. My soul sinks in God's delivering hands of soothing sweet hope…. This child is in a blinded dark way. I have fought moment after moment, minute after minute, hour after hour, day after day, week after week, month after month, year after year…I fight to try to hold on … my child was stolen and snatch ….

Oh my child caught on the dark deceiving rope strangling my child's life and my love for my child…

Oh each day running chasing pleading promising… pointing to hope …. Pushing pulling up this dark path. … Only my child's breath pants through … only the thin smile peeks through … only the sweetness peeks through…. Oh bring back my child,

Oh bring my child back to existence of the brilliant authentic being you created. Oh bring back for the beauty of your plan…

Yes, oh Yes, I never forget the promises of the ancient living covenant of your love knowing there will be a miracle of only strength in God's light.

The savages of the world snakes that crawl and strangle the beauty of innocence and pure life….

But death will come upon these deceiving demons digging their own holes in destruction forever the darkness of death they will remain…

I will call upon the forever Spirit upon the cross to soothe my faith… because my joy abounds because my faith proceeds all that I hope… holding on to the ancient promises of love…

---

[196] Day of Reflection, Dialogue and Prayer For Peace and Justice in the World "Pilgrims of Truth, Pilgrims of Peace." Address of His Holiness Benedict XVI at the Meeting for Peace in Assisi Assi, Basilica of Sain Mary of the Angels Thursday, 27 October 2011. www.vatican.va/holy_father/benedict_xvi/speeches/2011/october/documents

This was an innocent child not an adult that came to be stolen and snatched and deceived dragged by the neck strangling from life's darkness

Oh my child was young and did not know better… Yes, God always creates and sustains the beauty of the breath of the innocent… .Yes, only the joy of love and fighting for truth and holding the weak and choosing the right… and speaking for peace… and working for pure life… and caring for the hurting.. and hoping for the miracle… and never giving up…and living in miracle.

One of the security man, a warrior of God, protecting the Pope Benedicto, I see him many times he is a towering light of powerful heart of our Lord watching from overhead as protecting our smiling Pope Benedicto because our most Holy Blessed Pope is bringing the Truth and Life and Love in Peace of God to the hungry mouths and souls to the "children "of the world": Hungry for peace, seeking for justice, thirsty for life, yearning for love.

"Finally I would like to assure you that the Catholic Church will not let up in her fight against violence, in her commitment for peace in the world. We are animated by the common desire to be "pilgrims of truth , pilgrims of peace."[197]

------

[197] Day of Reflection. His Holiness Benedict XVI.

CHAPTER FOURTEEN

Dr. Professor Karl Jaspers

Brief understanding of Justice

"Politics must be for striving for justice the preconditions of peace."[198]

Pope Benedicto XVI recent writings used the words "authentic freedom!"[199] This is the freedom of each individual as a human being living their authentic self. This "authentic freedom" is justice for all human beings. Throughout Dr. Karl Jaspers' oeuvre illuminates the "authentic freedom" for each individual among the world. In freedom there is justice. Dr. Karl Jaspers sentient and brilliant mind help recreate a free and democratic Germany. In Jaspers revolutionary book , "The Question of German Guilt", opens a redeeming path for those Germans who want to protest against Hitler's Third Reicht atrocity of the Holocaust. Dr. Jaspers believes individually and universally justice can be brought when one takes a deep consciousness and faces the "metaphysical guilt" taking responsibility.[200] Then in his later works he finds justice in communication

---

[198] Benedict XVI Pope His Holiness, Listening Heart, Reflections on the Foundations of Law, Reichstag Building, Berlin Thursday, 22 September 2011

[199] Benedict XVI Most Holy Pope, Writings Vatican Website 2012

[200] Jaspers, Karl Dr, The Question of German Guilt Originally published as Die Schuldfrage in 1947. Translated by Ashton, E.B. 1965 Piper Verlag GmBH, Munchen, Germany Translation 1948 by The Double Broadway Publishing Group, a Division of Random House, Inc. All rights reserved. Int 2011 by Forham University Press. On the whole. . . Germans have come into the greats distress among the nations[Universally] -- Also bear the greatest responsibility for the course of events until 1945. p. 89

revealed in"Way to Wisdom: An Introduction to Philosophy". As a physician, psychiatrist, and philosopher, Dr. Karl Jaspers later works magnificently transform heralding freedom and justice as the "world, democracy, peace and justice world order."[201] Dr. Jaspers' political view, opposed vehemently, the totalitarian Nazi Germany regime. He championed a form of governance that guaranteed individual freedom and limited government yet was rooted in authentic tradition and guided by an intellectual elite.[202] Most Holiness Pope Benedict XVI and Prof. Dr. Jurgen Habermas in "Dialectic of Secularization" brings to illumination with urgency for the world for humanity, "reason" and "authentic tradition [religious moral precepts]" is paramount for the present and future governments to possess the "individual freedom in the world" of the principles of justice.

Dr. Karl Theodor Jaspers is a German born in Oldenburg (1883-1969). Throughout Jaspers oeuvre he embosses brilliantly an ongoing development of the meaning of justice to the atrocities of the killing of the Jews during World War II of Hitler's Nazi Germany. Hitler was given the Fuhrerprinzip ("leader principal"), by the German state which gave him all encompassing power, considering Hitler's word above all laws.[203] During the Great Depression, which destroyed the German's lives, the greatest fear struck all individuals. The Germans voted for Hitler in conjecturing that he could control and give them the desperate needed support. Dr. Jaspers tells us in "The Way to Wisdom" that the Germans

---

[201] Horn, Herman, Karl Jaspers 18883-1969 Published in Prospects: the quarterly review of comparative education (Paris, UNESCO: International Bureau of Education), vol. XXIII, no. 3/4, 1993, p. 721-739. ©UNESCO: International Bureau of Education, 2000, p.3

[202] Wikepdeia Karl Theodore Jaspers After the Nazi seizure of power in 1933, Jaspers was considered to have a "Jewish taint" (jüdische Versippung, in the jargon of the time) due to his Jewish wife, and was forced to retire from teaching in 1937. In 1938 he fell under a publication ban as well. Many of his long-time friends stood by him. But he and his wife were under constant threat of removal to a concentration camp until 30 March 1945, when American troops liberated Heidelberg.In 1948 Jaspers moved to the University of Basel in Switzerland.

[203] Wikipedia, Fuhrerprinzip, Nazi Germany http://en.wikipedia.org/wiki/Führerprinzip

chose fear or "nothingness" [death,void] above "being" [life,existence].[204] The fear brought silence upon the Germans impotent actions and the fear of communication was a silent yet screaming death for the history of humanity. This desperate fear and ignorance of mere needs of humanity, trusting Hitler's diabolical Third Reich, turned to the killings of there friends and neighbors and even integrated family members.

The Question of German Guilt?

Metaphysical Guilt - take responsibility

Karl Jaspers' nucleus question to find answers for justice to the "National Guilt" of the Holocaust is: "Are German people guilty?" Jaspers searches encompassing every magnitude of the substance of human guilt. Jasper identifies four chalices of guilt that must be redeemed:

Criminal guilt: those individually violating overtly the law natural and international law.

Political guilt: All citizens politically acquiescence to the Nazi regime and having to suffer for the injustices and criminal and moral acts of the regime.

Moral guilt: the personal responsibility one bears before the tribunal of ones own conscience for one's own actions done intentionally.

Metaphysical guilt: responsibility that survivors often feel toward those who suffered and died . Universally share the responsibility to protest against the Nazi government and atrocities of the Holocaust.[205]

---

[204] Jaspers, Karl, Way to Wisdom: An Introduction to Philosophy, translated by Ralph Mannheim (New Haven: Yale University Press, 1954) p. 29 It is also believed that the Germans realized that the Jews would be exterminated. However, the Jews thought differently that they would be joined together with their family's and relocate.

[205] Jaspers, The Question of Guilt, p. 9-10 The German Guilt is sometimes called the guilt of all: the hidden evil everywhere is jointly guilty of the outbreak of evil in this German place. p. 80

Dr. Karl Jaspers philosophy of justice appeals to the German's as a "metaphysical" desire to take responsibility. "But the ones who in utter impotence, outraged and despairing, were unable to prevent the crimes took another step in their metamorphosis by a growing consciousness of metaphysical guilt."[206] The question for every German is whether to go this way at the risk of all disappointments, at the risk of additional losses and of the abuse by the powerful. Jasper believes this is the only way we can save our souls from a pariah existence.[207] In ancient history Nicomachean Ethics Book V. 1134 a 18 documented as Aristotle's influenced justice as: "Proportionately equal,", as overcoming the injustice of disproportionate excess or deficiency of something beneficial or harmful. This ancient decree of Aristotle's meaning of justice yet so simply stated in a few words but yet so powerful when abused can destroy millions and kill a precious race of creation.

"Saving our souls", the German souls, for Jaspers, is the deep center of the individual inner being bringing justice. While remaining in Germany, Dr. Jaspers and his Jewish wife hid Jews from the concentration camps and extermination. This genocide brought him to an him to an intense realization that the Holocaust would affect humanity throughout the centuries. "Saving our souls," is as if he was awaiting redemption for the innocent lives. This is justice to overcome the abuse by the powerful, even if one risks oneself. Each one of us needs to act to be conscious in our daily walk in bringing justice. The atrocity of the Holocaust brought a deep deformity in world history, marking the heart of each human. This life-and-death appeal of taking "responsibility" will and has affected, (What it is to be human?) in the world. Dr. Karl Jaspers makes a life-and-death plea for all of us to work for the beauty of justice for human freedom, speak, and live in the heart and actions of the present and future generations of people. "In the end, Jaspers acknowledges that jurisdiction over metaphysical guilt lies with God alone. It is a disturbing and easily abused . . . how we may unknowingly (and sometimes knowingly) profit from the

---

[206] Jaspers, Karl, The Question of German Guilt, p. 81

[207] Ibid, p. 81

sufferings of others."[208] Dr. Karl Jaspers, in his time, foreshadower's today atrocities of oppression, threats, and fears humans to humans.

Let our daily lives be reminiscent of heartfelt happiness that we daily fought for freedom of justice.

What it is to be human? Why did German's think they were justified to fanatically created anti-semitism leading to the extermination of millions of Jews?

"Lebensunwertes Leben" Life unworthy of life

Hitler's Ethnic Cleansing:

Professor Bauzon reminds us Nazism believed they were "noble" race the Aryan master race all other races. What it is to be human for Hitler's Third Reich is obtaining development of humanity progression was only through keeping the dominance only if it retained its purity and the institute for self preservation. Nazism, believed that the Jews were the greatest threat to the Aryan race.[209]

When Propaganda arises seek for Truthfulness

"Truthfulness to genuine exoneration of the innocent and initiate the appropriate punishments, the need reparations, and eventually the full restoration of healthy living for individuals and even for nations."[210]

Jasper clearly states that there was "propaganda." Treacherous biased or misleading nature: chiefly derogatory information and even lies. Even today people accept things face value. Ryan Bomberg, brings to light, and

---

[208] Jaspers, The Question of German Guilt, p. 3

[209] Bauzon, Stephen Professor, Political Ethics Lectures, Pontifical Saint Thomas Aquinas, Rome, Italy, Fall 2011 The phrase "life unworthy of life" (in German: "Lebensunwertes Leben") Later the killing was extended to people considered 'racially impure' or 'racially inferior' according to Nazi thinking.[3]

[210] Jaspers, Jasper's steady respect for staying open to truth and for acknowledging responsibility for action and choice has is roots in the quest for an adequate philosophy of being .Joseph W. Koterski, S.J. Fordham University.

Catholic online: Obamacare has 2,700 pages of propaganda, the "gag rule" hidden with these treacherous pages are deformity of the human existence to "nothingness" and death . In Jasper judgment of justice he fervently inculcates that we need to "research which is true of cognition."[211]

It is foremost to be cognizant and aware of propaganda that possess no bases of "science nor philosophy" just void evil power of deceit.

Critical movement, didactic of a way of thinking. Critically analyzing in a rhetorical truth.

Research, intellectually and by supportive documents and information, a "true cognition."

Different science' paradigms are constantly in motion, forming new ones. The Aristotelian notion of the ten categories causes change.

Aspects of reality in new paradigms are unknown, or if someone has never entered into that experience, they do not see it as a" Great Master-craftsman."

From time to time, a translucent individual who has seen pristinely and honestly at that point in the paradigm needs to present it to the "Great Master-craftsman" or "Politician."

---

[211] i.The world. ii. the soul. iii God. Reason must be presented with the whole of reality and yet we constantly feel the hunger to think about such wholes. This point is deep into his Justice. Here Jaspers point is much like both that of Aristotle, who long before insisted that we know an object only by grasping its form or structure, and that of the long tradition of realism, which has regularly identified an object's form with transcendental truth, the fundamental intelligibility of every being as being. Ryan Bomberger: More Black Americans Calling for Obama to 'Get Out!' Obamacare Obama and the Democrats have been promising a whole lot of hope and change but, instead, have delivered higher unemployment, higher poverty rates and millions more welfare enrollees while aggressively promoting abortion in the black community," Bomberger explains. "Unemployment among Blacks was 12.7% when Obama took office. It spiked at 16.7% last August and remains at 14.4% today. Abortion, which has cultivated a culture of abandonment, occurs up to 6 times more in the black community than in the majority population. Yet, President Obama persistently promotes Planned Parenthood, the nation's largest abortion chain, which claims that 'abortion and food stamps elevate the black community'."Catholiconline By SoOutloud.com 7/16/2012 (www.sooutloud.com/)

We need to keep this in mind. Paradigms do change, and good and evil are seen in the eyes of the pristine innocence but wisely. The "Great Master" does not see and sometimes has a blindness of understanding. However, if he or she seeks many wise, just counselors, justice will prevail.

Today, we need to listen and "communicate" with each other to bring to light a clearness of truth for this time in human history. Things are lurking, using their leverage in a propaganda, luring, deceiving way. "Great Masters" need to listen with a "listening heart" to this truth.

Today, complexities have developed in all sciences that have never been recognized or occurred in human history.

Let our daily lives be reminiscent of the daily work to be a beauty. We fought for the freedom of justice.

The Way of Wisdom - communication, change of consciousness of being

Professor Bauzon reminds us that political powers control the economy and even control the Constitution. The political powers control the materialistic good, controlling the people's way of life. This is injustice. We cannot have justice without heart. If you do not have a heart, as Mencius says, using the inborn heart, we will have an unjust and even evil society. Judeo-Christian traditions also include the belief in "loving your neighbor as yourself." There will be happiness and justice. When one has a heart for others, there is justice. "Communication, but investigation and tender for examination on your part. The intellect must put the heart to work."[212] Intellect and heart, reason and faith, and moral traditions working together to bring justice define what it is to be human. What is it to be human? Bare beauties of treating humans with 1. Basic needs to exist

---

[212] Jaspers, Karl, Way to Wisdom: An Introduction to Philosophy, translated by Ralph Manheim (New Haven: Yale University Press, 1954), p. 25 " At the center of Jasper' philosophizing we find the notion of the Umgreifende. Some have translated this assignation of Jaspers as the "Comprehensive" others"; others gave found the English term, the "Encompassing," to be a more accurate rendition of the original German." Two centered is "Encompassing as Being-in-it-self and the "Encompassing which we-are." Both of these modes have their guard and animation in Existent.

and autonomous work. 2. Non-violence, physically, economically, and mentally. 3. Traditional culture and religious acceptance of the value of bringing peace and authentic, wholesome human beings and family. 4. Work in peace and productivity in the social law in the domestic community in unity and acceptance. 5. Political law in the constitution, Human Rights, and ongoing protection to bring justice. 6. The Right to Life of innocent lives. 7. Professor Bauzon teaches us that the essence of justice is social and political norms working in unity in one heart.[213]

In the science of genetics, we ask What it means to be human?:

Dr. Prof. Antonio Damasio, neuroscientist: The critical unique factor is language. Creativity. The religious and scientific impulse. Our social organization has developed to a prodigious degree. We have a record of history, moral behavior, economics, political and social institutions. We are uniquely unique in our ability to investigate the future, imagine results, and imagine photographic images in our minds. I like to think of a generator of diversity in the frontal lobe– and those initials are G-O-D.[Reflecting Dr. Dames's belief in God]

Renee Reijo Pera, embryologist: "We're uniquely human from the moment that egg and sperm fuse. A "human program" begins before the brain even begins to form."[214]

Interpreting above the scientific professionals, we see that identifying what it means to be human is based on communication of a language of

---

213 Bauzon, Stephen Professor, Political Ethics Lectures, Pontifical Saint Thomas Aquinas, Rome, Italy, Fall 2011 November 11,2011

214 Kelm, Brandon Wired Science: News for Your Neuron, Genetics Addresses Dr.Antonio Dames, University Southern California Professor of Neuroscience Director, Brain and Creativity Institute, June 2008 http:// www.wired.com/wiredscience/2008/06/what-does-it-me/;Dr. Renee Reijo Pear, Principal Investigator in Standford University. Director of the Human Embryonic Stem Cell Research and Education and a Professor of Obstetrics and Gynecology at Stanford University.

faith and religion of freedom and integration of the unity of fundamental family values and the right to life of organized social concepts.

Furthermore, these social concepts have moral, economic, political, and social truths accepted by the people. In all this, there is freedom of the individual to have an essence of being to think, and all this above is encompassed in God.

Communication is the primary aim of Philosophy. Jaspers calls such ultimate situations "boundary situations" (Grenzsituationen). These ultimate situations, such as death, suffering, guilt, wonder, and doubt, are situations that we cannot escape or alter. We may try to escape these situations in everyday life. Still, if we confront them, we become authentically aware of ourselves as human beings and become ourselves through the enlightenment in our consciousness of being.[215] Communication brings justice. Marked in history, many just counselors bring safety and life freedom to live as a flourishing human being in any situation. The quietness of "nothingness" was fear because they did not know how to begin communicating that first step, that first word, that first action stepping out of to be a revolutionary. We have leaders such as Christ, Socrates, Saint Thomas Aquinas, and St.

Augustine, Gandhi, Joan of Arc, Mother Teresa, Martin Luther King, Pope John Paul II, Ronald Reagan, and others took responsibility for bringing justice.

Jaspers argues that human freedom only comes from God. Human free choices perceived as independence from God are nothingness. If humans acknowledge that we trust in God for our being and accept responsibility [in the seeking of the will of God] for making our own free choices, then our awareness of our own freedom becomes an awareness of God.[216]

---

[215] Jaspers, Karl "Way to Wisdom": An Introduction to Philosophy, translated by Ralph Mannheim (New Haven: Yale University Press, 1954). p. 27 The term here translated as "ultimate situation" is Grenzsituation. This is a concept of central importance for the understanding ofJaspers' thought, as for the understanding of Existentialism

[216] Ibid, p. 29. Jaspers valued humanism and the continuity of integral cultural tradition in political spheres. He strongly opposed totalitarian despotism and warned about the

God was not in Hitler's Third Reich actions. There was nothingness (human freedom without God is nothingness), killing precious human beings. Jaspers' serious intent for us is to recognize a "boundary situation" (Grenzsituationen). The Germans put up boundaries. They would not go beyond their comfortable boundary or line. Also, they put up a boundary not only by the action of the hand and boundary of what was owned by them, but they put up boundaries in their hearts of "nothingness." Killing someone as their neighbor was "nothingness." According to Jaspers, we become ourselves by choosing between being and nothingness. If we decide nothingness, then we deny our authentic being. If we choose to be, we achieve authentic being and flourishing existence and permeate happiness to others, which is life.

Reason does not always consider God. Reason does not always consider the human being. Without God, there are injustices and death of the human being.

Expositions of authors - thoughts on Dr. Karl Jaspers Herman Horn -

From individual "Metaphysical Guilt" (existence and reason) to " World" (Democracy, peace, and justice)

Jaspers' initial philosophical concepts of "existence and reason" evolved into a new perspective yet integrated the political humanism of a just world: "democracy, peace, and justice." In his later works after 1957, Dr. Jaspers conceived a world history of philosophy in which the Near East,

---

increasing tendency towards technocracy, or a regime that regarded humans as mere instruments of science or ideological goals. He was also skeptical of majoritarian democracy. Thus, he supported a form of governance that guaranteed individual freedom and limited government yet was rooted in authentic tradition and guided by an intellectual elite.[2]48 Today the President ignores the world is hurting deeply the powerful America that heart intent is to help others throughout the centuries weeps of sorrows. The world weeps of sorrow. He, a man the President of United States, Obama did not speak of God and in the Constitution of America it is written in God we trust. He was criticized by not using God in his Thanksgiving address. It as if he is reflecting the limited human powers of boundaries. America as a whole always based their power in God!. There is no faith here. Just chance, cause and affect, positivism functional yet consider by many failure

India, and China are investigated, alongside the West, as original routes of philosophical thinking and their significance revealed. Dr. Karl Jaspers' philosophy of the world of democracy, peace, and justice as the space in which existence and reason move now acquires an inescapable importance.[217] For us to have a "world" of democracy, peace, and justice, we need to work individually, looking within ourselves in our actions, and then bring it to the community and, subsequently, to the world. Hermann Horn brings to light Jaspers' philosophy: vigorous advocate of democracy because it is an ongoing quest for all believers of human freedom by which human beings can attain their potential degree of autonomy and organize the world to enhance that freedom.

Steven Alan Samson - Jurisdiction over Metaphysical guilt lies with God alone.

Mr. Samson's view of Jaspers' metaphysical guilt "suffers from a lack of proportion." It is a political apparatus used by people to extort advantages from others or avoid accepting personal responsibility. In the end, Jaspers himself acknowledges that "jurisdiction over metaphysical guilt lies with God alone."[218] Mr. Samson seems to not recognize in Jaspers' work "The Question of Guilt Study Guide, Dr. Jaspers began to seek justice when he hid Jews from the concentration camps and exterminated them. Furthermore, Dr. Jaspers' work after the Holocaust developed a dialogue of deep identification of individuality to truth, being of life and nothingness of death. Subsequently, his work evolved into a job that considered the entire world of democracy, justice, and peace. For one to even identify a solution to a vast atrocity in history, such as the Holocaust, one would have to begin with individual acceptance to bring justice to the world subsequently.

---

[217] Horn, Herman, Karl Jaspers 18883-1969 Published in Prospects: the quarterly review of comparative education (Paris, UNESCO: International Bureau of Education), vol. XXIII, no. 3/4, 1993, p. 721-739 ©UNESCO: International Bureau of Education, 2000, p. 3

[218] Samson, Steven Alan, Karl Jaspers: The Question of German Guilt Study Guide, 1-1-1977 Liberty University, Faculty Publications and Presentations, Helms School of Government

Mr. Samson states, "For Jaspers, metaphysical guilt results from confining our solidarity to the closest human tie -- family, friends, neighbors -- rather than extending it to all mankind."[219]

To address the issue of this anti-semitism to attempt an "ethnic cleansing" genocide, one needs to start in the hearts of the people, individually responsible, "metaphysically." Because this historical atrocity has to be dealt with from generation to generation, it could be dealt with on a universal level. This is precisely what Dr. Karl Jaspers carried out. He sought to bring justice through "metaphysically individually" and then to "world, democracy, justice peace" and give it to God's hands. Secondly, Mr. Samson believes divine forgiveness was not addressed. Possibly, Dr. Kaspers means "jurisdiction over metaphysical guilt lies with God alone." Through "God's divinity alone," there is forgiveness of oneself and then humbleness to take responsibility.

Let us return to the fundamental concepts of justice of Dr. Karl Jaspers's authentic majestic stream of brilliance in times of the world's most tragic times of modern human history from which we set out. As we have seen, Dr. Karl Jaspers instructs the Germans to take "responsibility" for their "Metaphysical guilt." Secondly, Jaspers identifies actions to give those tools that want to take 'responsibility" and communicate and accept being of life and existence in opposition to the nothingness of Hitler's Third Reich "suicide" of the human being. Thirdly, the philosophy of Political Humanism works for a world of democracy, peace, and justice world order. Dr. Jaspers' requisitions for human rights were evident in his works. After the Second World War, the murderous events of the first half of the twentieth century revived energy to international triumph to define and protect human rights. Human Rights Bill was created] Universal Declaration of Human Rights (United Nations, 1948) embarks a list of over two dozen specific human rights countries should respect and protect. This Universal Declaration of Human Rights supports Dr. Jaspers' concept of justice for the well-being of humanity.

---

[219] Ibid, p. 1; Human rights are international norms that help to protect all people everywhere from severe political, legal, and social abuses.

Dr. Karl Jaspers was a forerunner and champion of justice and human rights. " He also argued that a human polity requires a constitutional apparatus, enshrining basic rights, imposing moral-legal order on the operations of the state, and restricting the prerogative powers of the political apparatus."[220] The power of the political system's technological, scientific, and economic strategies should be kept at a minimum. "Governmental control should be limited" is Jaspers' warning to the world seeking democracy in peace and justice. Today, we see a multitude of atrocities with governmental control, such as vast abortion, euthanasia, economic corruption, nefarious generational economic internal violence in some third-world countries, forced abortions, and many other sinister abuses of human beings.

There are enough resources for all people. Only if the individuals in power and political powers can share and follow the one simple precept, "love your neighbor as yourself." With globalization changing the world, we need a new, fresh eye for reason, an essential heart for humanity, and fundamental ethical justice in society to bring justice and let Justice live.

Today, we cannot succumb to the "cause and effect" and the "is" and "ought" of legal positivism. Hans Kelsen " an aggregate of objective linked together in terms of cause and effect" then indeed no ethical indication of any kind can be derived from it." " A cause and effect, the positivist view is purely functional. It banishes all other cultural realities. Most Holiness Benedict XVI gives us hope in our working for justice in the world when he points out that Kelsen, a great legal positivist at the end of his life at age 84, conviction that there is a Creator Spiritus?"[221]

In 2000, it was particular Swiss banks that were only now disclosing records of "looted gold" that Hitler's Third Reich stole from the Jews during the Holocaust.[222] Today, we have a Holocaust of economic

---

[220] Thornhill, Chris, "Karl Jaspers", The Stanford Encyclopedia of Philosophy (Spring 2011 Edition), Edward N. Zalta (ed.), URL =
<http://plato.stanford.edu/archives/spr2011/entries/jaspers/>.
[221] Benedict XVI Most Holiness Pope, Listening Heart.

[222] Jaspers, Karl, The Question of German Guilt, p. 8

oppression, humanistic oppression of people, and the abuse of political powers of the minds, hearts, lives, and dignity of the people.

One of the most violent atrocities in the present day is a hidden secret of the death of the American dollar and can put millions and millions into poverty! Our American dollar is worth less and less than the Chinese yuan is setting up to try to control the American economy. We need to act now to save our country.[223] Most Holiness Pope Benedicto enlightens us on how to keep justice: "a necessary relatedness between reason and faith and between reason and religion, which are called to purify and help one another. The basic principle must take on concrete form in practice in the intercultural context of the present."[224] Yes, as citizens, we shall make a wholehearted requisition! We shall take responsibility, not succumb to the precipice of the present political leaders in the power of nothingness, the human being, seeking to kill traditions and cultures, economic corruption, vast fallacies, blinding propaganda, and the injustices of today! We shall make a requisition in a powerful didactic "reason" of justice in our just communication and our just actions to protect our "being," our "faith," and our meaning of What it is to be Human bringing and living for justice!

"Success is subordinate to the criterion of justice. The will to do what is right and to understand what is right."[225]

"Live in Truth, seek Truth for the wellbeing of humanity." "Love your neighbor as yourself."

Justice is respecting individual rights in a republic with equal weight to the community. The weighted evidence is judged and balanced between society's law and the individual's right to pursue individual happiness. History shows that extreme movements for either individual rights or

---

[223] Edelson, Larry, www.weissresearchissues.com Newsman.

[224] Dialectical Secularization, p. 50

[225] Benedict XVI Most Holiness, Listening Heart

community rights always end in horrible injustices over time. Justice is respecting individuals and community normative standards to pursue the right to happiness and build a cohesive society with an emphasis on limiting abuse and empowering the republic (the individual).[226]

29 Barker, Brent Strata CEO at Strata Capital Group, Phoenix Arizona USA, www.stratacg.com

---

[226] Barker, Brent Strata CEO at Strata Capital Group, Phoenix Arizona USA, www.stratacg.com

John Philoponus

On

Aristotle's On Intellect
(de Anima 3:4-8)

Professor Fr. Albert Bagood

Pontifical University St. Thomas Aquinas

Rome

<u>Science of Philosophy Spring 2011</u>

Lisa Lucia Arden

CHAPTER FIFTEEN

John Philoponus

Introduction

John Philoponus is a phenomenon, the first Christian Philosopher, and the first to be given the golden keys to unlock and open up the "straightjacket" of Aristotelian concepts. As a yearning student to understand philosophy, I want to learn philosophy from John Philoponus from a Christian perspective and the monarch of ancient philosophy, Aristotle. Studying these ancient philosophers is not primarily for a lover of knowledge, but prima, a lover of humanity. Realizing that through reason of philosophy, we can explain and understand the Word of God and His relationship with society and how to apply it to our world is my wholehearted purpose. Also, we can come to the closest understanding of why Christ gives us revelation and mystical revelations through reason. In our humanness, Christ allows us to use his infiniteness for his purpose.

John Philoponus a Phenomenon in History

John Philoponus is a remarkable phenomenon. John Philoponus' life was filled with spiritual and intellectual, fact and mystery, faith and reason, classic and first Christian revolutionary philosophy, acceptance and controversy. He had classical learning of the forefathers of ancient philosophy. He had a relationship with Christ that was beyond the ancient philosophers. Christ's performing of miracles, the quintessential miracle of resurrection, and the sending of the Holy Spirit at Pentecost to the disciples and then to the believers was and is beyond the explanation of ancient classical philosophy. Philoponus had to go beyond the reason of the classic philosophy because faith is beyond reason, which is a realm of the unknown, and the knowledge is only given at a time not by humans but by God. "He hath made everything beautiful in its time: also he hath set eternity in their heart, yet so that man cannot find out the work that God hath done from the beginning even to the end." Eccl. 3:11[227] In John Philoponus' search for answers, his human heart, intellectual curiosity, and soul yearned to know the answers scintillating in his oeuvre. In his human frailty, he had piercing conflict because of his revelation, not marked by a human time of searching for answers, but only when the knowing is allowed. God marks time!

John Philoponus is known as "John of Alexandria," a grammarian, Christian philosopher, scientist, critic, and theologian living approximately from 490 to 570. Philoponus as an original thinker, withheld all the [sofi÷a][228] of the ancient philosophers before him and upheld by his fervent devotion to Christian faith delivered in his hermeneutical genius revolutionary concepts and disputes. Philoponus was known to have "cleared part of the way, which led to more critical and empirical approaches in the natural sciences. [Initiating and foreshadowing] the eventual demise of the Aristotelianism."[229] Philoponus' revolutionary motivation opened up the most genius treasures of Aristotle's philosophy and questions of philosophy in a Christian world, putting them together as a symbiosis. The classic concepts of philosophy Philoponus used to bring Christian ideas to visibility and truth. Philoponus

---

[227] American Standard Version of 1901 The electronic version of this text has been analyzed and corrected by OakTree Software

[228] Siedler, Horst, Metaphysics and Realism: Discussion on Modern Criticism of Traditional Roma: Angelicum University Press, 2008, p. 17 "The meaning of philosophy as " sophia"(sofi÷a) has again an old origin, namely a religious one (different from the above-mentioned meaning of expert knowledge). The divinity possesses that wisdom to which human beings only aspire as "lovers of wisdom."

[229] Wildberg, Christian, "John Philoponus", The Stanford Encyclopedia of Philosophy (Fall 2008 Edition), Edward N. Zalta (ed.), URL = <http://plato.stanford.edu/archives/fall2008/entries/philoponus/>. It is accepted that Philoponus is from a Christian family.

is known to be the first Christian Aristotelian. God's omniscient hand mixes the beauties of His wisdom of philosophy and Christianity, accommodating each philosopher and theologian. Each seeking to find the truth and to be " in truth"[e☐p' aÓlhqei÷aß]. Today we see in the contemporary world the enlightenment of theories and beliefs that philosophers contributed to, such as Philoponus, known as the "lover of toil": persevering to see the arché [aÓrch/]; to know wisdom (knowledge) [sofi÷a]; to know the truth [aÓlh/qeia] in the influence of the actuality of his masters. He was chosen to seek to find the truth in one of the most brilliant minds, Aristotle, in the light of Christianity. Philonopus was severely punished by the Council of Constantinople of 680-81 for his trinitarian philosophy "The three divinities of the Trinity are all the same, single divine nature."[230] On the other hand, Philoponus' magnitude of archaic toil, genius, and using his understanding of philosophy and his Christian faith, his œuvre flourished as a classical line clearing the path for a more critical and empirical method in the natural sciences. Philoponus' courageous faithfulness in the light of his purpose for the love of God contributed to the theological aspects of the unfolding of Christianity allowed in his century into the actuality of reason and truth. God marks time!

Where did Philoponus get his ideas? Christian Perspectives, Neoplatonist, Proclus, Ammonius

The grandfather and master teacher to Philoponus is Proclus, the Greek Neoplatonist of 411-85. Proclus' archaic travail was "to find a logical and metaphysical structure which embrace unity."[231] Proclus found that to identify things; he said, each has its own species, yet all species are one whole. 'One' is a primitive absolute where we continuously experience

---

[230] Ibid, Tritheism

[231] Helmig, Christoph and Steel, Carlos, "Proclus", The Stanford Encyclopedia of Philosophy (Summer 2011 Edition), Edward N. Zalta (ed.), forthcoming URL = <http://plato.stanford.edu/archives/sum2011/entries/proclus/>.Routledge Proclus

awareness, thought, and existence and parallel to a changing world together, working in ultimate unity.

Proclus' idea is to realize that philosophy and science go hand in hand in the process of understanding the human being. Exercising philosophy and science, Proclus' concepts developed from all his teachers, Plutarch of Athens and Syrianus, teaching him according to Plato, Aristotle, and the Neoplatonist curriculum.[232] All these monarchs of philosophy believed that reason, aided by imagination, lifts us to a transcendental state of religious and ethical values.[233] Ammonius, an Alexandrian Neoplantonist, the pupil to Proclus, and the father master teacher to Philoponus, seems to be Philoponus central influence. The book Metaphysics and Realism by Professor Horst Seidl enlightens us and brings to a center in reflection of Ammonius and Philoponus' philosophy in a Neoplatonistic school:

The Neoplatonists determine theoretical philosophy from its object as knowledge of being as well as of the human and divine things whereas philosophy is for them as for Plato's ethical understanding, guided by scope as 'care of the soul,' in view of death, and as 'becoming similar with God.'[234]

---

[232] Helmig, Christoph and Steel, Carlos, "Proclus", The Stanford Encyclopedia of Philosophy (Summer 2011 Edition), Edward N. Zalta (ed.), forthcoming URL = <http://plato.stanford.edu/archives/sum2011/entries/proclus/>.Routledge Proclus

[233] Routledge Encyclopedia of Philosophy General Editor Edward Craig Volume ,7, Routledge , London 1998

[234] Seidl, Horst, Metaphysics and Realism Discussion on Modern Criticism of traditional Metaphysics and Its Realism taken for Praechter refers to Ammonium, In Porph. Isag. 2,12 p. 18 Interesting to note that Ammonius is the son of Hermias friend, also influenced Aristotle. Routledge, Neoplationism Many of these works evolved out of the school practice of the Neoplatonists (see Neoplatonism §1) and conformed to several requirements: "(1) the commentaries consisted of an extremely detailed oral exegesis of a philosophical text, designed for the benefit of students; (2) not uncommonly, pupils were responsible for taking verbatim notes of their teachers' instruction, thus turning the lecture into a book; (3) each commentary constituted a step within a substantial curriculum of philosophical training which began with Aristotle and aimed at progressing towards Plato – a commentator was expected to demonstrate the agreement between

Philoponus uses philosophy, the superior to all arts, the highest knowledge known by philosophers, and his love for wisdom in his faithfulness in Christ, realizing that he will find this wisdom in the Lord. Ammonius' lost treatise of Aristotle's prime mover (aÓrch/) is both the final and the efficient cause of the universe was to bring Christianity to the forefront and neglect orthodox Neoplationism. This hypothesis was rejected. However, Ammonius's concepts influenced others to deduct this hypothesis and also in the eyes of Philoponus.

As Christians, "becoming similar with God" seeks to know His precepts about all areas of life and develop a "care of the soul" relationship, becoming one with Christ.

The comprehensive metaphysical panorama of Proclus' is congruent with his Neoplatonist collègues. He subscribes to realism in that he accepts a reality independent of what we individuals think about it. But the fact is not physical because what we grasp with the five senses is episodic and often illusory. The things that exist are of the intellect – with the provision that such intellect and its ideas are not just personal but objective and universal (this can be traced to the revision of Aristotelian nous by the influential Alexander of Aphrodisias (§2)).[235] Ammonius's Religious aspects are reflected in his known teaching to his students that "philosophy assimilates the soul to the godhead, separates it from the body, and turns it towards the source and highest Neoplatonic principle, the One."[236] This search for God in philosophy has been a form of the intellectual actuality that catalyzes Philoponus' belief system, intellectual potentiality, and religious and spiritual foundation.

Plato and Aristotle, indeed, to show forth the harmony among all ancient philosophers including Homer; and (4) philosophy in this way was viewed as education as much as pagan religious exercise by which human beings could perfect their intellect and character with a view to [become closer to God]."

[235] Routledge,V. 1.p. 209

[236] Ibid, Routledge V. 1p.209

Ammonius' stature of distinction is difficult to assess. Almost a hundred percent of Ammonius' works are lost. Philoponus as an amanuensis, based on Ammonius' seminars (ek tôn synousiôn Ammôníou), copied his master's seminars such as the commentaries on Aristotle's On the Heavens and Meteorology, Plato's Gorgias, monographs on logic and theology. One analysis survived on Aristotle's De Interpretatione. These experiences developed Philoponus' understanding as his magistrate was a praised commentator, mathematician, and astronomer.

Philoponus Magistrate's powerful views on the order of logic, ethics, physics, mathematics, and theology planted seeds for Philoponus' dynamic courage and brilliance to question the truth of Aristotle's mind and unlock philosophical concepts to illumination. According to Ammonius, a commentator should adopt a position of critical independence: the fact must be preferred to what Aristotle says.[237] Principal historians of logic "acknowledge that Philoponus was the first to render a satisfactory definition of the syllogism, which states that the significant premise includes the predicate term of the conclusion, the minor premise the subject term On Aristotle's Prior Analytics 67. Also, in On Aristotle's Prior Analytics 274 Philoponus, intellectual actuality instructed a schematic diagram facilitating the construction of valid syllogisms, later termed by the philosophy students, ass's bridge, pons asinorum.[238] We see and will see throughout his life that Philoponus was a revolutionary in his time, bringing the freedom of action to take Aristotle's genius and find the answers to truth and falsehood in Aristotle's work. As we know to be a revolutionary, one needs to prove the present complacency to a new level, and it may take a merciless fierceness or flow smoothly. But as we know, we never reach the final truth until we meet our Lord face to face.

The Life of John Philosopher

As stated above, Ammonius argued that Aristotle's prime mover is the universe's final and efficient cause in a lost theological treatise. The

---

[237] Routledge V. 7p. 372

[238] Ibid, Routledge, V. 7 p. 372

suggestion that the ideas put forward in the treatise was motivated by the influence of Christianity and amounted to a substantial deviation from orthodox Neoplatonism has been plausibly rejected.[239] As we can see, the philosophers continue to have a parallel between their philosophical findings and Christianity. Because there are similarities, this can be controversial because it brings them both to the same level of acceptance of the truth. Ancient philosophy was challenged with something beyond itself in the foundation of Christianity: Christ changed history, changed ancient philosophy alone by the historical resurrection, and sent the holy spirit into the hearts of the believers. God, for the ancient philosophers, is "the first cause, arché, (aÓrch/), principle cause, [the prime mover], "Heraclitus assumed it as fire, on the one side, and divine reason[on the other] (lo/goß, ratio)."[240] John Philoponus, the Christian philosopher, found answers for the aÓrch/. For the believer in Jesus Christ gives answers to the aÓrch/. The intense philosophical incompatibilities between pagan and Christian beliefs surface in Philoponus' work. Philosophy is seeking answers to life carrying the human frailties of the unknown. When walking into the puzzle, you will have unknown truth. Then when it is allowed, humans will know the truth, and for believers in Christ, it is known. But we know as Christians in our Catholic Faith that Jesus is the truth, the way, and the life, and now comes to the Father by Jesus Christ.

The cultural background of the time

In 529, Justinian, the Christian emperor, is believed to have sought to prohibit the ancient philosophy of unorthodox Christian principles. However, Platonist philosophers persevered even under self-imposed exile. Christianity outshined ancient philosophy under the influence of Justinian, dominating Medieval and Renaissance philosophy. This eventual eclipse between ancient philosophy and Christianity may reflect that philosophical creeds in late antiquity supported similar purposes as religious movements, with which they shared many of their intentions and

---

[239] Ibid Routledge. 1.p. 209

[240] Ibid Routledged I, p. 16

formal praxis.[241] We ask, what are the likenesses and differences between philosophy and Christianity? First, Etienne Gilson explains to us in his book The Spirit of Medieval Philosophy that there are two groups of philosophers, one is a rationalist, and the other is a neo-scholastic.

In essence, philosophy is independent of religion, and anything that has an intrinsic or necessary relationship to religion, and faith is not philosophy. While rationalists believe that religion can have no relation to philosophy, neo-scholastics believe that philosophy can be related extrinsically to faith, as facilitating religious belief, or as corrective for philosophical errors.[242]

Philosophy is knowledge built up by reason in the light of the dialectical agreement, as Aristotle tells us in Topics 1.1, 100a30-100b23: accepted opinion is the agreement of the majority or most famous and distinguished among them. Then the opinion has to be tested to be examined as accurate. (Nicomachean Ethics, VII.1).[243] For Christians, truth is known in Christ and Christian precepts and is used to build up truth to be found. Revelation is used as wings for a reason.

Through him are believers in God, who raised him from the dead. Purifying your souls in your obedience to the truth unto unfeigned love of the brethren loves one another from the heart fervently: having been begotten again, not of corruptible seed, but of incorruptible, through the word of God, which liveth and abideth. 1Peter 1:21-23[244]

---

[241] Routledge V. 7.

[242] Thomistic Philosophy Page Joseph M. Magee Ph.D. www.aquinasonline.com Unmixing the Intellect: Aristotle on Cognitive Powers and Bodily Organs was published by Greenwood Press in 2003.

[243] Ibid, Thomistic Philosophy Page Joseph M. Magee Ph.D. www.aquinasonline.com Unmixing the Intellect: Aristotle on Cognitive Powers and Bodily Organs was published by Greenwood Press in 2003.

[244] American Standard Version of 1901 The electronic version of this text has been analyzed and corrected by OakTree Software

We know by faith and others' witness that Jesus was raised from the dead. Giving us hope for the present and the future. Our souls are purified by "caring of the soul" in obedience to the truth. In our relationship with our Lord, the mystery of the Holy Spirit fills our "heart fervently" to love one another in the spirit of Christ. In Him, the community of believers, the sacraments, and the Holy Word of God, we are a new creation in Christ, abiding and living on earth and for His coming for eternal life.

As discussed above, according to Ammonius, a philosophical commentator should adopt a position of critical independence: the truth must be preferred to what Aristotle says.[245] This is why John Philoponus and others pursued their "critical independence," searching for answers "in their truth," in truth. Intellectual, religious, and cultural circumstances of human history at the time of John Philoponus opened new paths of understanding, allowing the particular veils of the unknown to be removed.

Works and Contribution

His œuvre comprised at least forty innovative works on many subjects such as grammar, logic, mathematics, physics, psychology, cosmology, astronomy, theology, and church politics; even medical treatises have been attributed to him. We need again to remind ourselves that a substantial work has been given to us; however, some treatises are only known by the author's quotation or translation Philoponus.[246]

Philosophical Commentaries

The Theory of Light

Aristotle's On the Soul is the primeval commentary comprising passages in which Philoponus deviates from the traditional exegesis, "outright rejection," and uses substantial interpretation. There is discord about

---

[245] Routledge, V. 1 p. 209

[246] Please see the John Philoponus list of works

whether the pieces exhibit a change of mind away from orthodox Aristotelianism.[247] The concept of light for Aristotle in On the Soul (II 7) is incorporeal, and its appearance is an instantaneous transition from the potentiality (dýnamis) of a medium to be transparent to the actuality (enérgeia) of transparency. The description fails to account both for the laws of optics and for the phenomenon that the region below the moon is warmed by the light of a celestial body, the sun. Philoponus proceeds to interpret the term enérgeia not as an actual state but as an 'incorporeal activity' capable of warming bodies, just as the soul is in the case of animals. Philoponus' substantial exegesis still holds the vein of the Aristotelian concept of light in changing the terminology from enérgeia not as a state of actuality but rather as an 'incorporeal activity.' Light is now understood as dynamic.[248]

Theory of Impetus

In Alexandria, Philoponus, the Christian Platonist, was accepted by the Neoplationists and influenced the transformation and development of Islamic and Western physics, structuring an unconventional alternative to Aristotelian physics. Many of his unorthodox ideas were included in his attack against Proclus, published in 529, but he also began introducing them in his Aristotle commentaries.

Philoponus' Commentary On Aristotle's Physics contains an exhibition of examples of his dynamic independence and genius. "One of his most celebrated achievements is the theory of impetus, which is commonly regarded as a decisive step from an Aristotelian dynamics towards a modern theory based on the notion of inertia."[249] Scientists have asked for

---

[247] The Cambridge Dictionary of Philosophy / ed. Robert Audi Cambridge: Univ. Pr., 1995. XXVIII, 882 pp.

[248] Wildberg, Christian, "John Philoponus," The Stanford Encyclopedia of Philosophy (Fall 2008 Edition), Edward N. Zalta (ed.), URL =
<http://plato.stanford.edu/archives/fall2008/entries/philoponus/
[249] Routledge, V. 7. Concepts akin to those deployed in Philoponus' impetus theory appear in earlier writers such as Hipparchus (2nd c. BCE) and Synesius (4th c. CE), but Philoponus nowhere intimates that he was influenced by any one of them.

years why a ball continues to "fly" in the air after the thrower throws it. First, Aristotle presumed that when there is motion, it is essential that something transmits the signal. Secondly, the mover of the thrower and move the ball must be in contact; the air is displaced like a "projectile," and the motion pushes around the ball, putting it in action. Philoponus advanced Aristotle's theory of the "projectile" and theorized that the projectile is a "kinetic force" that is impressed on the moved by the mover, exhausting itself during the movement. This theory of impetus or 'incorporeal motive enérgeia' Philoponus compares with the activity attributed to light 'incorporeal activity.'[250]

The impetus theory also "ties in" with the criticisms of Aristotle's general concepts of physics. Criticisms were projected with Aristotle's principle that void was a logical impossibility. Philoponus says that void or empty spaces in nature do not exist but in 'movement in a plenum,' replacing bodies in one position for the other.[251] Nature abhors a vacuum. These ideas were rediscovered approximately 1000 years later by Robert Boyle and Torricelli.

Space and Place

Philoponus' commentary, On Aristotle's Physics 675–94, presents a formidable defense of the void, connected to his conceptions of place and space. Interesting to note that Aristotle proposes that space is the "inner surface" of the body (Physics IV 4). Philoponus replies that place should be conceived as a three-dimensional extension equal to the fixed size of

---

[250] Ibid. See Motion §3 "Concepts akin to impetus theory appear in earlier writers such as Hipparchus and Synesius, but Philoponus never mentions them. . . Aristotle's theory was still in vogue among Aristotelians of the sixteenth century, despite the fact that a thousand years earlier Philoponus had demolished it.In this erroneous but insightful theory can be found the first step towards the concept of inertia in modern physics, although Philoponus' theory was largely ignored at the time because he was too radical in his rejection of Aristotle.

[251] Ibid, Routledge, V. 7

the body, which is its volume. Space is an indeterminate pure three-dimensional extension devoid of the body.[252]

Theory of Matter

The theory of matter joins in connection with the principle concept of space. In the commentary On Aristotle's Physics Commentary 687–8, Philoponus presents a parallel understanding of the theory of matter with Aristotle in Metaphysics VII 3. Aristotle's theory of matter: "prime matter" is undetermined, removing all the qualities from the body. The Neoplatonists define prime matter as incorporeal and formless, not having a body. Philoponus is opposite to the Neoplatonist defining matter as "corporeal extension", (sômatikón diástêma).

The sômatikón diástêma is a composite of Neoplatonic excellent matter and indeterminate quantity and must not be confused with Philoponian space. Following the Stoics, Philoponus's concept of excellent matter is 'the three-dimensional,' indeterminate corporeal extension.[253]

Treatises

John Philoponus' innovative and independent style also transformed the traditional apologetic commentary into open criticism of fundamental Aristotelian-Neoplatonic doctrines, most prominently the tenet of On the Eternity of the World. This independent approach to philosophical tradition and the solutions of his arguments antagonized Philoponus' colleagues, the classic philosophers; they may have compelled him to abandon his philosophical career.

Philoponus devoted the second half of his life to influencing the theological debates of his time. However, this dynamic genius went beyond the scripture agreement of the Orthodox Church: the Orthodox clergy condemned him posthumously as a heretic because of his

---

[252] Ibid. Routledge, V.7

[253] Routledge, V.7

Aristotelian interpretation of the trinitarian dogma, which led him to enunciate three separate godheads, tritheism.

The Critical Treatises

On the Eternity of the World against Proclus

Philoponus as a Critic against Proclus

Proclus, 411- 485, Philoponus' master teacher and headmaster of the Alexandria school of Neoplatonism, wrote a vindication of Greek tradition about the world's eternity against eternalism. Proclus disputed with eighteen arguments that Christian creationism was intellectually unjustifiable. Proclus interprets his view using Plato's Timaeus: the world is created by a divine 'demiurge,' which is a mythical foundation, not a philosophical principle. Rebuttaling, Philoponus embodied his independent criticism away from Neoplatonism and published a reply entitled On the Eternity of the World against Proclus. The sixth century brought an open door for refuting Christian beliefs when Emperor Justinian suppressed Greek philosophy in Athens. Philoponus took his innovative renegade approach and wrote a book as an anti-commentary against his grandfather's teacher, Proclus. The controversial argument of the Christian debater cleverly used a Platonic structure without biblical theology. Philoponus interprets Timaeus as an authentic creation account congruent with Christian doctrine. Also, Philoponus creates a new interpretation of the concept of generation and corruption in which an idea is viable, which Greek schools never accepted, creation ex nihilo. The first Christian philosopher, devotion to the Lord: "God is indeed more powerful a creator than nature and therefore capable of creation ex nihilo (IX 9).[254]

On the Eternity of the World against Aristotle

---

[254] Routledge. V.I 209-210 "Eventually, he transformed the usual format of apologetic commentary into a discourse of open criticism, in the course of which he examined and repudiated fundamental Aristotelian-Neoplatonic tenets, most prominently the doctrine of the eternity of the world. He was an inspiring figure and exercised his considerable authority politically both in and outside Athens. A proud defender of the 'Hellenic' values and religious multiformity, Proclus lived when Christianity became the state orthodoxy."

Philoponus continues his innovative hermeneutic approach, pointing out problematic tensions and apparent contradictions in the Aristotelian corpus and also highlighting salient instances of argument between Plato and Aristotle; in contrast, the program of the Neoplatonic tradition he grew up in ignores the problems or explains them away.

Philoponus has a battle against eternalism, presenting it in a triumvirate:

In 529, a treatise against Proclus as discussed above: Proclus openly endorsing Christian creation is intellectually unjustifiable.

In 530-534 treatise against Aristotle, a scrutiny of the first chapters of Aristotle's On the Heavens (his theory of ether as the fifth element, of which the heavenly bodies are made) and the eighth book of Physics (arguing for the eternity of time and motion).

The third stage is represented by one, perhaps two, non-polemical treatises that have survived in fragments, which indicate that numerous arguments against eternity and for creation were arranged in some systematic order. Here, Philoponus' center purpose is to eradicate the barrier for creationists. Simplicious documents in In Physic 1178,7-1179, 26 Contra Aristotelem Fr. 13:

The existence of something is essential to the preexistence of something else. The first thing will only come into existence with a prior something.

Infinite numbers cannot exist in actuality. Infinite cannot be counted over or increased.

If a being requires the preexistence of an infinite number, it cannot come into being.

Philoponus can't have a temporary infinite universe of a continuous successive chain. The anti-eternalize treatises exonerated that an endless power or potentiality(dúnamis) cannot reside in a finite body (Phys. VIII 10). The eternal view Philoponus exploits since the universe is a finite body; it cannot have the *dúnamis* to exist for an infinite time. Interesting to note in the relationship to eternity and light: there is a shift of meaning in the theory of light—Aristotle's argument in Phys. VIII 10, dúnamis meant 'kinetic force'; Philoponus incorporates the term in the sense of 'existential capacity' or 'fitness to exist.'[255]

Theological Treatise

On the Creation of the World

Philoponus's life changed around the end of 530. As mentioned, his Neoplatonist colleagues may have forced him to retire from philosophical work, and his theological works began to flourish.

Philoponus is acclaimed in the history of science as the individual who made the first attempt at a unified theory of dynamics. The unifying idea of dynamics was interwoven in his theological work written approximately 550 On the Creation of the World, as a commentary on the bible's story of creation incorporating the knowledge of Greek philosophers and the wisdom of Basil the Great. Using his theory of impetus, he explains the motion of the planets. The movement of the heavens could be explained by a 'motive force' impressed on the celestial bodies by God at the time of creation. The impetus theory is presented for the first time in forced motion, as when one shoots an arrow with a bow. He insightfully uses the idea of the regular and natural activities of the universe. Philoponus believes natural movements are attributed to the creator's divine force or energy with which a body moves or impetus. Unlike Philoponus, Aristotle presented two analytical concepts for moving heavenly and earthly bodies. In Arbiter, 52-A-B, it is interesting that by integrating his innovative brilliance of science and theology, Philoponus debated that all material objects' formation of being is by

---

[255] Wildberg, Christian, "John Philoponus", The Stanford Encyclopedia of Philosophy (Fall 2008 Edition), Edward N. Zalta (ed.), URL =
<http://plato.stanford.edu/archives/fall2008/entries/philoponus/>.
Influence: "His arch- enemy Simplicius, also a pupil of Ammonius, submitted the Grammarian's anti-eternalism almost immediately to thundering pro-Aristotelian criticism (in his commentaries on the De Caelo and the Physics, written sometime in the late 530s). It was that polemic which resounded through the ages; its shockwaves can still be felt in later thinkers

God.[256] Here, the Christian-Aristotelian philosopher opens the doors by giving examples of how God created the universe, reflecting the creation story coming alive. As we have seen, Philoponus, using his classical Neoplatonic training in philosophy and his faith and devotion to theology, used a symbiosis to build each position up.

Monophysitism

Philoponus' fervent devotion is mapped out in his position in 553 Constantinople when he became a partisan of the Fifth Council. His theological purpose was to present Christology as a partisan monophysite with an Aristotelian artery. In the eastern portion of the empire, monophysite Christology, within a century, became progressively affluent. The divinity of Christ was in the foreground; however, at the Council of Chalcedon in 451, monophysitism was "scandalized" by the convergence of other Christological positions. Chalcedon in 451 Christ of their Christological positions: 1. Christ is consubstantial (homooúsios) 'of one substance' with the Father; 2. Christ is consubstantial with humans; 3. one person and on hypóstasis (existence); and 4. 'discernible in two natures.' 'unitatem personae in outrage natura intelligendam". This proposition could be read as Jesus merely as a divinely inspired man.[257] Philoponus, a partisan for monophysite Christology, argued that the part of Christ is divine.

Philoponus claims, using the terms 'nature' and 'hypóstasis,' that the Nature of Christ is complex, and like Thomas Aquinas (1224-1274) and Zabarella (1533-1589), who carefully examined, though in the end rejected Philoponus' anti-eternalist arguments."

---

[256] Wildberg, Christian, "John Philoponus", The Stanford Encyclopedia of Philosophy (Fall 2008 Edition), Edward N. Zalta (ed.),
URL = <http://plato.stanford.edu/archives/fall2008/entries/philoponus/>
[257] Wildberg, Christian, "John Philoponus", The Stanford Encyclopedia of Philosophy (Fall 2008 Edition), Edward N. Zalta (ed.),
URL = <http://plato.stanford.edu/archives/fall2008/entries/philoponus/>

It is not as ordinary as the human nature of man or the particular nature of an individual. Also, according to the 'hypóstasis,' Christ is one. Christ, therefore, cannot have two natures. Philoponus presents Christ's divinity by preposing "we should speak of one complex nature (mía phúsis súnthetos).[258]

Tritheism

As we have discussed above, Philoponus was honored for his position on monophysitism, being a powerful theological movement in the Eastern Church; however, the orthodox clergy condemned him posthumously as a heretic in 680-81 because of his Aristotelian interpretation of the trinitarian dogma, which led him to enunciate three separate godheads (tritheism).

Tritheistic interpretation of the trinitarian dogma: By reading the relevant concepts in this debate (nature, substance) in a strictly Aristotelian way, Philoponus was led to enunciate not a single god in three persons (Father, Son, Spirit) but three separate divinities.[259] Philoponus' courageous and persevering devotion to present questions of transcendental theological complexity was accepted in most cases; unfortunately, the orthodox church did not theologically sound the tritheism doctrine he adopted. We have to celebrate and appreciate Philoponus for all his œuvre. He, the first Christian Philosopher, is the gneiss in the rock; he is the foundation of understanding a myriad of philosophical and theological concepts changing history.

"The eye hath not seen, O God, besides Thee, what things Thou hast prepared for them that wait for Thee" (Is. 66:4).

The consequences and the contribution to the succeeding generations.[260]

---

[258] Wildberg, Christian, "John Philoponus

[259] Bibliography also from direction from Dr. of Physics James Done, Pasadena, California June 2011

[260] Ibid, Bibliography entire.

We cannot list everything that Philoponus proceeded in consequence and contributed to the next generation because he is a remarkable phenomenon.

As stated above, Philoponus' eminence is known for the catalyst he produced with his independent enthusiasm, genius, and curiosity to unlock the doors of Aristotelianism. On the other hand, philosophers were antagonized by Philoponus's use of the symbiosis of ancient Greek philosophy to support Christianity and vice versa.

Today, in contemporary notoriety, Philoponus' prominence is heralded in that he is the first to reconcile Aristotelian philosophy, one of the greatest philosophical minds, with Christianity. In doing this, he honed the path to more critical and empirical approaches in natural science.

Today, we also see theologians, scientists, students, and many others seeking to find jewels of wisdom in precepts and sound doctrines to open and unlock all forms of knowledge, theological revelation, and insight.

As we have seen, Philoponus' characteristics of his thought deny a center Aristotelian influence. Still, on the other hand, he takes up a certain doctrinal harmony to Plato, and he did not take up the strict Neoplatonic interpretation.

His works were translated into Arabic, Latin, and Syriac, and he influenced later thinkers such as Bonaventure, Gersonides, Buridan, Oresme, and Galileo.

Simplicius was his fellow student under Ammonius and his enemy. He argued against Philoponus' anti-eternalism, which caused others, such as St. Thomas Aquinas and Zabarella, to misconstrue him.

His criticism of Aristotle in On Aristotle's Physics was widely discussed, and he persuaded diverse thinkers such as Giovanni Pico della Mirandola and, for different reasons, Galileo Galilei.

John Philoponus' Christological "opus magnum" stands in line with St. Cyril of Alexandria and Severus of Antioch.

He proclaimed the understanding of Christ as both divine and human, in opposition to Chalcedonian authors who strove to find a middle ground.

The Hellenic teaching of Aristotle influences Philoponus' view of space as homogeneous. However, Philoponus and his contemporaries, Simplicius of Cilicia and Strato, developed this concept further. This concept guided the Renaissance theory of perspective, particularly the one highlighted by Leon Battista Alberti and other architectural masters.

In the latter work, Philoponus became one of the earliest thinkers to reject Aristotle's dynamics and propose the 'theory of impetus.' An object moves and continues to move because of energy imparted to it by the mover, and movement ceases when that energy is exhausted. This erroneous but insightful theory can be found as the first step toward the concept of inertia in modern physics. However, Philoponus' idea was largely ignored at the time because he was too radical in his rejection of Aristotle.

Philoponus' work on motion revolutionized Galileo's quantitative understanding of relative motion and frames of reference.[261]

---

[261] Galieo: Galileo 1638 Discorsi e Dimostrazioni Matematiche, intorno á due nuoue scienze 191 - 196, published by Lowys Elzevir (Louis Elsevier), Leiden, or Two New Sciences, English translation by Henry Crew and Alfonso de Salvio 1914, reprinted on pages 515-520 of On the Shoulders of Giants: The Great Works of Physics and Astronomy. Stephen Hawking, ed. 2002 ISBN 0-7624-1348-4 The Galilean transformation is used to transform between the coordinates of two reference frames which differ only by constant relative motion within the constructs of Newtonian physics. This is the passive transformation point of view. The equations below, although apparently obvious, break down at speeds that approach the speed of light due to physics described by relativity theory. Galileo formulated these concepts in his description of uniform motion[1]. The topic was motivated by Galileo's description of the motion of a ball rolling down a ramp, by which he measured the numerical value for the acceleration of gravity near the surface of the Earth. www.wikipediaGalileo has been called the "father of modern observational astronomy",[6] the "father of modern physics",[7] the "father of science",[7] and "the Father of Modern Science".[8] Stephen Hawking says, "Galileo, perhaps more than any other single person, was responsible for the birth of modern science."[9]

His work on understanding the nature of the vacuum opens the doors for Robert Boyle and Torricelli.[262]

In his work on the nature of light, Philoponus influenced Christian Huygens to develop the wave theory of light. The wave theory states that light is composed of waves and not particles; it is incorporeal, as Philoponus theorized.[263]

26 Edelson, Larry, www.weissresearchissues.com Newsman.

27 Dialectical Secularization, p. 50

28 Benedict XVI Most Holiness, Listening Heart

---

[262] Boyle: McCartney, Mark; Whitaker, Andrew (2003), Physicists of Ireland: Passion and Precision, London: Insitute of Physics PublishingReading in 1657 of Otto von Guericke's air-pump, he set himself with the assistance of Robert Hooke to devise improvements in its construction, and with the result, the "machina Boyleana" or "Pneumatical Engine", finished in 1659, he began a series of experiments on the properties of air.[1] An account of Boyle's work with the air pump was published in 1660 under the title New Experiments Physico-Mechanicall, Touching the Spring of the Air, and its Effects www.wikipedia.com Torricelli, de Gandt (1987). L'oeuvre de Torricelli: Les Belles Lettres. www.wikipedia.com Torricelli's chief invention was the mercury barometer, which arose from solving a practical problem. Pump makers of the Grand Duke of Tuscany attempted to raise water to a height of 12 meters or more, but found that 10 meters was the limit with a suction pump. Torricelli employed mercury, fourteen times heavier than water. In 1643 he created a tube approximately one meter long, sealed at the top, filled it with mercury, and set it vertically into a basin of mercury. The column of mercury fell to about 76 cm, leaving a Torricellian vacuum above. As we now know, the column's height fluctuated with changing atmospheric pressure; this was the first barometer. This discovery perpetuated his fame, and the Torr, a unit used in vacuum measurements, has been named for him.

[263] Christiaan Huygens, Traité de la lumiere (Leiden, Netherlands: Pieter van der Aa, 1690), Chapter 1. (Note: In the preface to his Traité, Huygens states that in 1678 he first communicated his book to the French Royal Academy of Sciences.Huygens is remembered especially for his wave theory of light, expounded in his Treatise on light, 1678 (see also Huygens-Fresnel principle). The later theory of light by Isaac Newton in his Opticks proposed a different explanation for reflection, refraction and interference of light assuming the existence of light particles. The interference experiments of Thomas Young vindicated Huygens' wave theory in 1801, as the results could no longer be explained with light particles see however wave-particle

29 Barker, Brent Strata CEO at Strata Capital Group, Phoenix Arizona USA, www.stratacg.com

Isaiah 12:1   And, that day, you will say: 'I praise you, Yahweh, you have been angry with me but your anger is now appeased and you have comforted me. **2** Look, he is the God of my salvation: I shall have faith and not be afraid, for Yahweh is my strength and my song, he has been my salvation.'

Isaiah 12:3   Joyfully, you will draw water from the springs of salvation **4** and, that day, you will say, 'Praise Yahweh, invoke his name. Proclaim his deeds to the people, declare his name sublime. **5** Sing of Yahweh, for his works are majestic, make them known throughout the world. **6** Cry and shout for joy, you who live in Zion, For the Holy One of Israel is among you in his greatness.'

Isaiah 12:1   And, that day, you will say: 'I praise you, Yahweh, you have been angry with me but your anger is now appeased and you have comforted me. 2 Look, he is the God of my salvation: I shall have faith and not be afraid, for Yahweh is my strength and my song, he has been my salvation.'

Isaiah 12:3   Joyfully you will draw water from the springs of salvation 4 and, that day, you will say, 'Praise Yahweh, invoke his name. Proclaim his deeds to the people, declare his name sublime. 5 Sing of Yahweh, for his works are majestic, make them known throughout the world. 6 Cry and shout for joy, you who live in Zion, For the Holy One of Israel is among you in his greatness.'

Bibliography

Apply the Blood of Jesus,
https://www.youtube.com/watch?v=8byRiGaOrCk.

Arden Lisa, Lucia, MDIV, Our Need to Give to the World, Heal America and Love in God, Published Lisa Lucia Arden, 2016Our Need to Give to the World: America Love in God, Heal America - Kindle edition by Arden, Lisa Lucia. Politics & Social Sciences Kindle eBooks @ Amazon.com., Arden, Lisa Lucia, MDIV

Arden, Lisa, Lucia MDIV, Arise to God's Truth, Restore and Keep America's Freedom, Lisa Lucia Arden, December 2020, geopolitics https://www.amazon.com/ARISE-GODS-TRUTH-LUCIA-ARDEN-ebook/dp/B08T8LJ8TR/ref=sr_1_3?crid=6SLHFQ1ND2FV&dib=ey J2IjoiMSJ9.xtnuqkBr2JVwfsZJzfYFXvR9uvMZNWtuV_HxjEuwOv fGjHj071QN20LucGBJIEps.BdlOV17fMuCB5UaGKHXzRVhCRa Xwjn1uxaR_D-OW1R4&dib_tag=se&keywords=lisa+lucia+arden&qid=173148758 0&sprefix=%2Caps%2C213&sr=8-3, Arden Lisa Lucia, MDIV

Arden, Lisa, Lucia, MDIV, God First, America our Miracle Vote Freedom Vote President Trump The United States of America, Publisher Lisa Lucia Arden, October 2024GOD first, America Our Miracle: Vote Freedom, Vote President Trump: Arden MDIV, Lisa Lucia: 9798345121887: Amazon.com: Books, Arden, Lisa Lucia, MDIV

Arden, Lisa, Lucia, MDIV, Pillars of Power 2024, get the original date.. and copyright.

Bauzon, Stephen, Political Science Pontifical University Saint Thomas Aquinas, 2010

Biblia Hebraica Stuttgarenisa, edited by Karl Elliger, William Rudolph, et al. 4th corrected edition by Adrian Schenker. Copyright 1966, 1977, 1983 Deutsche Biblegesellschaft, Stuttgart. Used by permission. Verb consecutive masculine singular, covenant sign, pledge of the covenant, הַבְּרִית א׳ (v. ברית), e.g., circumcision, of Abrahamic covenant; the sabbath.

Børge Brende is the President and member of the Managing Board of the World Economic Forum https://inp.harvard.edu/people/b%C3%B8rge-brende.

Boyle: McCartney, Mark; Whitaker, Andrew (2003), Physicists of Ireland: Passion and Precision, London: Insitute of Physics PublishingReading in 1657 of Otto von Guericke'

BRICS grows, adding 13 new 'partner countries' at historic summit in Russia https://www.youtube.com/watch?v=wUdlzmk73Ns,

Brics https://en.wikipedia.org/wiki/BRICS#:~:text=BRICS%20is%20an%20intergovernmental%20organization,joining%20the%20group%20in%202010

BRICS New Members: 50+ Countries to Join BRICS https://www.youtube.com/watch?v=jH-dcOXiHs4

Carrier CPA NEWSROOM AUGUST 18, 2022 https://prosperousamerica.org/vanguard-blackrock-funnel-u-s-investment-to-chinese-shipyard-that-built-third-ccp-aircraft-carrier/

CATHOLIC CATECHISM (ENGLISH) The Catechism of the Catholic Church (English) (C. Catechism-E)©1997 Libreria Editrice Vatican, Vatican City Used by permission of Amministrazione del Patrimonio Della Sede Apostlica, Vatican City Electronic text hypertexted and prepared by OakTree Software, Inc.Version 1.5

Cobb, Don Agenda 21 Eliminating the Middle-Class http://www.renewamerica.com/columns/cobb/130219 www.freedom21santacruz.net

Crown Saudi Prince, Mohammed bin Salman Al Saud (Arabic: محمد بن سلمان آل سعود)https://en.wikipedia.org/wiki/Mohammed_bin_Salman,

Dams in California, Give us water Newsom, dams.

Declaration of Independence, Article 1 of the United Nations Universal Declaration of Human Rights (UDHR)[9 Human rights are commonly understood as "inalienable fundamental rights

Did George Washington have a vision of Our Lady? https://catholicherald.co.uk/did-george-washington-have-a-vision-of-our-lady/

Dr. Scholer, Fuller Theological Seminary, https://eewc.com/david-scholer-memoriam/

Dyvik, Einar H., Largest armies in the world by active military personnel 2024 Published Jul 4, 2024

EERDMANS DICTIONARY of the BIBLE David Noel Freedman Editor-in-Chief Allen C. Myers Associate Editor Astrid B. Beck Managing EditorWilliam B. Eerdmans Publishing Company Grand Rapids, Michigan / Cambridge, U.K. © 2000 Wm. B. Eerdmans Publishing Co. All rights reserved

Emmanuel, Mari Mari, stop Illuminati satan worshippers and pray for their salvation https://www.facebook.com/100005155443736/videos/526325873541348?idorvanity=1495743124559602.

Foreign Policy, https://foreignpolicy.com/2016/03/15/these-25-companies-are-more-powerful-than-many-countries-multinational-corporate-wealth-power/

Fortune releases list of top 10 biggest U.S. companies https://www.cbsnews.com/news/fortune-500-list-biggest-companies-walmart-amazon-apple/

Galileo: Galileo 1638 Discorsi e Dimostrazioni Matematiche, intorno á due nurse scienze 191 - 196, published by Lowys Elzevir (Louis

Elsevier), Leiden, or Two New Sciences, English translation by Henry Crew and Alfonso de Salvio 1914

Gould, Baring, S, Rev. Life of Saints, https://www.gutenberg.org/files/46947/46947-h/46947-h.htm

Greek-English Lexicon of the New Testament Based on Semantic Domains (Louw & Nida)Johannes P. Louw and Eugene A. Nida, Editors Copyright © 1988, 1989 by the United Bible Societies, New York, NY 10023 Second Edition. Used by permission. Landkarten zur Bible, prepared by Karl Elliger, revised by Siegfried Mittmann. Designed by Deutsche Bibelgesellschaft Stuttgart and Kartographisches Institut Helmut Fuchs Leonberg. Copyright ©1963, 1978, 1990 by Deutsche Bibelgesellschaft, Stuttgart. Used by permission. Electronic text hypertexted and prepared by OakTree Software, Inc. version 4.4

Hamas, https://www.linkedin.com/feed/update/urn:li:activity:7142340902252916736/

HEBREW STRONG'S DICTIONARY Strong's Hebrew and Chaldee Dictionary of the Old Testament (Hebrew Strong's) Public Domain Electronic text downloaded from the Bible Foundation e-Text Library:http://www.bf.org/bfetexts.htm Hypertexted and formatted by OakTree Software, Inc.Hebrew text added by OakTree Software, Inc.Version 3.3Melek Kreesis

Helmig, Christoph and Steel, Carlos, "Proclus," The Stanford Encyclopedia of Philosophy (Summer 2011 Edition), Edward N. Zalta (ed.), forthcoming URL = <http://plato.stanford.edu/archives/sum2011/entries/proclus/>.Routledge Proclus

Hillsdale, College, Hillsdale College - Developing Minds. Improving Hearts.

Horn, JASPERS (1883-1969) Prospects: the quarterly review of comparative education KARL JASPERS (1883-1969) Hermann Hom1 (Paris, UNESCO: International Bureau of Education), vol. XXIII, no. 3/4, 1993, p. 721-739. ©UNESC O: International Bureau of Education, 2000. This document may be reproduced free of charge as long as an acknowledgment of the source is made.

How India is making new roads from recycled old tires, https://www.dw.com/en/how-india-is-making-new-roads-from-recycled-old-tires/video-68857469,

https://calmatters.org/commentary/2022/08/newsoms-water-strategy-needs-to-go-a-step-further

https://ustr.gov/countries-regions, The Offices of The United States Trade Representative

Hurricane Helene storm [2024] https://www.britannica.com/event/Hurricane-Helene; https://www.cbsnews.com/news/hurricane-helene-conspiracy-theories-lithium-mining-weather-control-fact-check/

Hussel, Mausian https://www.youtube.com/watch?v=O30ufWni5UU November 7, 2023

Huygens,Christiaan , Traité de la lumiere (Leiden, Netherlands: Pieter van der Aa, 1690), Chapter 1. (Note: In the preface to his Traité, Huygens states that in 1678, he first communicated his book to the French Royal Academy of Sciences.Huygens

In-vitro=fertizalition https://www.mayoclinic.org/tests-procedures/in-vitro-fertilization/about/pac-20384716, In-vitro-fertilzation

Iron Dome,https://www.politifact.com/article/2023/oct/13/us-may-not-have-iron-dome-but-military/, Iron Dome

Jasper, Karl, Questions of Guilt,https://digitalcommons.liberty.edu/cgi/viewcontent.cgi?article=1230&context=gov_fac_pubs

Jasper, Karl, Questions of
    Guilt,https://digitalcommons.liberty.edu/cgi/viewcontent.cgi?article=
    1230&context=gov_fac_pubs

Jasper, Karl, Way of Wisdom,
    https://www.angelfire.com/md2/timewarp/jaspers.html

Joel S. Kaminsky https://www.iiss.org/press/2024/02/the-military-
    balance-2024-press-
    release/#:~:text=About%20The%20International%20Institute%20for
    ,Middle%20East%20Regional%20Security%20Summit).

Juna Grainer, Iranian, Persian Leaders, Junagranier4@ Instagram.

K. Koch, "Is There a Doctrine of Retribution in the Old Testament?" in
    Theodicy in the Old Testament, ed. J. L. Crenshaw. IRT 4
    (Philadelphia, 1983), 57–87; G. E. Mendenhall, The Tenth
    Generation (Baltimore, 1973).

LIDDELL & SCOTT (INTERMEDIATE) An Intermediate Greek-
    English Lexicon (Liddell & Scott) founded upon The Seventh
    Edition of Liddell and Scott's Greek-English Lexicon. Oxford, At
    the Clarendon Press, 1889. The print form is in the Public Domain.
    This electronic version of the Liddell-Scott Greek-English Lexicon
    copyright the President and Fellows of Harvard College and the
    Corporation for Public Broadcasting, 1996. Used by permission of
    Yale University Press. Accordance edition hypertexted and formatted
    by OakTree Software, Inc. Version 2.3

Maui, How rumors and conspiracy theories got in the way of Maui's fire
    recovery, https://www.npr.org/2023/09/28/1202110410/how-rumors-
    and-conspiracy-theories-got-in-the-way-of-mauis-fire-recovery,
    Maui Fire September 28, 20235:01 AM ET

Morerod Bishop, Pontifical University Saint Thomas Aquinas Rome,
    2010 Most Powerful Countries | U.S. News (usnews.com)

Most Holiness Pope Benedicto's writings. True wisdom that is of God
    comes from our love relationship with Jesus Christ and the Saints on

earth and as it is in heaven. Please note this is just an overview of expressions of our Christian aspects of wisdom.

Most Holy, Pope, Benedicto, XVI, 2009, 2010 Writings Most Powerful, Most Powerful Countries | U.S. News (usnews.com)

Most Holy, Pope, Benedicto, XVI, 2009, 2010 Writings Most Powerful, Most Powerful Countries | U.S. News (usnews.com)

MOUNCE GREEK DICTIONARY Concise Greek-English Dictionary of the New Testament (Mounce Greek Dictionary) edited by William D. Mounce with Rick D. Bennett, Jr. Copyright © 2011 by William D. Mounce http://www.billmounce.com/greek-dictionary All rights reserved. Greek Strong's Audio pronunciation, Open Source Accordance edition hypertexted and formatted by OakTree Software, Inc. Version 4.5 noble

Musk, Elon, X Social Media, interviewed by Tucker Carlson 2024

Netanyahu Benjamin ,
    https://en.wikipedia.org/wiki/Benjamin_Netanyahu Prime Minister
    of Israel, ⓘⒾ בל נולד ;21- באוקטובר 1949, בתשרי כ"ח י"(ה'תש
    הוא פוליטיקאי ישראלי

NIV GREEK DICTIONARY Greek to English Dictionary and Index to the NIV New Testament (NIV Greek) from Zondervan NIV Exhaustive Concordance Edward W. Goodrick, John R. Kohlenberger III, and James A. Swanson Copyright ©1999, 1990 by the Zondervan Corporation Grand Rapids, Michigan 49530 All rights reserved. Electronic text prepared by OakTree Software, Inc. Version 1.3, Noble interesting is an eagle that is a .. symbol for Americans.

Pope Benedicto, Listening Heart,
    https://www.cambridge.org/core/books/abs/pope-benedict-xvis-legal-
    thought/listening-
    heart/6C618CBEDA73C18DDB92708A47AE76DA

Prayer of the Continental Congress, 1774,
    https://chaplain.house.gov/archive/continental.html

Private Companies Black Rock, State Street Vanguard, BlackRock
    Funnel U.S. Investment To Chinese Shipyard That Built Third CCP
    Aircraft Carrier CPA NEWSROOM AUGUST 18, 2022
    https://prosperousamerica.org/vanguard-blackrock-funnel-u-s-
    investment-to-chinese-shipyard-that-built-third-ccp-aircraft-carrier/

Private Companies Black Rock, State Street Vanguard, BlackRock
    Funnel U.S. Investment To Chinese Shipyard That Built Third CCP
    Aircraft Carrier CPA NEWSROOM AUGUST 18, 2022
    https://prosperousamerica.org/vanguard-blackrock-funnel-u-s-
    investment-to-chinese-shipyard-that-built-third-ccp-aircraft-carrier/

Ratzinger, Habermas, Dialectic Secularization On Reason and Religion,
    https://books.google.com/books?hl=en&lr=&id=ERzoAPsS9usC&oi
    =fnd&pg=PA3&dq=ratzinger+and+habermas,+p.+33+dialectic+secu
    larization&ots=uBFPyS54Jq&sig=IBnDv16gES-kXbR-
    pomMKO4cwks#v=onepage&q&f=false

Reeves, C.D.C, Aristotle Politics Translated, with Introduction and
    Notes, Published by Hackett Publishing Company, Indianapolis,
    Cambridge, 1998

Routledge Encyclopedia of Philosophy General Editor Edward Craig
    Volume,7, Routledge, London 1998

Saint Faustina, https://www.thedivinemercy.org/message/stfaustina,
    Saint Faustina Saint Maria Faustina Kowalska: The Humble
    Instrument

Scobell Andrew Xi Jinping's Worst Nightmare: A Potemkin People's
    Liberation Army https://warontherocks.com/2023/05/xi-jinpings-
    worst-nightmare-a-potemkin-peoples-liberation-army/ May 1, 2023

Seidl, Horst, Metaphysics and Realism Discussion on Modern Criticism
    of traditional Metaphysics and Its Realism taken for Praechter refers
    to Ammonium, In Porph. Usage

Senator Robert Francis Kennedy,
    https://en.wikipedia.org/wiki/Robert_F._Kennedy_Jr.

Senner, Walter Epistemology 1 Pontificia San Tommaso D' Aquino, Spring Lectures, Rome Italy Fall 2011 Seidl, Horst, History of Ancient Philosophy Pontificia San Tommaso D' Aquino, Spring Lectures, Rome Italy 2011 Seidl, Horst, Metaphysics and Realism: Discussion on Modern Criticism of Traditional Roma: Angelicum University Press, 2008

Shoah is the Hebrew word for "catastrophe." https://www.google.com/search?q=holocaust+definition+stanford+university+definition&rlz=1C1CHZN_enIT1045IT1045&oq=&gs_lcrp=EgZjaHJvbWUqCQgAECMYJxjqAjIJCAAQIxgnGOoCMg8IARAuGCcYxwEY6gIY0QMyCQgCECMYJxjqAjIJCAMQIxgnGOoCMgkIBBAjGCcY6gIyCQgFECMYJxjqAjIJCAYQIxgnGOoCMgkIBxAjGCcY6gLSAQkxMTQxajBqMTWoAgiwAgE&sourceid=chrome&ie=UTF-8

Shoah is the Hebrew word for "catastrophe." Nicodemachean Ethics by Aristotle are the foundation of Justice in a Political Society. Refer to Book V. Also, refer to Aristotle's Politics.

Taitz, Sarah, Former National Security Fellow, News & Commentary Five Things to Know About NSA Mass Surveillance and the Coming Fight in Congress Congress must take this opportunity to rein in the pervasive government surveillance enabled by Section 702. https://www.aclu.org/news/national-security/five-things-to-know-about-nsa-mass-surveillance-and-the-coming-fight-in-congress

Ten and millions of Americans lost their homes https://www.prindex.net/news-and-stories/press-release-tens-millions-americans-expect-lose-their-homes/

The Difficult Realities of the BRICS' De dollarization Efforts—and the Renminbi's Role https://carnegieendowment.org/research/2023/12/the-difficult-realities-of-the-brics-dedollarization-effortsand-the-renminbis-role?lang=en

The Left's $7 Trillion Lie: Biden Far Outpaces Trump in Racking Up the National Debt Jul 2, 2024, 4 min read Commentary By Senior Visiting Fellow, Economics Research Fellow, Grover M. Hermann Center https://www.heritage.org/debt/commentary/the-lefts-7-trillion-lie-biden-far-outpaces-trump-racking-the-national-debt

The Military Balance 2024 spotlights an era of global insecurity, https://www.statista.com/statistics/264443/the-worlds-largest-armies-based-on-active-forcelevel/#:~:text=As%20of%20January%202024%2C%20China,the%20top%20five%20largest%20armies

The Military Balance 2024 spotlights an era of global insecurity, https://www.statista.com/statistics/264443/the-worlds-largest-armies-based-on-active-forcelevel/#:~:text=As%20of%20January%202024%2C%20China,the%20top%20five%20largest%20armies. 13th February 2024

The Offices of The United States Trade Representative https://ustr.gov/countries-regions

The rupee may be weaker, but the rich are richer https://www.forbesindia.com/article/india-rich-list-2022/the-rupee-may-be-weaker-but-the-rich-are-richer/81427/1

The Top 25 Corporate Nations https://theconversation.com/who-is-more-powerful-states-or-corporations-99616 BY DAVID FRANCIS

These 25 Companies Are More Powerful Than Many Countries https://www.google.com/search?q=WORLD+COMPANY+POWERS&rlz=1C1CHZN_enIT1045IT1045&oq=WORLD+COMPANY+POWERS&gs_lcrp=EgZjaHJvbWUqBggAEEUYOzIGCAAQRRg70gEJNTUxM2owajE1qAIAsAIA&sourceid=chrome&ie=UTF-8

Thomistic Philosophy Page Joseph M. Magee Ph.D. www.aquinasonline.com Unmixing the Intellect: Aristotle on Cognitive Powers and Bodily Organs was published by Greenwood Press in 2003.

Torricelli: Les Belles Lettres. www.wikipedia.com Torricelli's chief invention was the mercury

TRENCH: SYNONYMS OF NT Synonyms of the New Testament (Trench-Synonyms)by Richard Chenevix Trench, D.D. Public Domain Digitized by Ted Hildebrandt, Gordon College, Wenham, MA Electronic text hypertexted and prepared by OakTree Software, Inc.Version 1.5

US companies in China struggle with raids, slow deal approvals, anti-espionage law https://www.reuters.com/business/raids-exit-bans-us-companies-face-growing-hurdles-china-2023-08-29/

US companies in China struggle with raids, slow deal approvals, anti-espionage law https://www.reuters.com/business/raids-exit-bans-us-companies-face-growing-hurdles-china-2023-08-29/

WAR BRINGS DEATH IN THE LIFE OF THE NATIONS AR POINTS WHO ARE THE EMPIRES THAT WILL RULE THE WORLD AS REVEALED IN DANIEL AND IN THE BOOK OF REVELATION(32) WHO ARE THE EMPIRES THAT WILL RULE THE WORLD AS REVEALED IN DANIEL AND THE BOOK OF REVELATION - YouTube

WEBSTER'S DICTIONARY (19)Webster's Revised Unabridged Dictionary (Webster)Version published in 1913 by the C. & G. Merriam Co., Springfield, Mass., under Noah Porter, D.D., LL.D. MICRA, Inc. of Plainfield, NJ, prepared Public Domain This electronic version. MICRA, Inc. makes no proprietary claims on this version of the 1913 Webster dictionary—electronic text hypertexted and prepared by OakTree Software, Inc.

Who is more powerful – states or corporations? Published: July 10, 2018 11:14 am EDT https://theconversation.com/who-is-more-powerful-states-or-corporations-99616

Who is more powerful – states or corporations?Published: July 10, 2018 11:14 am EDT https://theconversation.com/who-is-more-powerful-states-or-corporations-99616

Wildberg, Christian, "John Philoponus," The Stanford Encyclopedia of Philosophy (Fall 2008 Edition), Edward N. Zalta (ed.), URL = <http://plato.stanford.edu/archives/fall2008/entries/philoponus/>. It is accepted that Philoponus is from a Christian family.

World News, Massive, Arms, www.lisaluciaarden.co https://www.msn.com/en-us/news/world/france-hands-ukraine-massive-arms-boost/vi-BB1kSYfp?ocid=msedgntp&pc=U531&cvid=9683b87b83014c13ac010a904fb2287b&ei=32